Michael Chugg is one of the music i[ndustry's leading]
music promoters and a public figure i[n his own right, running]
the PR machine for many of his tours and often being the
media's go-to man for an opinion on the industry or the state
of the nation.

Not shy to take hold of the microphone at a stadium event,
many concertgoers will have experienced Michael Chugg,
better known as 'Chuggi', during one of his legendary on-
stage rants, which all began with the now famous, 'Hey, you in
the black T-shirt – stop running!' that has given this book its
title. At a sold out Guns N' Roses concert in 1993, those words
stopped thousands of music punters in their tracks.

As Stuart Coupe succinctly said, 'Most people love
Chugg. A few hate him. Many are jealous of him. Everyone
respects him.'

Iain Shedden is music writer and critic for *The Australian* and
The Weekend Australian newspapers. Since taking on that role in
1998 he has interviewed some of the biggest names in popular
music and writes profiles, commentary, news, features, reviews
and a weekly column, Spin Doctor, in *The Weekend Australian*'s Review section. He is also an experienced commentator,
across all media, on the music industry and brings his expertise
to industry conferences as a speaker, panellist, interviewer and
mediator. Shedden is a trained journalist, but also spent many
years as a professional drummer, most successfully with Australian rock band The Saints. He lives in Sydney. This is his
first book.

Hey, you in the black t-shirt

The real story of touring the world's biggest acts

MICHAEL CHUGG
with IAIN SHEDDEN

MACMILLAN
Pan Macmillan Australia

First published 2010 in Macmillan by Pan Macmillan Australia Pty Limited
1 Market Street, Sydney

Reprinted 2010, 2011 (twice)

Text copyright © Michael Chugg 2010

The moral right of the author has been asserted.

All rights reserved. No part of this book may be reproduced or transmitted by any person or entity (including Google, Amazon or similar organisations), in any form or by any means, electronic or mechanical, including photocopying, recording, scanning or by any information storage and retrieval system, without prior permission in writing from the publisher.

National Library of Australia
Cataloguing-in-Publication data:

Chugg, Michael.

Hey, you in the black shirt: the real story behind touring the world's biggest bands / Michael Chugg.

ISBN: 9781405040228 (pbk.)

Chugg, Michael.
Impresarios – Australia – Biography.
Concert agents – Australia – Biography.
Concert tours – Australia – Management.

338.76178092

Typeset in 13/17pt Granjon by Post-Pre-press Group
Printed in Australia by McPherson's Printing Group

Papers used by Pan Macmillan Australia Pty Ltd are natural, recyclable products made from wood grown in sustainable forests. The manufacturing processes conform to the environmental regulations of the country of origin.

Hi Chris
enjoy the read, its not all lies

This book is for my brother Paul; for Nicholas, Sophie and Lucas; and for Harley Chugg and all that follow him. Dedicated to Mark Pope . . . and Buddha.

lots of Laughs & a few Tears.

keep on Rockin'

Chugg!

2015
xx

ACKNOWLEDGEMENTS

An Audience, My Life for an Audience

When Mark Pope first proposed I do this book, we spent a hilarious week at Trevor Smith's house recording the first tentative steps. It really felt like something I should do. Unfortunately, Mark, by his own admission, could not make the words 'laugh' enough on paper. With the help of Amanda Pelman, I met with many co-author candidates, waiting for the 'click' to happen. It was finally suggested to me by Gaynor Crawford that Iain Shedden should write the book. Two wonderful years later, here it is.

It has cost me a fortune in lawyers' fees! I have been as honest as I can through the hazy daze of the 70s and 80s. I have to say that if I had to come back again I wouldn't change much at all. It has been an incredible life.

We used to joke about making it to thirty. We now joke about making it to ninety. Even if you can't find yourself in the index, those who have helped to make me who I am *all* know who you are.

PROLOGUE

I am the king. I must be the king because I'm sitting in the king's chair. Down at the other end of the banquet table is the queen's chair, but it's empty. The twenty or so remaining seats on either side are also vacant. Whole pigs, sides of beef, shoulders of lamb, chickens, ducks, turkeys, vegetables, fruit and bread lie waiting, begging to be eaten, but no one enters. Champagne, brandy, wine and more crowd the parts of the table not occupied by food. Every night it's the same. I appear to be in a medieval tent, like something set up for a royal jousting carnival. It feels strange to be here alone, sad even, yet there's this amazing rush of wellbeing that comes and goes in my head. At its peak it feels like all I have to do is snap my fingers and anything I want – and I do mean anything – will be mine. When it subsides, futility and loneliness creep in.

This, you might think, is perfect fodder for the psychiatrist's couch; the recurring nightmare of a man who wants for nothing but who can't find happiness, a man too busy in the pursuit of money and power to appreciate the good things in life such as family or a few days lounging by the pool.

You'd be wrong. This is no dream. This is backstage at a Fleetwood Mac concert in Australia in 1977, nine months after their album *Rumours* went ballistic worldwide and just a few days after they arrived in the country for a tour that took in Sydney, Melbourne, Brisbane, Perth and Auckland. The man sitting alone is me, Michael Chugg, thirty-year-old tour director for Australian rock promoter Paul Dainty and the person in charge of supplying the members of Fleetwood Mac with their hearts' desires for the duration of their stay.

Top of their list is a medieval marquee, complete with flags, bunting and carpets, to be erected backstage at every performance so that they – Stevie Nicks, Lindsey Buckingham, John and Christine McVie and Mick Fleetwood – can indulge their newfound superstardom in a private and suitably excessive manner.

Also on their wish list is Gatorade, a drink almost unheard of in Australia at the time, which we have to import. They want limes, not readily available everywhere and, as with all fruit and vegetables, banned from certain interstate transportation. For the first and only time in my life I'm a lime-smuggler. Their tastes in alcohol, not surprisingly, are five-star – French champagne, Courvoisier cognac, Tanqueray gin and Pimm's, a drink I knew about only because my mum liked one on special occasions. And for every show there have to be six dozen bottles of Heineken beer – another exotic taste in 70s Australia – in the dressing room.

These requirements are above and beyond the security blankets they have brought along with them from the United States, such as a mobile gymnasium, two grand pianos and a masseuse. Only the masseuse and one of the pianos make it out of their flight cases during the tour. There was also cocaine – lots of it – although I wasn't aware of that at the beginning. An assortment of interesting people turned up with it. In Mac world, at the peak of their vacuum cleaner capabilities, whatever went up their noses was never enough.

In March that year we had toured ABBA, which was madness in its own way, but this was different. This was down 'n' dirty rock 'n' roll. 'The promoter's rep will meet the band's tour manager in the car park of Sydney Airport with two ounces of cocaine.' That was the instruction from the band's HQ in Los Angeles prior to their arrival.

I had made a rule, round about 1971 when I first started smoking marijuana, that I would never do powders. It was just a thing I had about heroin and all the other as yet unknown dangerous substances. When I was 18 and I had just moved to Melbourne from Launceston, guitarist Lobby Loyde gave me a purple heart one night and I didn't go to bed for three days. I talked everybody into delirium. I was a big enough loudmouth as it was without having all that shit in my body, so I never did that again. Marijuana was my drug of choice. I wasn't best placed to go skulking around Kings Cross in Sydney or anywhere else looking for marching powder. I knew a man who could and would, though, and his name was Ray Arnold. Ray was one of the best roadies in the business and a key figure in significant parts of my life. There wasn't much he couldn't do or fix.

I rang Ray and told him what I needed and arranged to meet him in the car park at Mascot the following Saturday morning. The deal was completed before Fleetwood Mac had left the baggage carousel. As it turned out, compared to the illicit drugs that followed them to Sydney, our stuff was pretty shithouse. I know that because the feeling of euphoria I had while sitting by myself in the marquee wasn't brought on by feasting on roast pork and sautéed potatoes. I broke my rule. I chopped a few lines of the good stuff. I bowed to peer pressure. If you didn't do it you weren't going to be part of the mob. You were going to be banished. So I did it and that was that. Cocaine remained one of my partners in crime for decades.

I spent quite some time in that marquee during the Fleetwood Mac *Rockarena* tour, either on my own or with various members of the 67-strong crew, or with some of Santana, Little River Band and Kevin Borich Express, who were also on the bill. I was managing Borich at the time, as well as working for Dainty. Every night a gang of us enjoyed the lavish spread of gourmet delights and copious amounts of grog that otherwise would just have sat there untouched. Courvoisier and Coke became my tipple of choice and I was drinking it for years afterwards thanks to the surplus from the band's ridiculous rider. Lighting roadie Peter Rooney and myself commandeered and customised a couple of road cases, which became the drinks stash that would be divided up between us when Fleetwood Mac had gone home. If you gave it back to the caterer, they would still charge you for it, so no harm was done. None of the band lobbed even once into that marquee, never mind that it was their idea. All of them were too wired to eat.

The excess was outrageous. There was just too much coke and too much weed.

Although they didn't touch the food, the Mac pack did make significant use of the Heineken. Before every show I would do the rounds of the dressing rooms and backstage area to make sure everything was in order. It had bothered me at the first show, at the Sydney Showground, that many of the bottles had been opened but the beer remained untouched. When I made the same inspection in Melbourne a few days later, the same thing had happened. In fact all 72 bottles had their tops removed but every one of them was full.

I went completely berserk, as I have been wont to do in stressful situations over the past forty-five years, screaming 'What the fuck is going on?' to anyone who would listen. Eventually one of their roadies took me up on stage, where they had two small tents, one on either side. In each of them there was a card table laden with bottle tops, sitting in neat little rows, with two caps pushed together, one on the bottom, one on top, to form a kind of capsule. I lifted one of the tops and saw the cocaine inside. During the performance, each of the band in turn would wander off to get a little card table action; all of them except drummer Fleetwood. His needs were somewhat greater than those of his colleagues, so he had his own card table within arm's reach just behind him.

I could have bought Fleetwood Mac enough bottle tops to fill ten dressing rooms for what they had cost with imported Dutch beer attached, but I guess that wasn't the point when you were as fucked up and successful as they were.

That was the most over-the-top, insane few weeks of rock 'n' roll debauchery I had been witness to in my career at that point, certainly from an act enjoying that level of success. That's not to say I had been a good boy myself up until then; far from it. I'd been living the life for about thirteen years, either on the road with bands or hanging out in the pubs and clubs of Melbourne or Sydney, working with people like Michael Gudinski, Roger Davies and Michael Browning, among others, all of us trying to mark some territory in the fledgling Australian rock business. But for me that 1977 tour was the beginning of a new era, the entree to many wayward nights on the rock 'n' roll circuit with Guns N' Roses, Bon Jovi, Billy Joel, Billy Idol, The Police and a thousand others. At its most outrageous, the nights rolled into days and just occasionally days turned into weeks. In the 70s, 80s and 90s any night could be party night and there was always something, or someone, on hand to make it go with a bang. Show me a joint and I'll show you a line of coke as long as your arm.

The *Rumours* tour was hitched to the back of an album that had its roots in the diabolical personal affairs of the participants. Nicks had split with Buckingham, the McVies had done likewise and Fleetwood had gone through a divorce with his wife Jenny Boyd Fleetwood. Their artistic expression of these break-ups made them rich beyond belief. They were crazy by then, mind you, but they had hit the ground running in that respect, if you ask me. And yet they were really nice people too. When I went to Los Angeles the following year to set up camp with Borich and Richard Clapton, whom I was also managing by then, they were incredibly helpful. Bob Jones and Richard Norton, the two Australian security guys on that Aussie tour, ended up going to the US to work with the Mac camp.

When I look back on that period, I can see a few parallels between Fleetwood Mac and my own career, although I've toured more often than them, flown around the world more often than them, probably slept with more people than them too. I've been just as reckless, probably more obnoxious and on the odd occasion just as drug-addled as they were back in the day. And, just like them, I've survived. I've toured some of the biggest bands in the world and taken drugs and gotten drunk with many of them. If my life were to be defined by famous albums it would be a blend of *Rumours*, *Highway to Hell* and *Blood on the Tracks*, with a nod to my best mate Billy Thorpe's 'Most People I Know (Think That I'm Crazy)'.

I've been promoting, managing, courting, bullying and championing rock acts since I was a fifteen-year-old know-it-all in Launceston, Tasmania, running dances and calling dog races to make a few quid. I've lugged gear, driven vans, collected door money, put up posters, nursed and endured egos, schmoozed, boozed, dined and done deals in every corner of the music world. I've made and lost millions on tours by international acts. I've helped raise millions for various charities. I've haggled over cents on a tour budget. I've abused people if I thought they weren't in the right and sometimes when they were, just because I could. I've made a habit of raising my voice to get my own way and I've earned a dubious reputation for invading the stage at hundreds of concerts I've promoted to mouth off at the audience. My singing voice is rubbish, but I can tell people in a crowd of 30,000 to sit down and shut the fuck up more effectively than anybody, if I think it's appropriate.

Oh, and I once had a gun pulled on me by a gangster, but I talked my way out of the situation. I'm quite good at talking.

That kind of résumé might slip perfectly onto the psychiatrist's couch at the beginning of this prologue, but that's just a small part of the story. I have spent a lot of time alone, in aeroplanes and hotel rooms, wondering what the hell I'm doing, but it would be wrong to paint myself as a solitary figure snared by my success. My life has been incredibly rewarding in all manner of ways. I have a young grandson. When something as wonderful as that happens, it puts everything else into perspective.

That said, doing what I do, promoting shows, I have been surrounded by the bizarre, the unscrupulous, the egotistical and the astonishingly talented, both on the stage and behind the scenes. I have seen excessive behaviour that you wouldn't believe, and half the time I was the ringleader. I have chased money for most of my life, but it has been incidental to what I love doing, which is putting on shows and seeing the excitement on people's faces. I genuinely love that. It gets me up in the morning.

I try to be as honest and straightforward as I can with people. It's not always the best thing to do, but if you don't, it just gets difficult. You tell someone what he or she wants to hear and it will come back and bite you on the arse every time.

I'm a poor boy from Tasmania who got lucky. I arrived on the streets of Melbourne in 1965, just at the right time, when rock 'n' roll was up for grabs and precious few people knew what to do with it. I still appreciate that opportunity and value it, just as I value many of the people with whom I started out and who are still around doing it because they love it.

I've been broke and I've been rich. In this business you can never guarantee anything. I've had bad times; times when I thought I had no future in the music industry. But I'm still here. And I love the limelight. I've been planning this book for a long time. I want to document my life and times. I want to be on the stage. That has got me into a lot of trouble in the past. This time, I suspect, will be no different.

1

An Education

The cycling track at Longford, twenty kilometres south of Launceston, attracted plenty of punters. It helped that you could park your car anywhere around the perimeter of the circuit to watch the races. As the amateurs' representative on the committee of Launceston City Cycling Club, I was a regular participant at events there, but on this occasion I was at the track, in a friend's car, for another reason. I was taking bets. Every few minutes someone would approach the window, hand over their cash and I'd place it on the rider of their choice. This, as you can imagine, did not go down well with my fellow club office-bearers, who were wary of me already because of my cocky attitude. It didn't help that I was fifteen.

That wasn't my first brush with the club authorities, nor was I confined to taking bets in the car park. I had some other dealings going on at cycling events down the coast and a scam selling programs at big events around Launceston. I remained a member of the club for another year or more after 'the Longford incident', but the committee, in its wisdom, got sick of me and said I had to become a professional cyclist or quit – I could no longer ride as an amateur because of my indiscretions. That's when I stopped cycling.

It was a tough decision. Cycling had been the focus of my early teenage years, but the rock 'n' roll business was starting to stir my soul. It's ironic that my cycling club was the sole beneficiary from my first effort at concert promotion. After that charitable deed, music took over my life.

I was born on 15 June 1947 in the Queen Victoria Hospital in Launceston. Mum and Dad were living with my father's parents, in a house that was also the kiosk of First Basin and Cataract Gorge, a sprawling parklands area on the outskirts of town. My grandfather was the caretaker and my grandmother ran the shop, which was always full of ice cream and lollies. I spent my first three years at that house. It was a great place to grow up. The bushland was incredible – full of kangaroos, wombats, peacocks, koalas and lyrebirds. There was a public swimming pool, one of very few in Launceston at that time. It was a magic kingdom for a toddler.

My earliest memory is from there, although it's not a particularly fond one. I was in my cot in my parents' bedroom and I can remember my dad, Victor, being woken up in the middle of the night. I was too young to understand what was going on, but my dad was a fireman and I learned later he was called out to fight the Ludbrooks fire. Ludbrooks was a department store in the centre of Launceston, on the corner of Charles and York streets. It was badly damaged and was later converted into a shopping arcade.

I used to love hanging out with both sets of grandparents. My mum's family, the Hancocks, had several acres at Invermay in north Launceston, with fruit trees, a dairy, chickens and an aviary. I'd spend a lot of time there, with my cousins Peter and Dennis.

Idyllic as it seemed to me, First Basin was only ever a temporary measure for my parents. It wasn't going to be big enough when kids came along. I was the first child, followed by my sisters Christine and Julie and finally, long after we had settled into our new home, by my brother Paul.

In 1950 we moved to Punchbowl Road, a new housing commission suburb that had been built in south Launceston. Ours was a single-storey wooden house with three bedrooms. It was on a big block of land with plenty of places to play, but it was a very working class area and it took me a while to adjust to it after all the freedom and tranquillity I'd been used to at the kiosk.

I went to Glen Dhu Primary School in south Launceston. It was one of the top schools in the area. I loved primary school. I was the patrol officer, helping kids across the road. I was in the Aussie Rules football team that won the premiership for the first time in fifty years. I used to sing in the choir. I had quite a good voice before my balls dropped; then I realised I couldn't sing any more.

Learning was a pleasure in my early school years. I finished in the top three all the way through my time at Glen Dhu.

English, history and geography were my favourite subjects. I spent hours in the Launceston public library, mainly reading non-fiction – biographies, history books. I read everything I could find on the fall of the Roman Empire. I became fascinated with Winston Churchill, a fixation that stayed with me, to the point where I began collecting and still collect Churchill memorabilia. I even visited his country house, Chartwell, in England a couple of years ago.

Anyone who knows me now would find this hard to believe, but back in the 1950s I was looked on by tough kids in the neighbourhood as a bit of a mummy's boy, the teacher's pet. I was a loner, too. I lived a lot in my own world. I'd play for hours on my own, with toy soldiers, or I'd just read. I used to have a lot of problems with some of the other local kids because they thought I was a smart-arse. I was well mannered, polite, talked to the teachers . . . a lot of kids couldn't deal with that. There was a family called the Rodens down at the bottom of Punchbowl Road and they terrorised me. They were scary animals. Then one day Dad, who could handle himself, showed me some moves. The following Sunday these kids came down the road looking for me. I walked over and kicked the oldest one of them in the nuts. He went down like a bag of shit. Then Dad bashed me up for doing it. I tried telling him that he was the one who had taught me, but that didn't seem to matter.

Of course the thugs really wanted my blood by then, so I had to be careful walking up Punchbowl Road to catch the bus to school. They'd be waiting for me, but I handled it. I wasn't a rough kid. I hated fighting. I didn't have many fights, but I won them. And I could talk down problems just by being aggressive and yelling a lot. That has served me well over the years, as many a roadie will tell you.

The most violence I experienced throughout my childhood, though, was at home, all of it from my father. He used to beat the shit out of me. Being number one son and possibly a mistake, I got the blame for everything. It might have been an accident, but I got the blame. A lot of grief got taken out on me, although I wasn't alone. I was born at a time when it seemed it was still cool to come home pissed and beat the crap out of your wife. I was four or five years old when I first had to try and stop that from happening. I made a vow then never to behave in the way my old man did towards his family. I used to hate the old prick.

My dad worked hard in a variety of jobs, sometimes working more than one at a time to make ends meet and studying as well; trying to better himself, he said. I learned a lot from him, although I didn't appreciate it at the time. One of his extra jobs was to round up workers, mainly firemen and policemen, to load or unload ships down at the docks. Sometimes the consignment would be wheat; other times it would be butter or dynamite. Prior to these shifts, I would hear Dad cajoling his mates on the phone, trying to convince them (almost always successfully) to come to work, while I played with my cars in the hallway. It was only many years later, well into my music career, that I realised I had picked up that persuasive manner from him. He gave me my wheeling and dealing instincts.

I got close to my father only in the last twenty years or so of his life. He died on 4 June 2002. When I reached puberty, however, our relationship was at its lowest point. My grandmother Ella, his mother, was my best friend. Whenever my dad beat me up, I could go there. I'd jump on my bike and ride down to the Launceston council yards where my grandparents were based after they moved from First Basin, just until he calmed down. His rage could last for days. I was a big disappointment to my dad in many ways when I was growing up. As I got older and smarter, his resentment centred on the fact that, through my various scams and part-time jobs, I was making more money than he was. I'd run a few dances in Launceston and when I had enough money I'd go up to Melbourne, stay in a hotel, go to gigs and spend everything I had. He couldn't deal with that and he couldn't believe that I'd become a long-haired bum involved in rock 'n' roll. His view, understandably, was that he had four kids and he was struggling to feed us all and here's his son pissing it all up against the wall. That was the subject for a lot of beatings for me as a teenager.

When my nan died, on New Year's Eve, 1961, I was scheduled to go to Burnie next day to a cycling carnival. I wanted to stay at home, because I was so knocked sideways by what had happened. Instead of letting me mourn and be there, my parents sent me off to Burnie to the bike race. I wasn't even allowed to go to the funeral. It was horrible, driving eighty-five miles to Burnie when my best friend was dead. She was everybody's vision of a wonderful grandmother. Her death and the way I was cut off from it scarred me. Since then, I have always been afraid of the agony of losing someone. That fear has had a profound, ultimately catastrophic influence on almost all of my relationships.

I loved my dad, though, and I have fond memories as well as bad ones. Radio was the centre of entertainment in our house. I couldn't get enough of it. You had to use your imagination with radio. You had to put yourself there. I remember listening to *The Goon Show* with my dad. We had an antenna, so we could listen to DJs such as Stan 'The Man' Rofe and Bob Rogers from the mainland. One of the first broadcasts I heard was the funeral of King George VI in 1952, again sitting in the lounge room with my old man. I can recall it as if it was yesterday.

If Punchbowl Road brought radical change to my early life, so too did starting high school. It marked the end of my interest in formal education and the beginning of sex, drink, rock 'n' roll and being able to look after myself.

In 1958 a new high school called Queechy High opened in the south-eastern suburb of Norwood, so the education authorities made up new boundaries to incorporate it. Because of where I lived, I was sent there and all of my friends, including all of the guys in the football team, went to Kings Meadows High. I was shattered. Queechy was full of kids from some of the other housing commission suburbs and they were pretty rough and ready. It wasn't a good time for me.

Mum really wanted me to go to a Catholic school, but we couldn't afford it. My sisters got to go because it was considered more important for them. That was okay by me. I was raised Roman Catholic, although my father's family were Protestant. My parents had visions of me being an altar boy, but I stopped going to church when I was thirteen. That was the reason for another beating from my old man. I stood up in church one Sunday – the whole family was there – and shouted that they, the congregation, were all a bunch of hypocrites and walked out. I got sick of all the gossip and snobbery that went on, not just in the church, but definitely the church seemed to be a centre for that sort of thing. My mum always saw herself as an upper-class sort of person. The Hancocks were quite well-bred stock. They weren't your typical blue-collar, suburban family. There was always a class thing going on around church. I guess I didn't handle that very well.

Just to prove thirteen wasn't totally unlucky for me, I had my first sexual liaison at that age, underneath the grandstand at the local cycling track. Girls loved cyclists, although I'm not sure why, so I had a lot of girlfriends when I was young. Much to my mother's disgust, I was a bit of a ladies' man. My first serious relationship was when I was sixteen, but from the age of thirteen until then, I had sexual relations with about thirty girls.

I was cycling a lot then. I had become friendly with a family called the Gilmores who lived around the corner in Bennett Street, a street that was also home to another gang that wreaked havoc on the neighbourhood for a few years. Graeme Gilmore was the wonder boy of Tasmanian cycling. He went on to be one of the best six-day cyclists in the world and held the world mile record in 1974–75. His son Matthew won a silver medal at the 2000 Olympic Games, although he was representing Belgium, his dad's adopted country.

When I started high school Graeme's father was training me. I won a few races. In my first year I made the final of the club championship. I played AFL as well and trained with the City Souths team. That was another point of contention with my old man. He was a rugby player from his boots up and played for northern Tasmania until he was forty years old. He wanted me to play rugby as well, but I knew all the chicks went for Aussie Rules players.

If you wanted to have prospects of leaving the island, you played football or you were a cyclist. No one ever said to run dances or manage bands or put on shows in order to get out of there. I learned that by myself.

In those first months of high school I would cycle to school with Graeme. Our houses were just next to Kings Meadows golf course, so we had to ride through there. It was a wonderful way to start the day.

My series of disasters at thirteen was completed when I fell in a bike race at York Park in Launceston and broke my arm in three places. The St John's Ambulance man told my dad it was just a sprain and so I tried to ride in the next race, but I couldn't grip the handlebars. Meanwhile my dad was telling me to stop being a sook. We went home and I had to sleep that night with my arm in a bucket of ice. He called me a big sissy. Next morning my parents took me to hospital, the doctor abused my old man and I was in the operating theatre within five minutes. That was the short-term nightmare. The long-term significance of my fall was that I couldn't write for three months and my schoolwork went to shit.

Not being able to write wasn't the only reason for my slide from top-three student at primary school to being bottom of the class at Queechy. I had turned into a smart-arse, but not in an academic sense. I thought I was a big shot. That's when I really dropped the ball at school. Because I couldn't write, I lost interest. When it came to mathematics, algebra, all that, I couldn't deal with it, although my arithmetic was strong enough for me to run a book on the Melbourne Cup from the school locker rooms. I got busted for that and had to stand in front of the administration building at school every lunchtime for six weeks.

I got huge grief at home when my education faltered, because I was the blue-eyed boy; I was the one who was going to be somebody. My mum sent me to elocution lessons. It was all about getting out of the 'burbs. I was going to go to university and I was going to be a doctor, but neither of these things were realistic prospects. I do regret not doing better at high school. Maybe if I had gone to university, I'd still be doing what I do, but I could have been a lot smarter more quickly, rather than learning by trial and error.

Part of the problem during those formative years, or part of the fun from my perspective, was that I always hung out with people older than me. I got a buzz out of being friends with older people. Most of my friends were from outside of school. When I was cycling, all the big bike carnivals would happen around Christmas time. All the international cyclists would come down for those – Syd Patterson and all the other legendary Australian cyclists of the time. My older mates from the club and I used to put our bikes on the back of an old Ford Customline and we'd drive down to Devonport, pitch the tent over the bluff and just sit there for two weeks, drinking and going to parties with all the older cyclists and picking up chicks.

At cycling meets back then, there would always be a commentator calling the races. One night at York Park, when I was fourteen, the regular guy didn't turn up and I volunteered to take over. I started doing that regularly and I enjoyed it. Maybe I liked the sound of my own voice, but it was also another string to my bow and a useful outlet for my yelling skills. Eventually Mac Sloane, a famous cyclist who called the professional races in Tasmania, took me under his wing and we'd go to the professional carnivals that had cycling, wood-chopping and various other events. Some of these carnivals attracted 20,000 people or more. Cyclists would come from all over the world. I'd call the amateur races and the foot-racing. Mac would sling me a couple of quid.

Prior to that I'd had a Saturday job for a couple of years at Launceston Trotting Club. My older cousin Dennis had done it before me and handed it on, along with his suit. I worked in the secretary's office taking nominations for the races and got the tea, coffee and sandwiches. Len Barker, the guy who was calling the horse races, let me call a few trials they had for the young horses before the main events. From there I started calling country gallops and trotting and greyhound races, as well as calling the cycling. I'd go to St Mary's or St Helen's or Scottsdale to call the races.

At one point, I was doing that as well as running dances all over Launceston, mainly in church halls. Sometimes I'd leave my father to run the dance, with his firemen mates working as bouncers, while I was calling the cycling, then I'd hurry back to the dance during the professional races, which I didn't call, to collect the money. It all got too much in the end.

I had a very brief career on radio as well, which came to an abrupt end when I swore on air. I said 'shitgun' instead of 'shotgun' during a cycling commentary. In the years since then the retelling of the story – not by me – has grown out of all proportion, to the point where I was saying something much worse after seeing a horse, or greyhound, that I had put money on fall while I was calling the race. Good story though it is, it never happened.

Even so, I had a reputation by then for being a loudmouthed arsehole, so when I fucked up on the radio quite a few people, one of them being the announcer I had replaced, went after me in a big way and I got the flick. My budding career at 7EX in Launceston went out the window.

So, at fifteen, I was commentating, I was cycling and I had girlfriends and I thought I knew it all. So many things were happening at once. I quit school. Then The Beatles came along and I really started to have an interest in music.

My first job was as a sales assistant in the soft furnishing department of Young's Furniture House in Launceston. That's where I met a guy called Rodney de Clerk, who was the bass player in a big local band called The Dominoes. The first dance I ever ran was a charity event, to raise money for the cycling club. I put on The Dominoes and another band called The Chevrons at the Launceston Trades Hall. Around 300 people turned up and we made 80 pounds. In those days that was big money. All of it went to the cycling club.

After that I started putting on my own shows. I became The Chevrons' manager. We'd do little tours, going to Burnie and Devonport. It was great fun. You'd load up the van on Thursday and drive to Burnie, get back Sunday to Launceston. It cost five shillings to get in at each show. One of the band's dads or my dad would come down and be the bouncer and collect the money and afterwards we'd divide it up between five or six of us.

Later, when I was eighteen, I started following visiting bands around Tasmania, groups like The Twilights from South Australia and The Loved Ones from Melbourne. They would come and play Devonport, Launceston and Hobart and I would tail them to every show over the three days. I'd walk to Devonport to see The Twilights. People in the family used to think I was an idiot, because no one did that. In those days 99 per cent of my family – and the Chuggs were a big family – had never been to Hobart a hundred miles away and here I was hitching to Devonport and Burnie on a Thursday, back for work by Friday morning and then hitchhiking to Hobart and back on a Saturday.

It was pretty safe in those days, but my mother used to be terrified. You could walk up the middle of the Midlands Highway at two o'clock in the morning and you weren't going to get murdered or attacked. Actually, it was a bit of a novelty for the truck drivers to pick up weirdos in the middle of the night. And I had a girl in every town, which gave me more of an incentive.

My ticket out of Launceston came from some of those early dances I ran in church halls. I saved the money I made to finance my trips to Melbourne. I was making a fair bit of money anyway from the cycling, the commentating, the dances, my day jobs.

My Auntie Barbara, my dad's older sister, was the first of the Chuggs to leave Tasmania, in the 1950s, to move to Melbourne. That caused quite a drama at home. Few people left their home town then. I was a little in awe of Auntie Barbara, inspired by her courage in getting out. She ended up doing really well, too, running the lingerie department of the Myer department store chain. When she moved, that was a big thing for me. She had been an influence on me in other ways as well. She had all the original Elvis Presley singles on the Sun label. I was impressed.

So, music was going to be my way out, but it was a good feeling also to be a big fish in a little pond for a while, that is until I got involved in a disastrous disco project in Launceston called Indigo. It was a club dreamed up by me and a few other locals, but we didn't have a licence. It went pear-shaped pretty quickly and I got left with the debts. That convinced me it was time to move on, although I did pay off the money I owed. I just realised then that it was okay taking a band around Tassie every few weeks, with a caravan of chicks riding along with us, but I didn't want to be doing that for the rest of my life. There had to be something more. I found it, initially at least, in Melbourne.

2

Well, La De Da

Many of us have pivotal moments in our lives that are defined by pieces of music or landmark concerts. My youth was littered with those and my early experiences of great rock 'n' roll deepened my resolve to make a career in the music business. The fact that I get a buzz now, standing side of stage watching a band or looking out into the audience, just as I did forty years ago, is what keeps me doing the thing that I do.

On those early trips to Melbourne in the mid-1960s, most of them just for the weekend, my sense of excitement and anticipation was wrapped up in the bands I was going there to see, many of whom were emerging from the burgeoning British rock and pop scene; acts such as The Rolling Stones, The Who, The Animals and The Yardbirds. I'd go to see as many of them as I could. It wasn't unusual then, nor is it today, for a number of big artists to play in Melbourne within a few days of each other. One night I might have seen The Seekers or Manfred Mann, the next it could have been The Dave Clark Five or Roy Orbison. Then I turned into an Easybeats tragic. I couldn't get enough of them. The only band I missed seeing in Melbourne in that period was The Beatles.

It's odd to look back and realise that only a few years passed between that Orbison show and my becoming his tour manager, but in the interim I established myself as part of the furniture – although not much more than that – in Australia's burgeoning rock 'n' roll industry. I wasn't sure which part of the business would be the most successful for me, nor did I care. It really was a frontier. I could be a manager, an agent, a promoter and a roadie in the space of a day. That might read as if I were a jack-of-all-trades and master of none – or worse, a complete chancer. The truth was a combination of those things and more, but I was always convinced that taking on anything to do with music – other than actually playing it – would serve me well in the long term, and so it proved to be.

I got into a routine on those Melbourne weekends. I'd fly in on Friday and get a room at the Victoria Private Hotel in Little Collins Street. That was the only hotel in Melbourne that anybody from Tasmania had heard of. It was in the heart of the city and handy for gigs and many of the happening nightclubs. There seemed to be one of those on every corner. I'd hang out at a place called 10th Avenue on Bourke Street, sometimes until 3 am. I had made a few friends through Melbourne musicians who had toured in Tasmania, so I wasn't always alone, plus I used these holidays, if that's what they were, as a way of sparking up my image – which up until then had been that of a long-haired lout.

I became a mod. I got into buying button-down-collar shirts and bright flares and Cuban heels and went to clubs where I knew I could find other mods. I would never have considered wearing that kind of shit in Tasmania, where I knew for sure the local bikies would have beaten the crap out of me. The sharpies in Melbourne gave that their best shot. I remember being chased down Little Collins Street by about eighty of them, a small gang of mod friends and me, all fearing for our lives as rocks flew past our heads and the mob with baseball bats loomed closer.

I never got into any really bad scrapes there, though, apart from that one. Only when I ran out of money a few times and had to spend the night at the Salvos hostel on Kings Way did the drunks make life a little scary. Living the dream was far from perfect then, but it was better than the reality I had back in Launceston.

I would have been a good travelling salesman. I liked travelling, I had the patter, the confidence and, by the time I was twenty, I owned a few decent shirts. That line of employment was my best option when I settled in Melbourne in 1967. I'd had a few sales jobs in Launceston, aside from the gigs I had selling myself as a broadcaster and promoter, so sales seemed like a natural first step to a career on the mainland. It started badly. As soon as I arrived in the city I took a job selling *Encyclopaedia Britannica*. I lasted two days. I soon found something more suitable, in another furniture warehouse, JP Harman and Sons, and that gave me a position to work from while finding something better in the music industry.

Melbourne's music scene was vibrant in an unprecedented kind of way in those days. I came in on the end of the pop era.

Things were changing. The tide of blues-influenced rock music from the US and Britain was becoming heavier in the hands of artists such as Jimi Hendrix and Cream and there was a rash of bands in Australia that were coming from the same headspace. Ida Mae/May Mack from Launceston was one of them. The band took their name from a 1920s Texan blues singer (Ida Mae Mack). I had started managing them in Tasmania but they soon followed me to Melbourne. Years later the band's guitarist, Tony Naylor, went on to be one of Australia's most in-demand session players.

One of the industry people I had met in Tasmania was Ronnie Burns's and The Flies's manager Gary Spry, who was one of the partners in a Melbourne booking agency called Ambo. I made my first trip to Melbourne, on the *Princess of Tasmania* (the first and last time I travelled by boat to Melbourne), with a young girl singer I was managing called Sue Garwood. I visited Ambo – where I also knew Ron Blackmore, who had brought bands to Tasmania – and they gave her a few shows. When I became a Melbourne resident, I wanted to get Ida May Mack on the books as well. Bill Joseph was another of the agents at Ambo and he helped me get Ida May Mack off the ground.

However, it was the young kid Joseph had taken on as Ambo's junior agent who proved to be a most useful ally, among other things, in my early career. His name was Michael Gudinski. I met him in the Ambo office. He was sixteen and he was different, I knew that. And he loved music. He had just started working there, while I would go and hang out there just to soak up the atmosphere and maybe learn something. Ambo had many well-known and up-and-coming acts on its books, including The Loved Ones, Bulldog and Chain, the last of whom Gudinski came to manage. He and I steadily got to know each other, although we didn't work together as such. I soon learned that he had ambitions way beyond his Ambo gig.

Gudinski was a Jewish boy from a Russian background. He had been to Melbourne High School and the Jewish, private Mount Scopus Memorial College. Like me, he had been running dances since he was at school. Some of his friends from there were musicians, including a few who would go on to form the successful band Madder Lake.

As a teenager, Gudinski was putting on shows in broken-down mansions around St Kilda and Balaclava in Melbourne. He called them 'Magic Mushroom'. He'd roll into these deserted houses, put in a PA and a band and charge a few quid at the door. Mostly he'd get away with two or three and then the police would send him on his way. Clearly we had something in common, if only an entrepreneurial spirit, an agenda of 'Let's do it and see what happens', although we came to share a lot more than that in the years ahead.

Such were the pioneering days of Oz rock that if you decided you were going to do something in the music business and you set your mind to it, it would happen, although of course there was no guarantee that it would be successful. I was hungry for an opening. Anything. I had different jobs to keep myself alive but I definitely wanted to be part of the business. I was doing everything to be involved; whatever it needed. If you were the manager, particularly a novice manager as I was, you had to do everything. I drove the van. I loaded the gear. I set up. I got to know the roadies, people like Ray Arnold, John and Norm Sweeney, John Highland and Wane 'Swampy' Jarvis, all of whom became legends of

Australia's wide open rock 'n' roll road. You couldn't do just one thing. If you were just a promoter or just a manager you would go broke, because there wasn't enough money around. You had to do more than one job to stay alive. So, in the process, you learned.

In 1969, I moved to a flat in Balaclava. At various points there were bands living above and below me, including The Valentines (featuring Bon Scott – later to be with Fraternity and then AC/DC – and Vince Lovegrove) and The Master's Apprentices. Lots of bands lived around Balaclava, St Kilda, Fitzroy and South Yarra. There was a real sense of community among musos there, something that I think has always existed in Melbourne more than in other Australian cities.

Ida May Mack did lots of shows and that kept me busy along with my day job. We had a little old van. I used to carry the gear in that. We'd do three gigs on a Saturday night sometimes, starting off at the Thumpin' Tum or Catcher in the city, then we'd move on to Dandenong Town Hall and follow that with a late spot in Frankston. I'd be our only roadie, with all the gear. You'd help the other roadies who were there and they would help you, so you were picking up knowledge and expertise from each other all the time. A lot of the people I learned from and worked with in those early days are still around. Some of them are still good friends.

Gudinski and his new partner Michael Browning, who was managing former pop star turned rock troubadour Billy Thorpe and who would later manage AC/DC, set up an agency of their own, Consolidated Rock, in late 1969. In its first few months of operation they were working from the front lobby of Sebastian's Disco, which was a big club in Exhibition Street,

Melbourne, run by the Knight brothers and Browning, who also ran Berties at the Prince Albert and Victoria's Discotheque. The area they were using was no bigger than a cupboard, but they had a phone and they were booking bands. Every lunchtime I'd go up there from work and just listen to what was going on. Browning was managing singer Doug Parkinson about that time as well and Gudinski was booking Chain, Bulldog and Healing Force, among others.

After a few months, once they had the business up and running, Gudinski and Browning rented a house in St Kilda Junction and launched Consolidated Rock properly. I got the job of putting up the street posters and being gofer, for £12 a week. I gave up the secure future at JP Harman and Co, where I was getting double the money, but I knew I had done the right thing. I felt certain my future was somehow tied up with being in the band booking business.

One Thursday night, Ida May Mack was doing a show, a regular dance I ran at the College Lawn Hotel in Prahran. There weren't many people at the gig so I couldn't help notice when two attractive young women walked in, particularly the blonde one with the big smile. Her name was Liselotte Reisner, or Lilo. She and her friend were from German families and lived at Glenroy, one of the outer suburbs of Melbourne that was a largely German expat community. We got talking and hit it off. Pretty quickly we started going out together. She was one of four kids, two brothers and two sisters. She had come to Australia as a baby with her family from Germany and settled in Glenroy. Lilo was a hairdresser.

I had just started at Consolidated Rock by then. Between that and meeting Lilo, I really thought I was on my way.

It was around then that I struck up a friendship with Billy Thorpe. I'd met Thorpie a few times when he had played in Tasmania, so I had no problem making myself known to him when he came into the Consolidated Rock office, which he did regularly. That's when he took me under his wing and got me involved in his career. He'd see me working away in my little poster area and ask me to sit in on marketing meetings he was having with the others. That didn't seem to please my employers very much, but of course I was delighted.

Lilo and I became inseparable. She helped me to put up gig posters around the Melbourne streets, sometimes in the middle of the night. I soon began spending a lot of time at Glenroy with her family. They were very close-knit. I would go to some public event in Glenroy, such as a fete, and there would be 1000 Germans there and me. That was an incredible eye-opener for me to German culture. I loved the food especially. Her mother cooked the most amazing meals, with red cabbage and delicatessen food that I had never tasted before. My Aunt Margot, Dad's youngest sister, had married an Italian migrant called Beppi, which the Chuggs thought quite exotic (some of them thought too exotic), so this was a similar leap into the unknown for me, but it was worth it. I was in love. We got married in 1970 in the Lutheran church in the city and had the reception at Monash University. My family came from Launceston for the ceremony. I was twenty-three.

Soon after the wedding we got a place in Clayton, halfway between the city and Dandenong, but our time in Melbourne was almost up. Later in 1970 Consolidated Rock decided to open an office in Sydney. Sydney and Melbourne were the two main territories for rock and pop shows at the time, so it seemed perfectly natural that they should want to have an office in both cities. I was asked to run the Sydney end with another agent, Phil Walker.

I headed to Sydney with Lilo and moved into a three-storey house in Underwood Street, Paddington, which had the Consolidated Rock office on the ground floor. It wasn't an auspicious beginning and as it turned out the whole venture was short-lived. There weren't a lot of venues in and around Sydney in 1970, or at least not established rock 'n' roll venues. In the city you had The Whiskey, Chequers and The Stagecoach, and further afield were Narrabeen Surf Club and the Ritz Ballroom in Parramatta. There was no scene as such. We ran some local dance gigs in the suburbs, places like Eastwood and Randwick, mainly in church halls. We had to do that because we were bringing bands up from Melbourne and there weren't many places for them to play. Sydney was tough.

One initiative Browning and Gudinski had in Melbourne was running shows at the Town Hall, imaginatively titled Consolidated Rock Concert... No. 1 and so on. In June, 1971 they held one featuring Billy Thorpe and The Aztecs, Daddy Cool and others and 5000 punters showed up. Browning thought it would be a great idea to stage another one at Sydney Town Hall, not an established rock venue by any means. The show was a shambles. The security people were angry that there was a rock show going on in their venue, so they were offside from the beginning. The show was beset with sound problems, not least by being incredibly loud. It also ran way over time. Johnny O'Keefe, the king of Aussie rock 'n' roll, was there in the audience, in his trademark white suit, sitting right above the stage, lording it over everybody. Thorpie, who was closing the show, came on very late and did two songs before the security turned the house lights up and it was all over. The crowd was livid.

A week later, *Go Set* magazine, the most influential rock mag in Australia at that time, ran a story with the headline 'Rock Con at Sydney Town Hall', criticising in great detail what had happened. One of *Go Set*'s main contributors at the time was Ian Molly Meldrum, who, throughout our forty-year friendship, has always denied that he wrote that story. I'm still not convinced.

As a result of this bad publicity and to avenge *Go Set*'s audacity at criticising Consolidated Rock, Browning launched another magazine in competition, *The Daily Planet*. It was run partly from Melbourne and partly from the Consolidated Rock office in Paddington, with a succession of editors moving in and out over a period of months. It was a great magazine, but it was doomed. Not only that, it sent Consolidated Rock broke. *The Daily Planet* ate up all the funds.

So at that point I was in Sydney with my new wife, we had no money, we didn't know anybody and Consolidated Rock was going out of business. It was a testing time. Fortunately a roadie friend was able to supply me with hash to sell occasionally in order to keep Lilo and me alive.

It didn't take long before another opportunity arose. Roger Davies was a roadie I knew quite well (but not the one who supplied me with the hash). He was from Melbourne and when I met him in 1970 he was tour managing the band Company Caine. He picked up some extra work from Consolidated Rock and when that folded we set up our own agency, Sunrise, in the same office in Paddington, late in 1971. It was during that period he started raving about a band he saw doing a residency at Jonathon's Disco in Sydney. That was Sherbet, which he guided to international success throughout the 1970s, before going on to handle the careers of Cher, Olivia Newton-John, Tina Turner and Pink.

Our new agency marked the parting of the ways for Gudinski and me for a few years. He started a new agency with another Melbourne agent, Ray Evans. He was also managing Chain, who had had a No.1 in Melbourne with the song 'Black & Blue'. Then in late 1972 he and Evans started Mushroom Records, which was the launch pad for Gudinski's music industry empire.

Sunrise did well initially. We built up a roster that included singer Jeff St John and the bands Tamam Shud and Pirana. We had eleven or twelve acts. One of them, The La De Das, I started managing in late 1971, taking over from Michael Browning. The group, originally from New Zealand, was well established in Australia by then. They were one of the most popular live acts in the country and the single 'Gonna See My Baby Tonight' had just hit the charts when I came on board. The line-up at that stage was singer Phil Key, bassist Peter Roberts, Keith Barber on drums and Kevin Borich on guitar.

One of the first gigs I did with them was on Boxing Day, 1971, with Billy Thorpe and Daddy Cool, both hugely popular at that time. It was held at the Rosebud Show at the Rosebud picnic grounds on Victoria's Mornington Peninsula, and run by Melbourne radio station 3XY. An estimated 50,000 people showed up, unprecedented numbers for an Australian rock show. Many people, especially rock historians, cite the inaugural Sunbury Pop Festival, also in Victoria and staged a month after Rosebud, as a turning point in Oz rock. Certainly it was a landmark event, but Rosebud, at least in terms of numbers, showed what was possible in the festival domain; not that I was particularly happy about the huge attendance just prior to the show.

There were so many people trying to get to the venue, essentially a large paddock, that the band and I, travelling by car, almost didn't get there on time. I had to get out, run up and down a few hills to reach the site and then walk on stage. Spectrum had already played by then and had come on again as Murtceps to keep the audience occupied. All I could do was gasp at Trevor Smith, the programming director at 3XY who was running the show, to tell him the La De Das were on their way. Unfortunately, in my haste running across the fields, I had lost the car keys. We had to force the boot open with a crowbar in order to get the guitars out. Then we had to flag down some Hell's Angels, who gave us a lift back across the hills to the stage.

The La De Das were part of that first Sunbury, as was another band that I had started managing, Sydney outfit Country Radio. We had no idea how significant an event it would be, but there was no doubt it was a great opportunity to be on an A-grade bill.

Gudinski and Evans booked the acts for Sunbury, but they took quite a few from Sunrise for the first one, including Pirana, The La De Das, Country Radio and Company Caine. The line-up over the three days also included Max Merritt and The Meteors, Chain, Wendy Saddington, Spectrum and, on the Saturday night, Billy Thorpe and The Aztecs.

Country Radio played the sunset spot that night, just before Billy. The bulk of the crowd was there for Thorpie, drunk and shouting his name. While this was going on, Country Radio's singer Greg Quill was hit by a beer can thrown by a drunken punter. Greg was a gentle giant of a man, so he wasn't looking for trouble. He saw me at the side of the stage and asked me what to do about the hostile reception they were getting. I told him to go up to the microphone and tell them to get fucked, which he did. He turned that gig around. The band really nailed it after that.

Thorpie's performance that night cemented his place in Oz rock history and sent 'Most People I Know (Think That I'm Crazy)' to the top of the charts. I'm proud to say I was there, but ashamed to admit that, due to a particularly wicked brand of grass known as 'Durban poison', I fled after the first song, fearing for my life.

Lilo and I had driven down from Sydney for the gig. Through a friend of hers, we had rented an old farmhouse up in the hills about ten miles from the festival for the weekend. Billy had arranged for the band to camp out by the river near the site. Everybody was either tripping on acid or at least doing something naughty.

Sunbury, aside from featuring six or seven of my acts, coincided with my earliest experimentation with marijuana. I wasn't a heavy user but I'd have a joint now and again, as did pretty much everyone I knew. I wasn't prepared for my next intake. Trevor Smith came up to me after Country Radio's set and said: 'I've just scored this.' It was a little brown paper bullet-shaped lump. It was called 'Durban poison' and a shipment had arrived into Melbourne, so there was a lot of it around. We rolled a few joints and had them just before Billy went on. Just as he walked out on stage, it kicked in. I was totally off my face. It came at me with such force that I started to get really paranoid. Thorpie had every amp he could muster on stage, all of them turned up to 11. It was as loud as loud can be and the crowd was going nuts. There was smoke and noise and lights. I couldn't handle it. All I could think about was how to get out of there fast. I imagined I was in a prison camp in Nazi Germany. It was terrifying. I've never been so frightened in my life. It looked like there were monsters coming through the fence backstage. Molly Meldrum was there, and he looked like a monster as well.

I grabbed Lilo. We ran to our car, got in and drove off doing about eighty miles an hour all the way to the farm, whereupon I jumped out, ran into the house, got into bed and pulled the covers over my head. I never touched dope like that again. Another lesson learned the hard way. There would be plenty more of those.

3

I`m the Leader of the Gang

If I can't account for Thorpie's performance at Sunbury 72, I can at least remember that The La De Das went down incredibly well that weekend. Their performance cemented their position as a major live attraction, so much so that two months later we joined Thorpie again for his legendary performance at the Sidney Myer Music Bowl in Melbourne, where an estimated 200,000 people turned up. It was an amazing sight and again The La De Das pulled off a great gig. I was the one who stuffed up. Being the ever-eager agent as well as manager, I had booked the band another gig later that evening at a club in Werribee, south-west of Melbourne. There were six people there. We'd just left a venue with 200,000 punters in it. Keith Barber wanted to kill me.

Still, I loved touring with The La De Das and I learned a lot managing them. In those days bands would go to Brisbane for a week, or even two weeks, then to Adelaide for a week and then up to Sydney for a week or two, the same in Melbourne. I started jumping the shows around, so we'd do a show in Newcastle, New South Wales, then the next night we'd be doing one in Tasmania and the night after that at the Adelaide Festival of Arts. I started bringing in that style of touring, but it didn't suit everyone in the band. Phil Key was married with a young kid; he didn't want to go on the road all the time The others were rock dogs; they were quite happy doing it. There were other issues between members that were starting to affect the band, however, particularly discussions over money. I ended my role as manager in August 1972 and Key and Roberts left to form a new group, Band of Light, a month later.

There were a lot of developments in the fledgling Australian music industry in 1972. Gudinski was making his move into the recording industry. Sunbury 72, which was soon compared to Woodstock, paved the way for three more annual festivals there and for many more around the country. Roger Davies and I bought into a Melbourne management company and agency, Let It Be, run by accountant Philip Jacobsen, Peter Andrew and John Pinda. They had Spectrum and Daddy Cool, among others, on their books. That deal folded Sunrise and Let It Be into a national agency, a move that would be mirrored by the Premier and Harbour agencies, in Melbourne and Sydney respectively, a few years later.

I also made a lifelong friend that year in Trevor Smith at 3XY. The station promoted a lot of shows in Melbourne to which I supplied talent. Trevor was one of the great innovators in Australian radio and had a huge influence on how commercial networks were run, particularly after forming the consultancy Digamae with fellow programmers Rod Muir and Jaan Torv, from 2SM in Sydney, to sell the More Music radio formula Muir had picked up in the US. Both 2SM and 3XY became so powerful in the early 70s that you could hardly do a gig in Melbourne or Sydney without having them involved.

I started spending a lot of time in Melbourne in the second half of 1972, running the Let It Be office there while Roger looked after Sydney. Lilo stayed in Sydney most of the time I was in Melbourne. That distance put a strain on our marriage, not surprisingly, but we got through it.

Country Radio also enjoyed huge success that year. They had a hit in August with what would become their best-known song, 'Gypsy Queen'. They were a great band. There had been a few personnel through the ranks during my time with them, but the 72/73 line-up of Greg Quill, Kerryn Tolhurst, John Bois, Tony Bolton, John A Bird and Chris Blanchflower was the best and developed their style from being overtly country to having a more pronounced rock sound.

The group was to be short-lived, unfortunately, but they left an enduring mark on Australian rock with 'Gypsy Queen' and the live album they released a few months later. Perhaps their crowning glory, however, was their performance at Sunbury 73. Country Radio's set was one of the highlights, judging by the crowd's reaction, on a bill that included Johnny O'Keefe, Madder Lake, Coloured Balls and Matt Taylor. Greg Quill, Country Radio's main songwriter, moved to Canada after the band split and became an arts journalist for the *Toronto Star* newspaper.

A few months after that second Sunbury, my career went off in another unexpected direction. A few days into it I was wondering if it had been a wise move; in fact I was panicking.

It was my first stint as a tour manager for an overseas act. A frenzied mob had gathered behind the stage, all of them desperate to get closer to the star performer, who had just finished his set. These young lunatics meant business. They were pushing each other as well as rocking the caravan that served as a dressing room, to the point where it was close to tipping over on its side. My roadie mate Graham Madigan, known to everybody as Scrooge, was doing his best to keep the crowd at bay, but it was a losing battle. Just as I began to freak out, there was a loud, despairing cry from inside the van: 'Scrooge, make sure they don't touch my hair!'

That was in April 1973, when the only things troubling Gary Glitter were his quiff and being able to get out of the venue in one piece. He escaped. At least he could justify having a sense of humour about his incarceration in those days. The concert was in Sydney's Moore Park, just a few weeks after Glitter had scored his third top-ten hit in Australia with 'Hello, Hello, I'm Back Again'. Even with those credentials and bearing in mind it was a free concert, promoted by radio station 2SM, no one had predicted that 27,000 people would show up to see the newly crowned king of glam rock.

It was a great show, but the drama afterwards illustrated just how naïve promoters were back then about the potential of crowd trouble at large outdoor events. There was nothing to stop all 27,000 Glitter fanatics from strolling into the backstage area at that show. Security, in terms of personnel, barriers and proper accreditation for artists, crew, industry people and the media was nothing like it is today.

I encountered several scenarios in the early 70s that had the potential to be fatal for fans or artists, but of course rock festivals were still in their infancy in Australia and there was still a hippie subculture. These events were largely 'gatherings', where everyone was there to smoke dope and chill out rather than cause trouble. Even with tragedies such as Altamont in the US casting a shadow over the new festival culture, it was the spirit of Woodstock that loomed largest in Australia's paddocks.

If you look at photographs of those early Australian festivals such as Sunbury, Myponga in South Australia and Odyssey at Wallacia in New South Wales, to name only a few of the significant ones, it's amazing to note how haphazard they all look, with a tiny stage and people parked in groups around tents and bongs. At the time it felt cutting edge to be there, but it looks astonishingly innocent now. Sunbury 73 and the Rosebud festival are examples of how the tide was turning towards a more testosterone-fuelled festival scene, but there was another one in 1973 that could have turned into our own Altamont.

It was held at Frankston Oval in Victoria. It was a free concert promoted by 3XY. Let It Be supplied most of the acts. Lobby Loyde's band Coloured Balls was the main attraction, which meant a significant part of the oval was populated by Loyde's sharpie fans. Our security guy Bob Jones was concerned about the high number of sharpies on the ground, over 1000 I estimated, and mid-way through the afternoon Bob's fears were justified when a fight developed between some of the sharpies and the bouncers. It was on and it was ugly. Innocent punters, including women and children, got caught up in the melee and within minutes it seemed like half of the audience were involved in the brawl. People were badly hurt and taken to hospital, but it could have been much worse.

When the fighting was at its height, I realised we had to try and do something from the stage to calm it all down. I figured that if anyone could talk these thugs into behaving themselves it would be Lobby, but he refused to go anywhere near a microphone. That left Trevor Smith, who could see his 3XY career disappearing down the toilet in front of him in a sea of thrashing fists, shaved heads and sharp attire. The situation was out of control.

Trevor got up on stage and screamed at everyone for five minutes to stop and eventually they did calm down. He was awesome. That's where I learned how to control a crowd, watching him yell for all he and his job were worth to get those idiots to control themselves. We learned through experience that day that you needed sufficient security staff and a significant police presence wherever there was any chance of violence, but that wasn't the only lesson Trevor and I got that weekend.

A few days before the concert, we came up with an idea to clean up on the soft drinks franchise at the event. We contacted a soft drinks company and got them to come down from Melbourne with a semi-trailer full of the stuff. It arrived the night before the show and Trevor, Philip Jacobsen, production manager Eric Robinson, assorted crew and myself spent hours unloading the truck and setting up stalls at various parts of the ground. What we hadn't realised was that there was a pub on every corner close to the oval.

Next day, show day, it was overcast. Straight into the pubs went the bulk of the audience. By the end of the day, we had sold about twenty cartons of soft drink. We had to put nearly all of it back in the truck. It was a disaster, and a costly one at that.

My entrepreneurial skills might have taken a battering on that occasion, but my career as a whole was branching out in all sorts of directions in 1973. Aside from being an agent and a manager, I was now a tour manager for international acts as well.

Glitter was the first of those overseas names I took on the road in Australia. The second, just a few weeks after Glitter, was English folk rock band Fairport Convention.

Both of these tours came about through a Sydney promoter called David Ginges. Roger and I met him at a club in Sydney we used to hang out at called Joseph's Coat, a weird bohemian joint also frequented by our mate Eric Robinson, who was in the process of setting up his lighting and production company, Jands. Ginges had promoted some shows in Sydney with Australian acts such as Daddy Cool and Spectrum, but he wanted to branch out into touring overseas artists, which hardly anybody was doing at the time. He approached us saying he wanted to bring out Glitter and Fairport Convention and asked me to tour manage them.

Ginges copped a lot of bad press for that first Fairport tour, mainly because all of the posters, handbills and newspaper ads billed the show as Fairport Convention with Sandy Denny. Denny, the group's original singer, had left the line-up in 1969, although she had made the occasional return in the interim, but there was no way she was going to be on that tour and the media had a field day when she didn't arrive. Just why Ginges had put it on the advertising in the first place I've no idea. He was never a big player in the industry. He went broke a year later and disappeared from the scene. I was happy, however, because I was able to give Country Radio the support slot on the Fairport tour.

Glitter's Melbourne show on his first tour was poorly attended. I think there were around 300 people inside the Festival Hall. Scrooge and I were sitting at the side of the stage, smoking a huge joint. The lights went down and . . . bang! It was the most incredible show I've ever seen. We were so stoned that 300 people sounded like 6000. Unlike my Sunbury 72 experience with Thorpie, I really got that gig. That show will stick with me forever.

Due to Ginges going bust, Sunrise picked up the next Glitter tour in 1974 and co-promoted it with Jands. We made a real killing. It was a big promotion. As a poster, I got a calendar made up for July 74, in black with gold letters and with Glitter exploding through it. 'Gary Glitter Is July', it said. We put the posters all over Australia. We sold out five Melbourne Festival Halls. Five Hordern Pavilions in Sydney. We sold 10,000 tickets at the WACA in Perth. We were away.

Glitter was the act that got me going as a promoter. He was fantastic. That was an amazing time. Glitter couldn't sing for shit, but he was such a showman. He was a great entertainer. He taught me a lot about show business, about image and selling records.

We were all young and doing things we shouldn't have been doing when Glitter mania was at its peak. Unfortunately, as the years went by, Gary didn't grow up. It saddens and appalls me how he became a paedophile and ended up in jail as an old man. I feel sorry for him, but I'll always look back on those 70s shows he did in Australia with a smile on my face.

You don't catch me smiling too often about the act that landed in my lap soon after those first tours by Glitter and Fairport Convention. Much to my surprise, one day in late 1973 former Easybeats guitarists Harry Vanda and George Young walked into my office and made me an offer I didn't feel I could turn down. They wanted me to manage their former Easybeats bandmate, singer Stevie Wright. Had I known then what I was getting myself into, I would have told them in words of one syllable where they could stick the devious little bugger.

4

A Really, Really Hard Road

I worshipped The Easybeats. To me they were the most exciting Australian band of the 1960s. I followed them all over Tasmania the first time they toured there.

That's why I was a little in awe when Vanda and Young asked to have a meeting with me. As much as I admired the band, I had never met any of them. Even more surprising was that the two famous musos considered me the best person to manage their former lead singer. My roadie buddy Ray Arnold, a recurring influence on my career for a variety of reasons, knew them and had suggested to them that I would be the perfect fit for Stevie. I loved Ray, but boy did he get me into situations.

Wright was between jobs. He struggled after The Easybeats split up in 1969, but his critically acclaimed performance as Simon Zealotes in Harry M Miller's stage production of *Jesus*

Christ Superstar, which opened in Sydney in 1972, had returned him to the spotlight.

Harry and George had spent the early 70s in England, working as producers and songwriters, honing their skills while using the proceeds to pay off some of the debts The Easybeats had incurred towards the end of their dwindling career. When they came back to Sydney in 1973, they were armed with a plan, to sign Australian talent and to make hit records.

The Albert Productions record label and Albert Studios was a partnership between the pair and Ted Albert, head of the publishing and production house that had helped launch The Easybeats in the 60s. Vanda and Young were already talking excitedly about *Hard Road*, Wright's debut solo album, when they approached me.

I agreed to manage him. The timing was important. For the first time since I had started at Consolidated Rock I had nothing going on. The La De Das were falling apart. Country Radio was finished. Sunrise wasn't getting much work. I was struggling financially and my marriage was on rocky ground. If I'd had a dog, it would have died. I was still buzzing from the tour managing experience with Glitter and Fairport Convention and I wanted to do more of that kind of work, but it was a great honour to be asked by Vanda and Young to look after Stevie. I was never going to turn that down. Besides, I thought it could be a golden opportunity.

While I had done well locally with some of the acts I managed, I was eager to work overseas. Stevie's success in the UK and the US with The Easybeats meant there was a better than normal chance of getting his solo career under way there, especially coming off the back of rave reviews for his *Superstar* performance. And of course he *was* a star. Few frontmen could command a stage in quite the way Stevie did with his backflips, tambourine slaps and his general charisma.

And then there was 'Evie (Parts I, II and III)', the Vanda/Young composition that was lined up to be the first single from the album. When I heard that song, all eleven minutes of it, I knew I was on to a good thing. As the months rolled by prior to the release of *Hard Road* in April 1974, so the inkling that I was about to become involved in a great Australian international success story grew more real.

The story began at Alberts. Stevie had left *Superstar* by the time Harry and George arrived back in Sydney and, for reasons that only became apparent later, was working in the warehouse at Alberts when they signed him to the label, Albert Productions. The idea of the new company was to build a roster of local talent and make hits, which they did with Stevie, John Paul Young, The Angels, William Shakespeare, Ted Mulry, Rose Tattoo, Cheetah and, of course, AC/DC, before the decade was done.

When I met Stevie he was very likeable, friendly and charming, and he was enthusiastic about rekindling his association with Harry and George and beginning a new phase of his career. Stevie had co-written many of The Easybeats' early hits with George, including 'Sorry', 'She's So Fine' and 'Come And See Her', before George and Harry's classic 'Friday on My Mind' changed the group's dynamic.

After *Hard Road* was recorded, at the new Alberts Studio in King Street in Sydney's CBD, all of the elements were put in place to make it an international success.

Chris Gilbey, an Englishman with a sound knowledge of the overseas markets, was managing director at Alberts and he took responsibility for negotiating with overseas labels for the release of *Hard Road*, which he did successfully with Atlantic in America and Polydor in Britain. Chris wasn't daunted at all by the English or the American scene, whereas many of the rest of us were.

Alberts was an institution in Australian music long before The Easybeats, with a history stretching back through generations of the Albert family all the way to Jacques Albert, who migrated to Sydney from Switzerland in the late nineteenth century and set up a business selling violins and, later, sheet music. There was a strong family tradition within the company. When I arrived in the Wright camp, Jacques' great-grandson Ted, one of the true innovators of the modern Australian music industry, was running it.

When Ted launched Albert Productions in 1963, a lot of Australian artists were still content to record cover versions of overseas acts' material. Ted wanted to break that mould. He wanted to sign acts, such as The Easybeats, that could write their own songs.

After teaming up with Harry and George in the 70s, Ted wanted to take that philosophy to the next level. He could see the potential and the huge financial rewards for an Australian act if they could get their songs in the overseas charts, especially from publishing, which could be more lucrative than any other part of a songwriter's career. Not everyone realised then that the real money for a band's songwriter(s) lay in publishing and not so much in record sales, although that could be lucrative also.

The atmosphere within the Alberts organisation was decidedly close-knit. It had the feeling more of a cottage industry than of a major record company such as EMI or

Festival, both of whom I had worked with through my management of The La De Das and Country Radio. For all that I was central to Stevie's career throughout the *Hard Road* phase and during the recording and release of the subsequent album *Black Eyed Bruiser*, I never felt totally at home in the Alberts environment.

Fifa Riccobono, the young woman who in the 70s did pretty much everything at Alberts, from making the tea to handling publicity and answering the phone, exemplified the company's united front. Fifa was Alberts through and through, which is why she went on to be the company's head of artists and repertoire (the A&R department at a record company is responsible for signing acts and developing their recording careers) and eventually CEO. When I entered their world, Fifa was the cottage gatekeeper. We didn't get on particularly well. As time went on, the more she seemed to dislike me. I thought then it was because I was loud and arrogant, but it turned out to be something else.

I got on well with Harry and George. I think they thought I could be really good for Stevie, with my connections and my background in a few different branches of the industry. I was excited to be working with them, too. George and Harry were across several areas of the business as well. They had come back from England with all the latest production knowledge. They had absorbed a lot of what was going on in London in the early 70s.

There was a general consensus in the months before *Hard Road* was released that something special was about to happen, so the early part of 1974 was spent structuring a plan for Stevie's long-term future, although I had to direct my attentions elsewhere for a weekend in January. That was when I made my own little mark on Sunbury. I didn't go running to the hills this time, I went running on to the stage instead. Not for the first time, my big mouth went ahead and all I could do was go with it.

It was the year Sunbury promoter John Fowler ended the Aussies-only policy in the festival line-up and flew in relatively unknown English band Queen. The resentment among some of the local acts was quite high. There were others – punters, crew and indeed myself – who were upset that this foreign band was coming to play at *our* precious Sunbury. So, just before Queen came on, I wound up the crowd by screaming 'Go home, you Pommie wankers' and worse into the stage microphone. They walked on and everybody screamed abuse at them.

There has been a lot of debate and numerous versions written about what happened after that, most commonly that Queen went down like a lead balloon, vowing never to return. What I remember is that after about three songs they turned the gig around and won over the crowd. Even so, singer Freddie Mercury was pissed off at the end of their set. He did promise that next time Queen came back to Australia they would be the biggest band in the world. And that's exactly what they became. I heard that on subsequent visits they would ask after me because they needed to 'talk' to me. Needless to say, it wasn't to offer me a job as their PR man. I never worked with Queen in any capacity.

My making-a-fool-of-myself commitments over with, I settled down to fully concentrate on making little Stevie Wright into a very big star. 'Evie' was scheduled for release a few weeks after the album in early May. Radio was a big concern. No one played an 11-minute song on commercial radio, even if it was split into three parts. We needn't have worried. It went to No. 2 nationally in July and stayed at No. 1 in Melbourne for seven weeks. By then the album had gone to No. 5 nationally and to No. 1 in Melbourne.

We had put a cracking band together for Stevie called The All Stars. It was a bit of a floating ensemble, with various musos added or substituted, but the nucleus was drummer Johnny Dick from the Aztecs, Kevin Borich on guitar, Ronnie Peel on bass and keyboards player Warren 'Pig' Morgan.

With the album and single both in the charts the foundations were set for Stevie to build on that success with heavy touring, which we did.

In August he did a national tour supporting Lou Reed, with George's little brothers Malcolm and Angus's band AC/DC doing the opening slot. Around that period people at the Sydney Opera House contacted me about the possibility of putting on a rock show in the concert hall there, something that hadn't been done since the venue opened a year before. We did it, once again with AC/DC supporting. George and Harry joined the band for that show, aided on guitar by Malcolm. The sound was pretty terrible, but no one seemed to mind.

By the end of 1974, we had also done the bulk of the recording of *Black Eyed Bruiser*, again with Harry and George at the desk in Sydney and contributing most of the material.

There was no definite release date for the album, since it would depend on how things went overseas with *Hard Road*. We released a single from *Black Eyed Bruiser*, 'Guitar Band', in November 74 and that did pretty well over Christmas, getting to No. 8 in the national charts.

So we had a record in the charts; we had just done well-received shows and, really, the world was Stevie's oyster. And yet, for all his charisma and stamina, there was something missing from inside him. He was doing everything right, but he wasn't engaging the audience as well as I would have expected. Stevie was a nice guy, but he had his insecurities and other stuff going on that I could never quite figure out. I had no idea what was behind it until we were doing a show at Myer Music Bowl in Melbourne. By that stage, early 1975, The All Stars had moved on to join John Paul Young, whose career really took off that year with the album *Hero*, written and produced by Harry and George, and the singles from it, 'Yesterday's Hero' and 'The Love Game'.

The new line-up of The Stevie Wright Band, as it was called, included Country Radio's Tony Bolton and Russ Johnston on drums and guitar respectively, plus percussionist Larry Duryea, keyboards player Peter Deakin and bassist Billy Rylands.

We were running late for the gig. We'd been smoking a lot of pot, as usual. Stevie was missing so I went to his hotel room and found him with a mate, sitting in the corner, next to the wardrobe, with a straw. I thought they were spotting hash, so I went over and ripped the straw from Stevie, had a hit and said: 'Let's go, we're late.' An hour later I was lying on the floor of the Myer Music Bowl spewing my guts up. I had taken heroin.

That's when I figured out why Stevie was walking out in front of thousands of fans at Melbourne Festival Hall or wherever to absolute hysteria and then walking off to complete stunned silence. He just wasn't connecting with the audience. He was a great entertainer and he worked hard. He was still doing the handstands and backflips, all of that, but it just wasn't working and I hadn't realised why. I'd never put it together. Lilo and I were living in McMahons Point in Sydney by then and I could never figure out why Stevie would come by the house at regular intervals and ask me for $30 for groceries. I felt stupid. I was so close to it, but I didn't see it.

Apart from the shock and the health implications of this latest development, the timing of the discovery wasn't the best. The release of *Hard Road* in the UK and America was imminent and we had promotional tours lined up in both places. This was the shot at managing an artist who could have a No. 1 all over the world.

I didn't tell anyone about what had happened at the hotel. Certainly no one at Alberts knew what was happening. God forbid Harry and George found out about it. They had seen Stevie nearly destroy himself once before, on alcohol, during his Easybeats days. They had learned a lot of hard lessons – not just with Stevie – from their move to London with the band and it was clear that their mission in the 70s was not to repeat any of their mistakes. This solo comeback was Stevie's best chance of superstardom, but it was also his shot at redemption in the eyes of his two mates. I thought it better to take care of it myself, so I helped Stevie to get on a methadone program and he settled down. Problem solved, I thought.

The overseas promotional trip, which began in late January 1975, was as exciting for me as it was for everyone else involved in Stevie's career. The furthest I had been overseas at that point was New Zealand, so when Stevie and I arrived in London to meet up with Chris Gilbey, I could see a world of opportunities and possibilities opening up. It wasn't especially intimidating, because Chris knew his way around the city and the industry. We stayed at the Inn on the Park in Mayfair, one of the most expensive hotels in the city, which only added to the sense of wonder.

We went to Polydor's offices in the West End and plotted a marketing and promotions strategy for the album and 'Evie'.

Lots of TV and radio appearances were lined up, as well as press interviews. A buzz began to build. We went over to Amsterdam to do a TV show. Everything was starting to look great, so great in fact that Gilbey and I realised that it would be better for everyone if Stevie secured management in Europe as well as me looking after his affairs at home. We needed someone who had international experience. The Dutch band Focus were huge in Europe at that time, so we went to meet their manager, Yde de Jong.

We spent three or four days at his house outside of Brussels in Belgium. Nothing came of it. Then we went back to England to do more press.

I went to London and Stevie took off to Manchester by himself to do an interview. I caught the train up there the following day and as soon as I walked into his hotel room I knew he was 'on'. He'd scored. I lost it. Here we were sitting on the verge of worldwide success and this little prick was out of it. I destroyed the hotel room around him, smashing chairs and I even smashed him a few times, I was so angry. Eventually I calmed down and he promised me it would all be fine. We went to London and did a photo shoot with a top photographer for the cover of *Black Eyed Bruiser*.

The rest of the British and European commitments went to plan. In all, we were there for two months. The next step was

America, where Chris and the people at Atlantic, who were totally behind Stevie, had arranged a fairly heavy press schedule to coincide with the release of the album. Unfortunately (and then some) I wasn't able to go with Stevie. Paul Dainty had booked me as tour manager for Irish guitarist Rory Gallagher. He was flying into Perth from Japan on 1 April and I had to be there to meet him. I missed my flight, and Gallagher had to find his own way to his hotel. Dainty didn't let me forget that one for a while.

So Stevie flew off to New York without me. He was behaving and seemed pretty pleased with how the media jaunt had gone in Europe. I wasn't unduly concerned. I figured the American record company would look after him and he'd do the methadone and it would all be rosy. Atlantic had taken out a two-page ad in Billboard to announce his arrival in the US. Television, radio and press interviews had been set up all over the country.

Two days into the Gallagher tour, I was in Adelaide for his show at the Festival Theatre. At the hotel, I got a call from Ray Arnold, who was in Sydney. He told me he thought he had just seen Stevie, walking down the street in Randwick in Sydney. I figured Ray had had a smoke or something. 'Don't be daft, Stevie's in America,' I said. 'It's going off over there. He's going to be huge.'

Stevie was in Randwick. I discovered later Randwick was where his smack dealer, a woman called Desi, lived. I could not believe it. I got to Sydney the next day – Gallagher's next show was there anyway – and got the full, sad, pathetic story.

He had gone to America, got off the plane, met a few people from the record company, hung round for a couple of days and then got on another plane and flown home, straight to the door of his drug dealer. This time I was beyond furious. In one fell swoop, Stevie's overseas career was dead.

Once again I kept the truth to myself. I made some ridiculous excuse to Alberts about why Stevie was back home, but already there were signs of resentment and mistrust coming from them, particularly from Fifa. Everyone thought that I was fucking up their boy's career. The truth was that Stevie had been doing heroin since *Jesus Christ Superstar*. He was just so good at disguising it, deceiving everybody, not least Harry and George, who would have parted company with him on the spot if they had found out.

A few weeks after it happened, they got their chance to see the reality. We were back in the studio in King Street, doing some final vocals on *Black Eyed Bruiser*. I was in the control room with Harry and George. I got up to go to the toilet and walked past the vocal booth. You couldn't see in there very well because it wasn't that well lit, but I could make out what was happening. Stevie was sitting in there chasing the dragon, inhaling heroin through a tube made from a piece of silver foil. I'd had enough.

I went and got Harry and George and brought them around to the window and pointed at Stevie and said: 'Look. That's what's really going on. He's a heroin addict.'

They freaked. That saved my relationship with George and Harry, but then we had to try and save Stevie and that wasn't easy. It was the beginning of the end for him as a rock star, just at the point where it could all have come good.

We did a country tour with JPY after that and another end of year show at the Opera House to coincide with *Black*

Eyed Bruiser's release. That show was significant for a couple of reasons. First, Stevie opened for AC/DC, the unknown band that had supported him a year earlier. Second, it was his last performance of any note before the drugs really took hold. He overdosed in August 1976 and it was all over. That began a terrible spiral into rehab and mental health problems. Poor Stevie suffered even more after admitting himself to the Chelmsford Private Hospital in Sydney. He was one of many patients there subjected to the controversial deep sleep therapy, a combination of electro-shock treatment and drug-induced comas that left Stevie irreversibly damaged. The man behind the treatment, Chelmsford's director Dr Harry Bailey, later committed suicide.

I know some of the Alberts people blamed me for what had happened, that some of them thought I was responsible for getting him onto heroin, or they thought that because I was there with him I could have prevented it. There was a lot of ill-feeling towards me, for years in some cases, from Alberts' employees. Fifa, I know, couldn't stand me and would have nothing to do with me. Eventually she came to understand what had really happened and we have got on famously ever since then. She still thinks I'm a prize arsehole when I set my mind to it, but she's now a close personal friend.

To watch it all disappear for Stevie like that was unbearable. I admit that at least some of my anger towards him was due to my own investment, personally as well as professionally, in his ability. I wanted to manage the No. 1 act in Australia. I wanted to have a hit worldwide. I had goals. We were so close to it, so very close. Everything was set up for him. He could have been a superstar. Perhaps that was what drove him to do what he did. He had a self-destructive nature. It was like he couldn't handle the thought of success. I wish I could have done something to help him, but I couldn't.

It would be twenty-six years before I worked with Stevie Wright again. He was a part of the *Long Way to the Top* tour in 2002 that so successfully reviewed and in some cases revived the careers of many of the Australian artists who had been Stevie's peers in the 60s and 70s. The other artists treated him like royalty. He and I got along just fine.

5

Bittersweet Symphony

Much to my surprise and delight, in August 1974 I found myself promoting the Sydney glam rock band Hush through Tasmania, a gig given to me by my friend, the band's manager Peter Rix. Hush were one of the first Aussie bands to pick up the mantle of English groups such as The Sweet and T Rex, playing catchy guitar pop complemented by eyeliner, lurid satin flares and platform shoes. I had just begun sharing an office with Peter in Sydney. He was aware that I knew Tasmania and its touring circuit back to front and because we worked together he knew for sure I needed the money. I wasn't particularly busy then and I certainly wasn't getting rich.

We were doing a gig in Launceston. It was a sell-out show at the town hall, just as the glam-rock phenomenon in Australia was taking off. Supernaut, still almost unknown outside of their native Perth at that stage, were the support act and their set went down well and without incident. Halfway through Hush's show, however, fire brigade trucks pulled up outside the front door. Firemen started pouring into the building. The venue operator saw what was happening and figured, logically enough, that the hall was on fire, so he switched on the house lights. Hush were oblivious to what was going on and kept playing, but from where I was standing there were so many firemen in the room that there had to be something seriously wrong.

The firemen moved swiftly from the back of the hall. The crowd, which was mainly teenagers, parted to let them through. Peter was standing looking bewildered at the front of the stage. The band in quick succession stopped playing their instruments until there was an uneasy silence. Everyone was wondering what the hell was going on. A burly fireman in his yellow helmet strutted forward, pointed at Peter and shouted: 'YOU! WHERE'S CHUGG?' Peter didn't have an immediate answer for him, but I could see from his expression he was forming a few questions of his own. Before he had a chance to air any of them, the fireman was in his face. 'WELL, YOU'D BETTER TELL 'IM HIS DAD'S HERE!'

It was my dad, the deputy chief of the Launceston Fire Department, pulling a stunt. Five minutes later he and his mates were back in their trucks and the gig went on as if nothing had happened.

After nearly fifty years in the music business there isn't a lot that surprises me. If a fire department turned up at one of my gigs today, just for a laugh, I'd be shocked, but I know it'll never happen. Everyone is way too accountable, even in Launceston.

In the 70s, surprises came at me from all directions, some of them bad, like the Stevie debacle, and some of them fortunate, such as meeting Peter Rix. He became a lifelong friend and supporter and in that Hush era got me out of several holes financially when it seemed the world was conspiring against me.

I met Peter in Melbourne at the beginning of Hush's success in 1973. I was managing The La De Das and we crossed paths staying at the Chateau Commodore Hotel in Lonsdale Street, a regular haunt for visiting bands in Melbourne. Peter was naïve about the music business. He'd never been out of Sydney with a band. I could tell from the start we were entirely different people. He was a gentleman, all rugby union and social graces, while I was the loudmouthed, working class opportunist. We are both Geminis, I discovered, something I felt brought us together in some weird way.

Peter is a few years younger than I am. When I met him he had only just quit his first proper job as a lawyer in the offices of book retailers Angus & Robertson in Sydney, in order to manage his friends in Hush. He came into the music business by accident. Peter booked gigs at university in Sydney and at a gay club in Kings Cross called Aquarius to give himself an income while he was studying law. Hush rehearsed in a garage attached to Peter's flat in Paddington. The band, from the Hills district in Sydney's west, were offered a recording contract by Warner Brothers after reaching the final of a Hoadley's Battle of the Sounds competition in 1972, which prompted them to make a demo. They asked Peter to look at the contract, which in effect handed him the manager's role.

Hush had their first hit, 'Get the Feeling', in late 1973, just around the time Vanda and Young were dangling Stevie in my direction. By the time I got to take Hush around Tassie, they were one of the biggest bands in the country. Stevie wasn't doing so badly either, but none of his earnings, or at least very little of them, were trickling down to me, even though 'Evie' and *Hard Road* were in the charts. Royalties always took months to appear, plus having a band such as the All Stars on the road wasn't cheap, so there wasn't a lot of money being made from his tours. I was glad to have that Hush tour just to pay the rent.

There were other problems at home. Lilo and I moved into a semi-detached house in McMahons Point in 74, but we were struggling – and not just because of cash flow. Money was an issue, but it didn't help that I was only there with her half of the time. Even when we moved to Sydney in the beginning, I was on the road a lot. I loved travelling and touring, but it wasn't the ideal arrangement for a marriage. I should have realised that before we got married. Instead, I'm ashamed to admit, I tried to have it both ways.

My motto then was you lived your life wherever you were. When I was in Sydney with my wife, that is what I did. When I was on the road . . . well, what went down went down. In those days on the rock 'n' roll highway there were women everywhere. It wasn't as if I was having full-on affairs or mistresses. It was nothing like that. It was just opportunity, one-night stands. I was driving up and down the highway to Melbourne at least once a fortnight. I got lonely. It's hard to look at that now and justify it, but that's how it was then. I married too early. If I had that period over again, I would never have done it.

Getting married when I did, so young, was a hangover from the establishment. You got married, you got a job and that was your life. I suppose part of me believed that's how things should be, but my views changed. The 60s spawned rebellious youth, the sexual revolution and a rock 'n' roll culture that was evolving every minute. By the time I was in my mid-twenties that was the norm in my world. I was right there in the middle of all of that, trying to grab as much of it as I could. Being a Gemini didn't help either. There are supposed to be two of us, but I think there are about ten of us. Not that I'm making excuses. I hurt people with my behaviour and I regret that. It wasn't until the 80s, when I went to a health farm for the first time, that I really came to grips with that side of my psyche.

Peter Rix and I opened an office at 128 Blues Point Road in McMahons Point and called it the Great Australian Sound Company, the GAS Company. Peter ran his business and I ran mine, but it wasn't too long before we were working together.

For many years now Peter has been a well-respected producer of corporate events, community outdoor concerts and stadium sports ceremonies and has worked in television and theatre as well as in music. He produced the ARIA Awards for fourteen years. He was never a rock 'n' roll animal, though. He was intrigued by some of the shady characters, such as myself, that he met when he hit the road with Hush. The rock 'n' roll scene was new to him and he couldn't really relate to it. Not that he had to relate. Peter had the Midas touch from the beginning.

In June 1974 Hush were scheduled to appear on a TV show being recorded by the ABC at Paddington Town Hall. It was a variety show called 'The Rock and Roll Ballroom of the Air'. Jon English, the singer and actor Peter would later manage, was the host. Peter and I, plus Trevor Smith and a mutual friend, Tony Hogarth from Wizard Records, all went along to watch the recording. We weren't prepared for what we heard that afternoon, although not from Hush, who were fine, but from the voice of Marcia Hines. Marcia, a young American singer and actor, made her name in the same musical Stevie had done so well in, *Jesus Christ Superstar*, although she had also earned rave reviews for her performance in the Sydney production of *Hair* immediately before that.

Marcia sang what would become her signature song that day, James Taylor's 'Fire and Rain'. The four of us – Tony, Trevor, Peter and me – were in tears. It was one of those great moments when you felt you were there at the beginning of something big. She signed to Wizard, which also had Daddy Cool and Rick Springfield on the books, soon after. 'Fire and Rain' and her debut album, *Marcia Shines*, were both huge hits. Peter, to his credit, saw a great opportunity and became her manager, a role he continues to perform today. His connection to Marcia was another reason I stayed in work in the mid-70s. In late 1975 Peter asked me to promote Marcia's first tour.

I had a lot riding on Stevie, so when it all went pear-shaped in mid-1975 my long-term future veered off course. I still had Dainty offering me tour manager gigs, fortunately, and some of his tours that year, among them Status Quo, Wishbone Ash, Roxy Music and Leo Sayer, kept me alive. As has always been the case with me, as soon as one chapter of my life collapses in a heap, so another one rises up. September of that year shaped considerably my professional life for the rest of the decade.

I had met a guy called Steve White, who had been the lead singer in a band from Sydney's western suburbs called Stonehenge. Steve was a young gun promoter, a bit like I had been ten years earlier. He wanted to run a show at Castle Hill Showgrounds, so I set it up with him. We called it 'A Day on the

Green' and we booked Marcia, Norman Gunston and Brisbane band the Silver Studs, among others. We didn't get rich out of it but it was okay and we did a few more, including one with Midnight Oil in their early days. That's when we formed the show promotions company Marquee Attractions. The company's first nationwide commitment was Hines's debut tour.

It was all class with Marcia. The shows were lavish affairs, mostly in theatres, with a big line-up – horn players, backing singers, stage sets, the whole bit. And she was easy to work with. The only down side for me was Robie Porter, who owned the Wizard label that by then was also home to Hush. He and I didn't see eye to eye, particularly on that first tour, because he was overly critical of Marcia's show. To my mind, it was a great show by a great performer and I couldn't see why her record company boss didn't like it. A couple of times I came close to decking him. That didn't stop me from enjoying the tour and we did two more with Marcia across Australia that were equally successful over the next few years.

Also in September I got a call from Gudinski, one that would influence my career direction for the next twenty-five years. He asked Philip Jacobsen and me to have a meeting with him, along with Frank Stivala and Ray Evans, to discuss a new company. It would be a partnership between the five of us called Premier Artists and it would combine our talents to establish the leading music agency in the country.

For a few years, Gudinski, Evans and Bill Joseph had been in partnership, but a dispute developed over Joseph wanting to bring in another partner, John Finch. Evans and Gudinski were against it, so they asked us in, along with Frank, who was working for them already as a booker. On 16 September, we had a long lunch in Melbourne at which alcohol and pot were in great abundance and the deal was done, although Frank I think was uncertain up until the last minute whether to stay with Premier or move to the new operation Joseph and Finch had set up, Nucleus.

Certainly on paper Premier looked strong, but initially it was tough for us because Nucleus, through Joseph's long-term associations, had all the venues in Melbourne sewn up. We had plenty of acts, but they had all the gigs. It became very competitive. We were also up against A.C.E., which was another Melbourne promoting/touring company run by Michael Coppel and Zev Eizik. Nucleus was able to steal bands from us because we didn't have anywhere for them to play. In order to try and fix that, we started another company called Pub Rock to find venues that would take our bands. It was heavy for a while, but we got through it.

We all had other things going on at the same time to keep us busy and to help with cash flow. Philip was managing Spectrum and The Captain Matchbox Whoopee Band. Gudinski had a few scary years getting Mushroom Records up and running, but in 75 he was on top after the release of Skyhooks' debut album *Living in the 70s*, which became the highest-selling Australian album in history to that point. I had my Dainty commitments, which would move up several notches in the coming years, and I was about to take on Kevin Borich's management after The La De Das had folded. I thought that perhaps, where I had failed with Stevie, I could turn it around with Kevin. Over the next year I concentrated on laying the foundations for his solo career as well as getting Marquee Attractions established out of Sydney and building the Premier Artists roster with my new partners.

Not long before Stevie had his breakdown in 76, Lilo and I went on holiday to Fiji. It was a significant break for a couple of reasons. The lesser of the two was that we were sitting on the beach one day when Billy Thorpe, his wife Lynne and their young daughter walked past. It was a fluke meeting. Thorpie's moment in the sun as a rock star had faded since the Sunbury days of 'suck more piss' and blues rock. The launch of the 'Countdown' TV show on the ABC in 1975, with my mate Molly Meldrum as the host, heralded a new wave of home-grown pop music from the likes of Sherbet and indeed Hush and Supernaut, as well as bringing much greater access to a wide range of pop and rock from overseas. There wasn't much room for Billy in there. That's why, when we met him on the beach that day he was on his way with his family to start a new life in Los Angeles, a move that brought him amazing success a few years later when his album *Children of the Sun* went top twenty in the US. It went to No.1 in some southern states.

The most important development in Fiji was that Lilo became pregnant. Starting a family hadn't been on my agenda; in fact at that point in my life I was beginning to question whether Lilo and I should be together. That issue became more pronounced a few months after we got back from holiday. I fell in love with someone else.

Her name was Margaret White. She was the wife of Stan White, who had been the keyboards player in Pirana, one of the bands Sunrise had on its books in the early 70s. I had met Margaret seven years earlier at the Australian Entertainment Exchange, Ray Evans's booking agency in Melbourne. We were both single at the time, but nothing happened, although there was definitely a vibe between us. She and Stan went to America after getting married, so I didn't see her for a few years, but I didn't forget her.

Then she turned up again. I was in Christchurch with The La De Das in 1974. I walked into a hotel lobby and there she was. I was with someone else, not Lilo, so the situation was awkward for all manner of reasons, but we got talking. I visited her again two years later just after she had had a baby with Stan.

When we reunited in Melbourne, Margaret had split up with her husband, who was living on the Gold Coast in Queensland. She was working for Propaganda, one of the first music publicity companies in Melbourne. I was spending a lot of time in Melbourne and one thing led to another and I started seeing her. Every chance I had to be with her, I took. I know some people will say what an unfaithful son of a bitch I was, but that was how it was. I lived for the moment. It's who I was then. It's not who I am now.

Margaret knew I was a manager as well as a promoter. At the time she was friendly with a couple of bands from Adelaide that she thought I might be interested in managing. One of them was called The Stars, a country rock band. I met them and liked what I heard. They were a great band. Beeb Birtles from The Little River Band produced their first single, 'Quick on the Draw'. They signed to Mushroom in 1977 and released three albums before disbanding in 1979. Sadly the band's guitarist and main songwriter, Andy Durant, died of cancer, aged 25, a year later.

The other band Margaret introduced me to was Cold Chisel. I could only afford to take on one new act, so I had to choose between them and The Stars. I chose The Stars.

Steve and I were doing well in early 1977. We had done all of AC/DC's early tours until Michael Browning took them to England. Steve was working a lot with The Little River Band. He tour managed them for a long time and eventually we would split up due to his commitments with them, particularly as their career began taking off overseas. Marquee had lots of work coming in, including gigs co-promoted with radio stations. We needed someone else in the office to take on some of the workload.

Kathy Howard, who was not long out of high school, was working for Tempo Records in Sydney, a distribution company that had helped with the launch of Kevin's solo debut album, *Celebration*, in March. She did such a good job on the publicity for that album that I offered her a job at Marquee. It was one of the best career moves I ever made.

Kathy and I got on really well from the beginning. Something clicked. We were both driven people, although she was the opposite of me in that she shied away from the excesses of the rock 'n' roll lifestyle, a plus as far as the business was concerned. By then, we had moved into another office, in the Man building in Alfred Street, North Sydney. Peter was in the same building. It was a steep learning curve for Kathy initially. Aside from looking after all the paperwork to do with Marquee, she had to be in regular contact with agents, radio stations, venue operators, record companies and a whole lot more. She was also handling some of the work for the Paul Dainty tours I was doing as tour director, which were getting more frequent and larger in scale. The first one she had to work on was ABBA, which was bigger than Ben Hur and with more drama.

Some of the local tours Marquee did, such as with Marcia Hines and Jon English, were enormous. The touring circuit had really opened up across Australia and you could spend months on the road if you wanted to do that. Between any two cities there were lots of towns with venues opening their doors to rock concerts. You could easily have a hundred dates on a tour itinerary. This style of touring was strongly pioneered by Roger Davies and Sherbet, who had become a huge success.

When it came to putting on a show, we did everything at Marquee. We booked the venues, did the marketing, put out the handbills, the posters, put a crew on the road. We were doing a lot and through that I was getting better at my job. Kathy's background in PR was a great help. She knew how to work the press, radio, TV. She was young but she was smart. We made a good team, which is what we were essentially for about eight or nine years.

I was starting to get my head around the business side of things with Marquee and with my management commitments. I still flew by the seat of my pants to a certain extent, but I took more of an interest in the fine print of touring, recording and publishing contracts, the small details in a tour budget, the money an artist could make from touring just from registering with APRA, the Australasian Performing Right Association. I learned that particular lesson from Richard Clapton when I began managing him in 1976. He received substantial cheques from APRA, which (among other practices on behalf of songwriters) paid out royalties based on how often and to how many people your material was performed on a tour or on radio. I was always learning, I suppose, although I didn't see it that way. I was just hungry for the life I was living; most of it anyway.

My son Nicholas was born on 7 April 1977. It was a happy occasion. I was delighted to have a son, of course. I felt that Nick's arrival could save my marriage, but it wasn't to be. It got very messy. Lilo and I were fighting a lot over nothing. A few months after Nick was born I moved out. Then I asked Margaret to move to Sydney with me, which was a huge mistake.

In the midst of setting up our move, in September, I had to go on the road with 10cc for Dainty. When the tour rolled into Melbourne, I was staying at the Hilton. Margaret came to see me. She told me she was going back to her husband.

I was numb, destroyed. I locked myself in my hotel room for three days and didn't get out of bed. The 10cc tour moved on without me. I started sending letters to Margaret from the hotel, to no avail. Somehow, probably through Margaret, word got out to one of the members of Stars, guitarist Mal Eastick, about what had happened and he called Gudinski. Michael turned up at the hotel, made me let him in, then read me the riot act; he told me to wake up to myself and pulled me out of there.

I went back to Sydney a few weeks later with my tail between my legs and apologised to Lilo and begged her to take me back. We got back together and stayed together until 1983. I have maintained a good relationship with her since we divorced and I have a wonderful relationship with Nick, even although I wasn't there for him as much as I should have been when he was growing up. That could be said of my other two children as well, with whom I also have great relationships, but I'll come to them later.

It was terrible what I did to Nick and Lilo. Nick hated me for it when he was old enough to understand. Although we have a loving relationship now, whenever we have a blue that subject usually comes up. I was very good at destroying relationships. More of that was to come.

6

California There We Went

My management of Aussie rock legend Richard Clapton began on the evening of my first son Nicholas's birth and came to an abrupt halt two and a half years later on the roof of the Sheraton Marquee Hotel in Potts Point, Sydney, from which my disgruntled client was about to jump. I like to think that I wasn't totally responsible for this drastic course of action on his part, but it would be fair to say that over those two and a half years I made a number of decisions that contributed to his state of unease.

Just before I went to hospital to be with Lilo for the birth, Richard was at our house in Blues Point Road, where I was trying to convince him that I should be his manager. Chris Murphy, head of the Solo Premier agency in Sydney, was looking after him then, but was eager for someone to take over. I genuinely believed I could do a good job of taking Richard to the next, international stage of his career. He agreed.

This was just a few months before the release of *Goodbye Tiger*, Clapton's most critically acclaimed and commercially successful album to that point and one that remains among his best. By then, he had enjoyed chart success with the album and single *Girls on the Avenue* and the single 'Capricorn Dancer', but there was an even stronger vibe about *Goodbye Tiger*. It was released in August 1977 and went top five in November. It was the album that combined perfectly Richard's early folk troubadour songwriting with edgier pop/rock dynamics. 'Deep Water' from the album, one of his landmark songs, also made the charts. If ever he was going to have a chance at making it overseas, this was the time.

Kevin Borich's album *Celebration* had also done incredibly well locally that year and he too was keen to extend his popularity as far as Britain and America. So in May 1978 the three of us headed to Los Angeles to set up camp there. They were going to write and record new music. I was going to spruik them to every agent, promoter and record company executive in town.

This meant deserting the family home once again, leaving Lilo to look after the baby. It wasn't the best move for our marriage, but for numerous personal and professional reasons I thought it was what I should do. Part of me wanted to get away from the mess I had made at home. I wanted to get lost in work and I wanted to break new ground for myself and for Richard and Kevin in America. I came back regularly to work for Dainty and to see the family.

I first heard Richard, or Ralph as he is known to his friends, when he was a young pup, doing his first gig outside of the

Sydney folk circuit, at Sunbury 72. He was one of the acts Sunrise had on the Sunbury bill, although few people knew who he was at the time. I met him for the first time when he came into the Sunrise office a few days later to collect his fee. He thought I had paid him less than the amount he was due, but he didn't make much of a fuss about it, so it went no further.

Next time we saw each other was when he did a solo slot supporting Billy Thorpe on a country tour in the mid-70s. It wasn't a perfect match. Billy's aggressive stage presence was in sharp contrast to Ralph's mild-mannered, almost timorous, approach to performing. When we began working together, I realised he was a rather insecure person. It would take a while to convince him to do things, or for him to make a decision on something.

One night towards the end of 1977, with *Goodbye Tiger* in the charts, I got the opportunity I'd been waiting for to try and get Richard to be more assertive on stage. He was playing at the Bondi Lifesaver. There were 2000 people in the room. Some drunken hoon down the front was giving him a hard time. I was standing at the side of the stage drinking a bottle of Courvoisier, one of the bottles left over from the Fleetwood Mac tour I'd done a few weeks earlier. In between songs, Richard kept coming over towards me, gesturing as if to ask what he should do about the idiot in the audience who wouldn't shut up.

This was the road I had been down a few years earlier with Country Radio when singer Greg Quill got hit with a beer can at Sunbury. Gradually I was becoming the go-to guy for sensitive singer–songwriters with crowd issues.

Each time Richard came over, he'd take a swig of the

Courvoisier. The moron kept heckling while Richard was doing his nice introductions in his gently spoken manner: 'Thank you. I'd like to do a song for you now that I wrote about some friends of mine,' he'd whisper, and so on. It was very folky. The next time the hoon mouthed off, Richard looked at me again for guidance. 'Tell him he's a fucking prick and to get fucked!' I kept shouting that at him, over and over. By the next outburst from the floor, the Courvoisier had seeped through to Richard's brain. Much to my amazement, 'Hey! Fuck you, arsehole!' were the next words to come out of his mouth. The crowd was totally onside after that and the idiot was put in his place. That was a life-changing moment for Richard, he told me later, one of the better ones in which I had a hand.

By the time *Goodbye Tiger* was a hit at home, Richard already had a following in parts of Europe, particularly Germany. He spent a lot of time in Berlin when he wasn't on the road. It became his second home for a while. Early in 1978, he flew from there to London, where I had set up a meeting for him with Island Records. They wanted to sign him. A deal was in place, but there were problems.

Just after *Goodbye Tiger*'s release, I had renegotiated Richard's recording contract with Festival Records in Australia. His relationship with them was fairly volatile. Nevertheless, he was signed to a new worldwide, three-album deal. The difficulty for us was that in those days the chances of a record company in Australia getting another one overseas interested in its product was virtually nil. Acts from here were up against the volumes of new releases coming in from everywhere else in the world onto executives' desks in London, New York and Los Angeles. Worldwide didn't really mean worldwide at all.

Perhaps I shouldn't have committed Richard to that kind of worldwide deal, but I figured that, if there was money in it for Festival, some kind of agreement could still be made overseas, which is why the Island opportunity came about; indeed, several companies in England had expressed an interest in *Goodbye Tiger*. If Festival would agree to license the album and to take a percentage of the overseas profits, everyone would be a winner.

Richard arrived in London and met up with Island's head of artists and repertoire, Phil Cooper, but the meeting did not go well. While they were standing in the street outside Island's office, the label's owner, Chris Blackwell, rolled up across the road in his Aston Martin, beckoned Cooper over to talk to him, whereupon they had a heated argument and Blackwell sped off. An hour later, in a nearby pub, Cooper told Richard the deal was off. Festival wanted too much of a cut — points as they're known in the trade — so Blackwell pulled out of the deal. That was the first of several disappointments for Richard and myself over the next eighteen months.

Los Angeles began with lots of promise. It was exciting to be based somewhere new. Richard, along with his singer girlfriend Diane McLennan and bass player Michael Hegerty, set up in a house in Van Nuys in the Valley, a nice little cottage. Kevin Borich, bass player Paul Christie, drummer John Annas, sound man Gerry Georgettis, stage manager Mark O'Donell and I ended up in a house in Agoura, which was almost as far out of LA as you could get before you hit the tumbleweeds. It was a reasonable, three-bedroomed house with a swimming pool. We bought a car, which, among other things, meant I could drive into town to have meetings with record company executives and agents. It also made it easier to pick up regular supplies of pot from our Mexican supplier in the Valley.

Early on in LA, I met a guy called Merv Goldstein, who booked acts for different promoters and who knew the scene really well. I liked Merv a lot. He had a few different things going on, not all of them in music. He had a deal as an on-the-ground producer for Barbara Walters, the TV journalist and interviewer. He also had a great deal going with the Beverly Wilshire Hotel, one of the hip places to stay and to do business in LA, so now and again I'd stay there.

From the beginning, I knew it was going to be difficult getting Richard and Kevin recording or touring deals. Just getting a foot in the door with record companies and agents was hard, but I figured that, to have any chance at all, we had to be there. I'd just have to chip away at it. To try and stimulate some interest, Merv and I formed a company, Oz Rock International Incorporated, which was registered and set up with the idea of introducing and developing Australian talent in the US. Just quite how we were going to go about it was yet to be determined, but to begin with it was about managing Richard and Kevin.

Merv was a great ally and a good operator. Sometimes the last dollar in his pocket would go towards buying dinner. We had no real money coming in, other than the occasional royalty cheque from back home. Life was made easier by the fact that I still had my Dainty commitments, so every month or two I was flying back to Australia to do a tour. Dainty was paying me $2000 a week plus expenses, which was great money then. Whatever I earned from doing those tours helped to keep us all afloat in LA when there was no other money coming in.

My view was that everything I made had to go back into the business in some way. It would pay off in the long term, I thought.

Most of us, in our household and Richard's, found LA intimidating in the beginning. Australians were something of a curiosity, so our accents stuck out quite dramatically. Some of us were too scared to open our mouths when we went to the supermarket or had a meeting. Our main problem, however, was that we couldn't get anyone interested in what we were selling.

We got an early break with Richard. One of his biggest fans at home was Double J presenter George Wayne, who had worked at radio station K-Rock in LA and who had many friends in the industry there. He had sent a copy of *Goodbye Tiger* to some of them, including a few people at Elektra/Asylum. Peter Burke, a publisher who befriended us and who did his best to help us, also knew people there, as did Merv, so from all of that, particularly some connection one of them had to singer–songwriter Jackson Browne, one of the biggest acts on the label, we scored some studio time from Elektra/Asylum.

Aussie singer–songwriter Brian Cadd, formerly of The Groop and Axiom, had been based in Los Angeles for four years by then, working mainly as a songwriter for other artists. We asked Brian to produce some demos and through his contacts we lined up A-grade session players to play on the songs, including bass player Reggie McBride, Billy Joel's guitarist Richie Zito, drummer Mike Huey and a couple of great female backing singers. The six tracks, among them 'Thorn in the Saddle', 'Steppin' Across the Line' and 'When the Heat's Off', sounded fantastic. Everyone worked really hard to get them sounding perfect.

We had another ally in Carol Thompson, who had just been newly promoted to the A&R department at Elektra/Asylum. She befriended Richard. He had carte blanche to walk into the record company office and hang out. The signs were good that we could secure a recording contract, but time flew past and nothing happened. As is often the case in the music industry, a personnel shake-up at the company took Thompson out of the picture and, after months of optimism and free coffee, we were back on the street.

Richard, not surprisingly, was extremely upset at this development, not least because he had gone through a similar trauma in London only months before. He remembered that Alan Hely, the head of Festival Records in Sydney, had boasted to us many times that he was on buddy terms with the chairman of Elektra/Asylum, Joe Smith. Richard urged me to call Hely and make him do something to rekindle our relationship with the label. Hely didn't return the calls. Richard wanted to fly home and confront him personally. He was very angry, but I doubt that there would have been anything Hely could have done to remedy the situation.

Kevin was writing some great songs, one called 'New City Lights'. Peter Burke, who loved Richard and Kevin, got this song covered by an American singer–songwriter, Ian Lloyd, on his album, which helped bring in some money for Kevin.

I was making slow progress, trying to build an American profile for my two artists. I asked a favour of AC/DC's manager Michael Browning, when they were playing in town, and got Kevin the support spot. Then Merv put us in touch with a heavy rock agency in Detroit that had Ted Nugent and Bob Seger, among others, on their books. We went there and had a meeting with them. They took on Kevin and set up a tour for him. It was something.

From the Valley, we got a keyboards player called Tim Schafer, who played in American singer Gary Wright's band. Kevin Borich Express began rehearsals. They played one great gig in Seattle and then spent weeks on the road travelling thousands of miles playing in really terrible places. Kevin was pretty unhappy by the end of it. Frustration was beginning to set in at both camps. It was tough.

I had a great relationship with Ross Barlow, who was the head of Polygram Australia. We had become friends after a big night out in LA. Kevin and I figured we needed $30,000 to do a new Kevin Borich Express album. When I was back in Australia for a Dainty tour, I went to see Barlow and convinced him to give me some money so Kevin could record.

When I got back to LA, we found two producers, Ross Salomone and Jim Taylor. Taylor had worked with a few name acts in the States and had a deal with Cherokee Studios on Fairfax Avenue in Hollywood, one of the top LA studios. The band for the album was the same one that had just been around the fleapits of America.

The recording sessions went well. Rod Stewart was recording there in another studio. I knew some of the roadies who were around from Australian tours they had done with various acts. It was a good vibe. *No Turning Back* was a good record. The single of the same name was released in November 1978 in Australia and the album a few months later.

By the time the single was released, Kevin had had enough of the US and returned home in December 1978. The album was released on Mercury, a subsidiary of Polygram, and the band went on the road to promote it. Tim Schafer was with them, but didn't stay long and the Kevin Borich Express became a trio for the remainder of the tour. There were more line-up changes over the next couple of years.

I continued to manage Kevin and in 1979 we switched our attention from America to the UK. By then, the punk explosion in London had changed the musical landscape completely and there wasn't much room on it for a hot guitar player singing blues-based rock. We parted professionally in 1981.

Richard was another matter. As the months rolled by, he got increasingly disillusioned with America. He had left home a pop star and been plunged into obscurity in a new, strange environment. That began to take a toll on our relationship, as did cocaine. If our house was pot paradise, his was toot central.

To keep interest high at home and to create more cash flow, we used two of the tracks from the demo sessions and put together a kind of Richard Clapton greatest hits package album called *Past Hits and Previews*, which was released in November 1978. It sold well, but Richard was beginning to feel compromised by the inactivity he had to endure in LA. Tension had built up already between us. I remember him being upset when I presented him with the cover artwork for *Past Hits and Previews*. We started arguing and I punched the wall.

It was a frustrating period for both of us. I was failing. Americans didn't want to know about Australians. The whole thing was starting to fall apart. Merv lost interest. He didn't want to pour any more money into a project that offered no return.

Richard stayed on in LA in 1979 and recorded the *Hearts on a Nightline* album with producer Dallas Smith. Through Zev

Eizik, I set up a tour in Australia for him to promote the album, starting at the Sydney Opera House. That tour was when our fractious relationship reached the point of no return.

Richard had a few hot musos with him from LA on that trip. One of them was sax player Raphael Ravenscroft, who was much in demand after playing the distinctive sax parts on Gerry Rafferty's monster hit 'Baker Street'. He had some problems on tour, though, and had to be sent home. From there, the tour developed into a disaster. We kept adding dates because the costs of doing it were so high, but the longer it got the more exasperated Richard became. He felt I was touring him into the ground. He'd had enough. He described the tour as a travelling loony bin and he wasn't far wrong.

There were other issues. Richard was resentful of the fact that almost all of his efforts in moving to America had come to nothing. I think he also felt he had been manipulated by me into doing it. He had other problems with my style of management. I played my cards too close to my chest and I wasn't the best at keeping tabs on finances, in his opinion.

From my perspective, I thought it was important, to any manager of any act, for the artist not to listen to too many opinions from outside. There were too many people in Richard's ear. I think musicians took advantage of him as well, over money. Richard was very easygoing in that respect. That didn't stop him from trying to sue me, mind you, although eventually he realised he didn't have the money to go through with it.

Crunch time came on the roof of the Sheraton Marquee Hotel in Potts Point, late in 1979. Richard was indeed threatening to throw himself off, although I didn't believe for one minute that he was serious. He was clearly distressed about a number of things, including our working relationship. We were finished. We had destroyed our friendship.

While the two of us were up there having our showdown, I called Peter Rix. I figured he might be the person who could help Richard to calm down. I also thought that he could be the one to take over Richard's affairs. Peter was doing incredibly well with Marcia at the time. 'I've been on the roof of the Sheraton Marquee for the past three hours trying to convince Richard not to jump off,' I told him. 'Can you get over here? And can you take over managing him? You're the only person I know who won't give a fuck if he does jump. I can't take it anymore.'

It was pretty late at night by then, but, as the situation demanded, Peter got in his car and drove over. He had only been on the roof for a minute or so when he screamed at Richard: 'Dick, jump for fuck's sake. Get it over with.'

He wasn't going to jump. Peter knew that. Richard was depressed, but he wasn't suicidal.

Peter took over Richard's management from that night, overseeing the release of the follow-up to *Hearts on the Nightline*, *Dark Spaces*, which marked the end of his three-album commitment to Festival. Richard dedicated that album to the memory of guitarist Andy Durant (from the Stars), who had joined his band only months before his death from cancer.

Peter managing Richard wasn't a match made in heaven either and they parted soon after *Dark Spaces* was released. A succession of managers followed in his wake, as did another album, *The Great Escape*, in 1982, released through Warner Brothers.

Despite our acrimonious split, I felt I still had unfinished business with Richard and in 1983, while he was being managed by John Blanchfield, I started pursuing him again, turning up at gigs and trying to persuade him that I could do better things for him second time around. He agreed, again, and I negotiated a new recording contract for him with Mushroom Records that resulted in the album *Solidarity* in 1984. Working with Gudinski wasn't the best business decision he ever made. Gudinski was more interested in his new signing – Jimmy Barnes – than he was in Richard.

By 1984, I had tired of management altogether, after years of banging away at local and overseas record companies with a number of acts. Richard and I parted again. Our second business relationship didn't last as long as the first one, but we remained friends, as we do to this day.

Thank God Peter got it right up on the roof.

7

The Show Really Must Go On

I owe Paul Dainty a great deal for being in the position I am in now, even if, at various times over the past thirty-five years, I have wished him harm. I've mellowed with age. Dainty taught me some important lessons about the promoter's gig when I was working for him in the second half of the 70s, lessons that I embraced and enforced for the rest of my career.

First among them was something I learned from the early gigs I did with him working with overseas artists. His attitude was that you should treat those acts impeccably from the moment they got off the plane until they left the country. It might seem obvious, but it's not always easy to put into practice when you're dealing with a large entourage and artists' egos. Nevertheless, I have done my best to make visitors feel at home. It has paid off in building long-term relationships with bands, singers, managers and agents. I took Dainty's advice on those first tours working as tour manager with Status Quo, Leo Sayer and Wishbone Ash and I have applied it to every tour I have done since then.

It's strange now to think that our working relationship was for only seven years; stranger still to acknowledge that it was thirty years ago when we went our separate ways, not long after Dainty threw a bottle of red wine at me in a restaurant in Christchurch. I hardly talked to him after that. Nevertheless, that journey I had with him, from 1974 to 1980, was an incredible learning experience and one that I will never forget.

Dainty is a significant player in the Australian music industry and has been so for longer than just about anyone else. He came here in the early 70s as an employee of an English agency which brought Roy Orbison to Australia. Dainty was English, but he moved to Australia because he could see an opportunity for someone who was prepared to bring big-name overseas rock acts down under. Few people were doing it. In the 60s, Lee Gordon had done it with the early package tours of American rock 'n' rollers. Sydney entrepreneur Kenn Brodziak was the first to bring out British acts such as Cliff Richard and the Shadows, Lonnie Donegan and The Dave Clark Five. I saw some of the acts he toured in Melbourne, such as Manfred Mann and The Seekers. He'll be remembered most of all as the man who brought The Beatles to Australia. Harry M Miller was another early player, bringing The Rolling Stones here for their first two tours, but in the early 70s there was room for someone who could deliver top-drawer touring American and British acts into Australia.

After a spell of moving back and forth between Australia and London, Dainty rented an office from Brodziak and set about creating the Paul Dainty Corporation. By the time I became involved with him he had toured some of the biggest names in rock and pop, including Cat Stevens, The Bee Gees, The Jackson Five and The Rolling Stones. I met him at a Black Sabbath/Status Quo concert at Memorial Drive in Adelaide in November 1974, which was part of an event called 'British Rock 'n' Roll Month'. I was working for him and Status Quo on that tour. He was a very reserved kind of guy, although I was pretty shy too in my own way. We got on well and from then on, whenever he had two or three tours on at the same time, I would get a tour.

Ironically, it was the man who introduced me to Dainty, Ron Blackmore, who tried to cut me out of the Dainty Corporation several years later, all because of Leo Sayer. Blackmore was a bit of a legend in rock 'n' roll circles by the time he became Dainty's right-hand man in the early 70s. I had known him for years. He had been a muso first, then ran dances in Melbourne in the late 50s and early 60s. He was a real doer. And he loved to talk. He could tell stories for hours. He used to bring a lot of acts to Tasmania in the 60s and I would go to the gigs to see the bands, but also to watch how he operated.

Ron was Dainty's man on the ground, the original tour manager/tour promoter when Dainty was still flitting between the UK and Australia. He had lots of experience and everyone looked up to him. He was the one who rang me and offered me the Status Quo tour that included the one-off show with Black Sabbath (the rest of the dates on the *Sabbath Bloody Sabbath* tour were with AC/DC in support).

I've known Leo Sayer for thirty-five years. I helped launch his career in Australia and we have remained friends since then. He sang at my sixtieth birthday party in Phuket. That first meeting, when he toured here in 1975, was significant for a number of reasons. It was the first time I had taken an idea to Dainty and convinced him he should tour someone. It was the first time I had taken a financial interest, other than my tour director fee, in one of Dainty's projects. Philip Jacobsen and I took a percentage stake in the tour. I did that because I was so confident that the tour would be massive.

Dainty agreed to do the tour. In late 1974 we did a huge poster campaign around the country, long before tickets went on sale, with just the image of Sayer's face in his Pierrot guise, the one that had helped launch his career internationally with the song 'The Show Must Go On' a year earlier. It went to No. 7 in the Australian charts and he had another Australian hit in 1974 with 'Long Tall Glasses (I Can Dance)'. The time was right for him to tour Australia.

The tour, in May and June 1975, exploded. It was one of the biggest tours of the year.

Blackmore wasn't happy, I think because this punk Chugg, whom he and Dainty had brought in as a tour manager, was running the biggest tour of the year. He had tried in vain to get me out – so that he could do the gig himself – before Sayer got to Australia. He was telling Dainty I couldn't handle such a big tour and that he should be doing it. It came to a head when we were all sitting on the top floor of the Southern Cross Hotel in Melbourne the night before Sayer arrived. I was emotionally involved in that tour. I had helped set it up with Festival Records. I did everything. It was my tour.

Blackmore was belittling me, putting me down in front of the others. I was shocked and embarrassed. We were sitting with Judy Nichols, the publicist for the tour, and a girl from the office called Sally. At midnight I was sitting on the couch by the lift and I was upset and they were comforting me because I was distraught at what was happening. I was a wreck. I ended up doing the tour, although I suspect I didn't make as much money out of it as I should have.

Blackmore left Dainty Corporation a year later, after we had done a Skyhooks national tour together. He set up his own company, Artists Concert Tours, using the highly respected Clair Brothers PA system that Dainty had acquired and used for all of his big tours. He died in the late 90s.

Ron's departure was a turning point for me. It placed me at the top of Dainty's list of reliable tour managers and from then on I took on all of the big jobs. Over the next four years I worked with some great acts, including Linda Ronstadt, David Bowie and Fleetwood Mac. We had a team in place that did all of those tours. My friend Eric Robinson's Jands company did all of the production. Sydney publicist Patti Mostyn did the PR. I was tour director. In all, there were about a dozen people who worked together, very efficiently, for the rest of the 70s, although a couple of the biggest tours were tests of patience and endurance.

I missed the chaos that engulfed Australian cities when The Beatles came to play in 1964, but I got an idea of what it must have been like thirteen years later, when I was Dainty's tour director for ABBA. The scale of ABBA-mania was more than The Fab Four enjoyed, or rather endured. No tour I had done up to that point prepared me for the two weeks of madness with Bjorn, Benny, Agnetha and Frida.

ABBA arrived on 27 February 1977. They had been in Australia a year before on a promotional trip, so anticipation of a concert tour had been building since then. They were enormous here, thanks to the promo trip and the way 'Countdown' had championed them in the two years it had been on the air. They were a staple on the show, not least due to Molly, who was one of their biggest fans.

I wasn't sure what to expect of them or the tour. I'd done a few large festivals by then with big-name acts, but a whole tour, with screaming fans of all ages waiting around every corner, was a new experience. It was by far the biggest tour, in terms of audience numbers and the level of production, I had been involved in. There were more than a hundred people on the road for dates in Sydney, Melbourne, Adelaide and Perth, thirteen shows in all. Fans followed us everywhere, plus a film crew shooting scenes for *Abba the Movie* accompanied the entourage for the entire trip.

I was stressed before the tour started, in Sydney. When the doors of the plane opened and they marched out in their white outfits, it was like a football team arriving. Hundreds of fans had been waiting for hours for the plane to land, but to avoid a frenzy we arranged to be diverted through a private section of the airport to waiting cars.

It took about a week to erect the site at Sydney Showground, mostly in torrential rain and strong winds, which didn't let up for the first night performance. The weather made rehearsals and sound checking extremely difficult. There was a heavy press schedule as well. It seemed every journalist and photographer and TV crew wanted a bit of ABBA. The morning after they arrived, we held a media call at the Sebel Townhouse, the famous rock 'n' roll hotel in Kings Cross where everyone was staying, but that wasn't enough for the eager media. They wanted to keep tabs on ABBA twenty-four hours a day. Everybody wanted a piece of them. A lot of talk was about how the first night show might have to be cancelled. I had my fingers crossed.

We had 25,000 people standing getting soaked while we counted down the minutes backstage wondering if we should go ahead with that first show. There was a lot to worry about. We had thirty-four musicians on stage, including a twelve-piece band and an Australian seventeen-piece orchestra that rose out of a revolving hydraulic platform. The four stars were nervous about going on in the conditions and it was a last-minute decision to proceed.

If you were there, or if you've seen *Abba the Movie*, you'll know just what a shocker of a night it was. It poured down and the stage got soaked. Water and electricity combined are a promoter's nightmare. We had acquired a couple of hundred towels from the Sebel. The crew, myself included, spent half of the performance mopping up water from the floor to avert disaster, or at least to avoid broken ankles. That didn't stop Frida from falling over during 'Waterloo' and making the papers next day sprawled on all fours. That and Agnetha's bum grabbed most of the headlines. The show, however, was a success and the crowd didn't seem to mind the rain. By the end of it, I was a wreck — and I wasn't the only one.

That's one of the reasons the after-party at the Sebel went off in the way it did that night. Everyone had been working so hard in the lead-up to that first show, not knowing if it was going to happen, that when it was all over something had to give. The party started in the basement ballroom of the hotel straight after the show. ABBA weren't there, but a lot of the other musicians were, along with the crew and various guests. It was a drunken affair, although that wasn't the only indulgence. I got to bed at around 4 am. The show next day was at the Showground as well, so I didn't have to worry too much about being on the move early, or so I thought.

At 7 am I got a call from one of the production people telling me in a panicky voice to get straight out to the venue. I could hardly speak and I didn't really know where I was, but what I was confronted with out at the Showground soon woke me up. I was fiercely hung over, with the sun burning into my eyes.

Among the technology Abba had brought with them from Europe was a large inflatable roof. In terms of staging, it was quite a revelation. At 6.30 am that day, a security guy had noticed that the roof had a huge dip in it and was hanging just above the stage. It was full of water, rain that had built up during the night as we were enjoying the afterparty. The sag was so severe that it was in danger of collapsing, so the security guy had let the air out of the roof so that it didn't sink the whole structure and everything underneath it.

I felt so ill standing there, looking at thousands of chairs around the stage floating in about three feet of water, but I was relieved as well. If it hadn't been for that security bloke's quick thinking, we could have lost the whole tour.

Then it was on to Melbourne. Anticipating how big the crowds would be there, since their performances were also part of the hugely popular Moomba Festival that weekend, we had asked the group if they would take part in a parade through the city on the Saturday they arrived. They weren't keen on the idea and in retrospect, given the kind of hysterical attention they received in Melbourne, it was probably for the best. We also turned down a request for a meeting in Canberra with Malcolm Fraser, although that had more to do with the strict schedule than the prospect of them being mobbed by the prime minister and his staff. Instead, Fraser brought his family to one of the Melbourne gigs and was introduced to them backstage. We didn't do the parade, but we reached a compromise. There was a mayoral reception at Melbourne Town Hall as soon as we arrived in the city. Thousands of fans gathered outside on Swanston Street just to get a glimpse of them on the balcony after the ceremony.

My main concern was getting them from their hotel, the Old Melbourne, to the show at Sidney Myer Music Bowl, with a minimum of fuss. I was mulling over that problem in my hotel room, aided by a large joint, when I got a message to say that the deputy commissioner of police was in the lobby and wanted to discuss with me just how ABBA would get from point A to point B for the evening performance. I said I'd be right down.

Smoking a joint was as common to me in those days as smoking a cigarette, so I didn't think anything of going down there with one in my hand. The band and crew were assembling in the lobby to go to the show when I got there. They really were like the Swedish soccer team, with their doctors and masseuses in tow.

I walked into the courtyard where the deputy commissioner and his offsider were waiting for me. I shook his hand and introduced myself. He said the city was gridlocked. We began discussing which route the band and crew should take to get to the show and what to do if we had problems. All the while, I was smoking the joint and inadvertently blowing the smoke in their faces. It seemed they had no idea. We finished talking and I stamped the joint out on the ground. As I walked back through the foyer, all the crew, who had been watching developments, started cheering and clapping. 'Gee, they like you,' was the deputy police commissioner's parting comment. An hour later, he may have been wondering why he felt so floaty.

The Melbourne shows went off without incident. The Myer Music Bowl held about 14,000, but there were just as many people assembled in the nearby Kings Domain to hear the performances. It was the same for the one show in Adelaide, at the West Lakes Football Stadium, with thousands of extra fans listening in the car park.

Finally, we did five concerts in Perth at the Entertainment Centre and the first one was subject to a bomb scare; another great opportunity for me to have a chat with a police commissioner. He told me we had to evacuate the hall. I had to walk onstage while ABBA were mid-song and whisper into Benny's ear for him to tell everyone to leave the stage. Then I had to ask the crowd, without telling them why, to leave the room in an orderly fashion, which they did in just a few minutes. After a police search of the building, the show went on as normal. ABBA flew back to Sweden the day after their final show.

When the tour was over, I went back to Sydney, back to work in the office and back to the imminent arrival of my first child.

The next six months were full of drama, including Nick's birth, my decision to leave home, my failed affair and my return to Lilo. Compared to all of that, going on tour with a bunch of cokeheads called Fleetwood Mac in November didn't seem so demanding, although it had its moments.

American promoter Bill Graham has had a powerful influence on me in my career, so I was pleased to learn that Dainty was bringing him out to compere the *Rockarena* shows that featured Fleetwood Mac, Santana, Little River Band and Kevin Borich Express. Dainty had modelled the shows, outdoor affairs, on the Day on the Green shows Graham had staged in America. Graham was also Santana's manager.

During the first show, again at Sydney Showground, a fight broke out at the front of the stage. It was pretty vicious, with about twenty guys all going for it. Bill decided to try and calm the situation by walking out and saying something like: 'Hey, guys, cut this out, you know? We're here to rock 'n' roll.' Fists kept flying. I grabbed the microphone. 'You fucking arseholes, stop that now or I'm coming down there with security and you'll all go out the door. How dare you do this to one of the greatest promoters of all time? I'm going to come down there and rip your heads off.' I didn't have much effect either, but then the police arrived and formed a big circle with the security people and threw out all of the troublemakers.

I came off stage and Bill walked over to me. 'Chuggi,' he said. 'I think you should compere the rest of the tour.' As if I needed any encouragement.

Events conspired to end my run with Dainty at the end of the decade. I was in London for six months in 1979 with Kevin Borich. One night he asked me to go and see a band he liked at the Lyceum. They were called The Police. That night was a tipping point for me. I was excited already by all of the punk and new wave music coming out of London and New York; bands like The Clash, The Ramones, Talking Heads and The Stranglers. It was a great time for new music. When I came back to Australia I tried to convince Dainty that The Police and all of those other acts were the ones we should be bringing over. He didn't see it and was particularly dismissive of The Police.

By then, however, I had another connection to Gudinski, having become a partner in the Harbour Agency, which became the Sydney sister agency to Premier in Melbourne. We talked about forming a touring company as well. Marquee Attractions was floundering by then and I was looking for a new source of income. Those new wave bands looked like the perfect incentive to set up a new touring partnership, one that was willing to take on The Police and anyone like them. Frontier Touring was born.

In March 1980, I was Dainty's tour director for Fleetwood Mac's return visit to Australia and New Zealand, even though I was now a director of Frontier Touring, potentially Dainty's competition. The tour was more shambolic than the *Rockarena* one had been three years earlier. Drug abuse was starting to take its toll on the band. They weren't performing as well as they could. They were fighting. The tension was unbearable. It wasn't fun to be around. Crowds were down.

Simultaneously, Frontier had The Police on the road with their *Regatta de Blanc* tour, which went through the roof. It started in Christchurch, but Sting got sick and the remaining dates had to be reshuffled while he recovered. I was in Christchurch with Fleetwood Mac. After the show, I was in a restaurant with Dainty and some of the crew. Dainty obviously wasn't happy that I was in effect now a rival promoter, so my days as a tour director for him were numbered.

The Police by then had become huge in America, so Fleetwood Mac's crew, including their tour director John Courage, were pretty impressed that I was touring them and of course loved reminding Dainty of that fact throughout the night. That's when the wine came flying at me and my relationship with Dainty was over. As ever, when that adventure ended, another one began.

8

Unguarded Moments

The Farewell to Double J concert at Parramatta Park, New South Wales, in January 1981 was a salute to a much-loved, pioneering radio station, but it was a reflection also of the changes that were sweeping through the Australian music industry. The new decade shepherded in new ideas as well as the new technology of FM radio, which saw Double J turn into 2JJJ on 1 August 1980, introduced Fox FM in Melbourne on the same day and brought 2MMM in Sydney into the world a day later.

I staged that concert at Parramatta. It was a wonderful gig, headlined by Midnight Oil, but the show is significant for me because it was there I met my future wife, when I picked her up and threw her off the stage.

The 80s was party city. It was the decade of excess and

innovation, when so many doors opened and success knew no bounds. Every day was an adventure, although some of those adventures got me into deep water. I was still living for the moment back then.

At the start of the 80s, I was a partner in the Premier/Harbour agencies. I was also a director of the Frontier Touring Company, which would be my second home for the next twenty years. I was still committed to being a manager as well, despite – or perhaps because of – my failure to launch Stevie, Kevin or Richard overseas.

The idea of starting Frontier flowered at a Premier directors' meeting in Melbourne, not long after I had come back from seeing The Police and several other new wave bands in London in 1979. Those were the bands I thought we should be bringing to Australia. I saw it as a great opportunity for me to build the foundations of something big and lasting in the industry. Dainty wasn't interested.

Gudinski didn't need much convincing. He had just come back from a trip to London and New York, where he'd had a meeting with Ian Copeland, brother of The Police's drummer, Stewart Copeland. Ian had founded the talent agency Frontier Booking International (FBI) in New York and was in the process of building a roster of acts, such as Squeeze, The Police and many of the new wave acts coming out of Britain and the US that I saw as having touring potential in Australia. He also helped bands such as Split Enz and Hoodoo Gurus to break into the US. Ian was to become a great ally of Frontier throughout the 80s and 90s. It helped my cause further that Gudinski's Mushroom Publishing had contracts with half of these new bands we wanted to bring over.

'We'll call it Frontier,' Gudinski said, and off we went. The company had nine partners at the beginning: myself, Gudinski, Philip Jacobsen, Frank Stivala, Ray Evans, Glenn Wheatley, Steve White, Sam Righi and Robbie Williams (not the singer). Righi had been a booker at Nucleus in Melbourne before he and Williams came to Sydney to run Harbour. Wheatley, who was managing Little River Band, was brought in because he promised us he could secure big-name acts from the US through LRB's success there. None materialised and Glenn eventually left. Before that, Steve sold his interest to go full-time working for LRB. I tried to convince him to stay as a partner. It seemed to me like a more secure future than LRB – and so it proved. He's still very much in the music business today, however, as manager of Lee Kernaghan and Leo Sayer.

Frontier wasn't – and still isn't – an equal partnership. Gudinski had a slightly bigger share than Philip and me. The others had lesser shares. The more hands-on you were, the bigger the share. The crux of it was that Gudinski did the deals; I put the acts on the road and Philip – the old man, as we called him – looked after the money side. It was an exciting beginning and no one had to worry about losing his investment because nobody put any money into it. We just started doing it.

The first tour, in January 1980, was by the English band Squeeze, although we had to call them UK Squeeze because there was an Aussie band called Squeeze at the time. UK Squeeze was a great band and the tour did well for us, as did the one that followed in February by The Police. Those tours sent out a message to the world (not an SOS) that we were the promoters to come to if you wanted to tour new wave acts in Australia. That message was underlined a year later through the good fortune of landing Gary Numan's first Aussie tour. Dainty had gone after him initially. That was probably about as left-field as he ever went in his choice of artists.

A couple of months before the tour was scheduled to start, Numan's English agent Steve Hedges contacted Frontier and asked us to take over the tour. We did and it was a huge success. The memory of young Gazza riding in the tour bus with his mum and dad and stopping at McDonald's at every opportunity will stay with me forever.

Steve's departure to LRB also spelled the end for Marquee Attractions. In its place came Michael Chugg Management, which was essentially Kathy Howard and me. The company logo was a wombat, with 'Kicking Arse Around the World' written underneath. We stayed in the office in the Man building, although not for long. By then Harbour had set up there as well, with Righi, Williams and booker Colleen Ironside. My office served as the Sydney branch of Frontier. It was a good time. I had a fairly loose approach to office etiquette — that's when I was there, which wasn't often — so there were always people coming and going, dropping in. It had the vibe, an expression that caught on around Frontier in the early days.

Kathy was the organisation behind the madness and chaos. She was under a lot of pressure, working long hours and running the office herself half the time, but she was extremely efficient and never complained, although my ears burned regularly when I was on the road.

It helped at the start of Frontier that I had already built a team of reliable road crew around me. I had done that by trial and error, but also by showing loyalty to those who put in the hard yards on the road. If you were brilliant at what you did, I was incredibly supportive, but if you fucked up you were out.

That's how it was. I had benchmarks, having done just about every crew job myself in the early days. If you didn't meet my standards you were out, but I gave people I trusted the freedom to put their stamp on things.

There were other landmark events in the industry as the 70s ended. Dirty Pool, the management company founded by John Woodruff, Ray Hearn and Rod Willis, changed the way the local live circuit operated by insisting that the bands they managed, such as Flowers, The Angels and Cold Chisel, were paid 90 per cent of the door takings at gigs rather than being paid a set fee by the agent. They did all the promotion and marketing themselves. It was a radical departure from the way touring had worked before. This had a financial impact on Premier, Harbour and every other agency in the country, but to be honest it was a fairer system. From that initiative, artists got what they deserved rather than what the agent or promoter thought they were worth.

In 1980, with the help of Righi, Ironside and local promoter Harry Della, I launched the giveaway gig guide *On the Street* in Sydney. It was little more than a two-page advertising sheet to help promote our shows, but it paved the way for the later tabloid magazine version of *On the Street* and for the street press we see around Australia today. We'd charge venues $10 for a 10-centimetres-square advertisement. Most of the covers were of our artists. Nine months later, publisher City Express bought it from us and turned it into a full-scale magazine. Years later the journalists from that magazine left and started their own after a financial dispute with the owners of *On the Street*. They called the new one *Drum Media*.

I'd suffered a few hard knocks in management, but I was by no means over it. I still believed there was a future for me as a manager if only I could make an act successful overseas. The next one to come along and excite me was fronted by a man who enjoyed spilling offal on the stage, setting fire to dolls, beating up an effigy of the prime minister and putting sticky tape on his nipples. His name was Ignatius Jones and he was the lead singer in what I first thought was the worst band in the world, Jimmy and the Boys.

They had been around for a few years in Sydney when I first heard about them. Sometime in 1979 John Tag, who managed Sydney band The Radiators, suggested I go to see them, so one afternoon I found myself in the upstairs room of the Rex Hotel in Kings Cross listening to them rehearse. Jones and his keyboards player mate Joylene Hairmouth (which I discovered wasn't his real name) had been to Cranbrook and Riverview respectively, two of Sydney's most expensive private schools. They were playing this very theatrical kind of electro-pop, a million miles from what I had been dealing with up until then. It seemed to me like a joke band, but they had a steady following, thanks to their outrageous and unpredictable stage show.

They really were awful at that rehearsal, yet something kept bringing me back for more and – after seeing how well they went down live a few times – I convinced them to take me on as manager. Around then, Philip Jacobsen and I became partners with a Melbourne record company executive John McDonald in a new label, Avenue Records. We had a publishing company as well. Kevin's albums *Celebration* and *Lonely*

One were released on Avenue, as were both Jimmy and the Boys albums – *Not Like Everybody Else* in 1980 and *Teddy Boys' Picnic* the following year. By then, they were one of the biggest bands in the country. I still didn't quite get it, but they were making good money and I quite enjoyed the fact that they were completely different from any other band I had come across in my career. They had moderate success with an early single, a camp version of The Kinks' 'I'm Not Like Everybody Else', and made the top ten in 1981 with a Tim Finn song, 'They Won't Let My Girlfriend Talk To Me'.

I knew from the beginning that Jimmy and the Boys wasn't a long-term proposition. It was too quirky. By January 1982, it was all over for them as a band, but Iggy reinvented himself, starring in the revamped Rocky Horror Show before launching a solo career. These days, he has a great reputation as a designer of entertainment events at sporting ceremonies. He was behind the opening ceremony of the Sydney 2000 Olympic Games, and close inspection of the opening of the Winter Olympics in Vancouver in 2010 would have revealed to a few old fans some relics from the Jimmy and the Boys stage set.

Moving from the ridiculous to the sublime, although no less weird in its own way, I took up the offer of managing The Church in 1981. I had worked with Chris Gilbey at Alberts during the Stevie Wright era; he was then head of ATV/Northern Songs publishing and was running the Parlophone record label. He had found The Church, produced their first album and got them deals through EMI/Parlophone in Australia, Capitol in the US and the independent label Carrère in Europe. He wanted me to take charge and I agreed to do it. That first album, *Of Skins and Heart*, had done well in Australia, partly on the strength of the great single 'The Unguarded Moment', which reached No. 22 in the charts. It was one of the first Australian albums to be released simultaneously in Australia, the US and Britain. I liked their songs and their image, a throwback to 60s psychedelia, with their paisley shirts and tight jeans. I could see potential for worldwide success.

The line-up was singer/bassist and chief songwriter Steve Kilbey, guitarists Peter Koppes and Marty Wilson-Piper and drummer Richard Ploog. We headed to America first to do promo for the album. That was a disaster. When we got to the Capitol building in LA, all the people in the office wanted to talk about was Little River Band, who had been Capitol's Aussie darlings for a few years by then. Not surprisingly, all four members of The Church were horrified to be mentioned in the same breath as LRB.

We had recorded the follow-up to *Of Skins and Heart*, called *The Blurred Crusade*, which I thought was a fantastic record, but Capitol had a different opinion. They wanted to change everything about the album. That seemed to be how they worked. Already they had released an edited version of 'The Unguarded Moment', much to the annoyance of the band. The atmosphere wasn't good. A&R man Bruce Raven even gave me a hard time for turning up late for the meeting that day. It felt as if we were second-class citizens. Nor did it help that the band were pretty weird about doing media. Kilbey was particularly hard to deal with in that respect. In Australia, Kathy found it difficult to get him to do interviews. He was always too busy meditating or writing poetry to spend an hour on the phone talking to journalists.

We came home and did some shows, including the Tanelorn Festival, near Stroud in New South Wales, on the October holiday weekend in 1981. That gig was memorable for a couple of reasons. I was stage-managing the event as well as having three of my acts on the bill. The Saturday night, when The Church performed, had Billy Thorpe as the headline act. He had come back from Los Angeles just for the festival, his first Australian show for several years. I introduced him with a big rap, before adding, 'Of course, everybody knows he's a little cunt'. He was always LC to me after that night. I was BC. Thorpie played into the wee small hours.

It was a great line-up at Tanelorn. Split Enz played, as did Max Merritt, Sunnyboys, Mi Sex, Kevin Borich and Midnight Oil. Men at Work had just had their first Australian No. 1 with 'Who Can It Be Now?', so when they played on the Sunday night they went down a storm. The reaction was so amazing that the crowd was screaming for more when they came off. Their tour manager Ted Gardner came up to me telling me they had to have an encore. I said no. 'But they're going crazy out there,' he said, and they were. 'They have to go back on.' I was having none of it. 'Look, when you've got a No.1 in America, not Australia, then you can have an encore,' I shouted. 'They're not going back on.' A year later, they had a No. 1 single and album in the US. That was the last time I worked with Men at Work.

Early in the new year Capitol announced that they weren't going to release *The Blurred Crusade* and that they were dropping the band. That was a tough blow. However, Carrère, run by a likeable English guy, Freddie Cannon, was happy to release the album in Europe and so, after much discussion, it was agreed that England would be a good environment to work in for a while. We moved to London, with the aid of some funds from ATV/Northern Songs.

Robbie Williams was managing Rose Tattoo as well as working at Harbour and Carrère had released Rose Tattoo's albums in Europe, so we found ourselves working together out of Carrère's London office now and again in 1982. By then I had taken on another Aussie band at MCM – Sunnyboys. They arrived in London full of hope after the success of their debut album at home and of its successor, *Individuals*. They toured in Europe and did two great shows at London's Marquee. Then they went off to record their third album, *Get Some Fun*, with English producer Nick Garvey at Ridgefarm Studios in Surrey.

I was sharing a basement flat with The Church in Notting Hill, just off Portobello Road. The building was owned by an Arab sheik. He had a luxury penthouse on the top floor. Now and again, when the owner was away, the caretaker would let us enjoy the luxury upstairs for a few days.

So I was sitting in London with two hot Australian bands, one of which, Sunnyboys, really wanted to make it overseas and the other, The Church, who wanted to make it overseas but on their own terms.

The best illustration of The Church's uncompromising agenda came late in the year. London agent Rob Hallett was a huge fan of the band. Out of the blue he rang me one day and asked if The Church would like to do a British tour with Duran Duran. At that point, Duran Duran were the hottest band in Britain. Their second album, *Rio*, had spawned four hit singles including 'Save a Prayer' and 'Hungry Like the Wolf'. They were everywhere in the media. They were Princess Diana's favourite group. I said yes.

We had to buy onto the tour, which was common practice for a support act in the UK. I got the £8000 from ATV/

Northern Songs, although I didn't pay the agent up front. On 30 October the tour, which was sold out everywhere, started in Dundee, Scotland. The Church got a polite but not ecstatic reaction. It was great exposure nonetheless, but I could see Kilbey wasn't happy. By the second show, in Glasgow, I could sense his discomfort on stage, playing to a largely young female crowd desperate to get their hands on Simon Le Bon, Nick Rhodes and the Taylors.

After that gig, the band decided they didn't want to do the rest of the tour. They wanted to do their own tour of Europe instead. I tried to talk them out of it, but it was pointless. They were hard work. All four of them were strong-willed and had their own ideas about how things should be, so it was never an easy gig for me. I could see yet another great opportunity slipping from my grasp.

We played Edinburgh the next night and then two nights at Hammersmith Odeon in London. After that we pulled out of the tour. We used the money I got from ATV/Northern Songs to fund a short European tour of our own, playing to a lot fewer people than we had been doing, but to people who were there primarily to see The Church.

That, I figured, was another chance to break a band overseas blowing up in my face. Nor did anything happen for Sunnyboys. *Get Some Fun* was never released in Britain, although it did reasonably well at home, but by then singer and songwriter Jeremy Oxley was having mental health problems and the band slowly disintegrated from there.

The Church, of course, went on to much bigger things a few years later when the album *Starfish* and the single 'Under the Milky Way' put them on the international map. I had sold my management to a US combine less than a year before that. I had remained their manager for a couple of years after the Duran Duran tour, but probably I shouldn't have stuck around for that long. They could have got where they did a lot more quickly and I don't know that they would have achieved their success if I had stayed their manager. They were hard to like as people, that was their biggest problem as far as I was concerned. Steve was really hard work. You could guarantee that if you set them up with some situation where they had to be nice, it wouldn't happen. You can't win as a manager in some situations and that was one. If something worked it was all their idea and if it didn't work it was my fault. That was a manager's lot.

The parting, when it came, was amicable. I've had very few really bad splits in my professional life. One thing I worked out is that you can be the greatest manager in the world, but too many managers stay with a band long after the thrill has gone, after the vibe you once had for them has died. I had nothing left to give to The Church or Sunnyboys. I was exhausted.

A year after those first two tours Frontier did with Squeeze and The Police, the latter came back to Australasia on their *Zenyatta Mondatta* tour. I flew into Sydney from New Zealand with the band. There had been crowd trouble at the last show in Auckland, unbeknown to any of us, when fans had crashed through the safety barriers at the gig, the Logan Campbell Centre. It had sparked a lot of media coverage in New Zealand, so when we arrived at Sydney airport there was a media pack waiting for us, asking us lots of questions to which we didn't know the answers. Fortunately we were able to get out of there without too much hassle, since I had to take Sting to a meet-and-greet function at 2SM.

We got there and it all went well. I was standing around chatting in the boardroom. I had just eaten a tuna vol au vent and had somehow managed to get a significant amount of it all over my face. Just as I was about to fix it, I looked up and this amazing woman in a red dress was heading towards me. It was the woman I had thrown off the stage at the Double J show in Parramatta a month earlier. She was more a girl than a woman. Her name was Lisa Slattery and she was 17.

I'd had a hard time with her at the Double J show. Apart from my having to throw her off the stage a few times, she had somehow kept getting backstage, trying to talk to the artists and being a general nuisance. Now I was seeing her in a completely new light. I was besotted with her. In her role as a junior assistant on work experience at Double J, she had won a wet T-shirt competition at Manly beach and the prize was the opportunity to meet The Police. We got talking. She was beautiful, a feisty, happy kind of person. She came to The Police show at Sydney Showground the next night and I saw her there.

Of course, I was still married to Lilo. We went off on holiday to Thailand a few weeks after The Police tour. We were still trying to make our marriage work, but it wasn't easy. It was never the same after the mess I had made several years before. Even Nicholas, who was nearly four, knew something wasn't right.

I started seeing Lisa a few months after that. That didn't go down particularly well at work. I made no secret of my feelings for Lisa and everyone liked Lilo. For the remainder of 1981, I saw Lisa a lot, until it reached a point early in 1982 when it became clear that we were serious about each other. I had some decisions to make. I decided I had to clean up my act, so I told Lilo I was moving out. That was a tough couple of months. It took a long time for me to realise that the only way to live life is to tell the truth.

9

A Slippery Slide

I get carried away when I have a microphone in my hand (if only, some might say). I've gained a reputation over the past forty years for getting on stage and making my feelings known on a variety of topics, mostly with expletives attached, before, during or after an event in which I have a financial or charitable interest. I bide my time, then I march onto the stage and do a rant. It might be to introduce an act. It could be to urge punters to dig deep into their pockets and give generously to a worthy cause at a benefit concert, or it could be to try and quell a volatile crowd situation with a few well-chosen words, such as, 'Sit the fuck down'. Whatever the reason, it's not something over which I have much control. Maybe it's the frustrated rock star in me, but I can't help myself.

I hope Jimmy Barnes understood that when he found me kneeling at his feet crying, screaming into the microphone and begging for him to go back on stage at Narara Festival in 1983. He and his Cold Chisel colleagues probably thought I was mad. I wouldn't have argued the point, nor would any of my partners in that venture.

Narara 83 is, like Sunbury 72, one of the landmark festivals in Aussie rock history. I'm proud to say I was one of the organisers of that concert, held on the Australia Day holiday weekend, not at Narara in New South Wales but at Somersby, a few kilometres from there, just off the Pacific Highway. As with the first Sunbury, it boasted a wonderful line-up of great Australian-only talent. Australian Crawl, Cold Chisel, Rose Tattoo, INXS, Mental As Anything, The Angels and Men At Work were just some of the acts on the bill.

For all that it was a celebration for most of the 30,000 people who were there, including those backstage, for me the vibe I experienced on stage and off it, with and without chemical assistance, was overshadowed by the ill feeling I suffered from people close to me during it and afterwards. It came as a shock. That was a crazy time, one way and another.

The details of Narara were hammered out by the promoters at a series of meetings at Benny's Bar in Potts Point in Sydney. Benny's, named after one of the alley cats in the cartoon series *Top Cat*, was legendary in Oz rock in the 80s. Every roadie, muso, groupie, manager, record company employee or agent who ever played or worked or succeeded in getting a backstage pass in Sydney rang the bell on the wooden door there at least once in their lives and waited for the bouncer to check them out through the peephole. It was a vibrant, feel-good little bar. It stayed open late and the atmosphere built as the night went on.

Just about every famous act that came through Sydney in the 80s ended up at Benny's at some point, including U2, Duran Duran, Tom Waits, Queen, Bon Jovi and hundreds more. It was a regular haunt for many Australian bands. Musos and crew arrived at regular intervals as soon as their working night was over. Roadies would go there even before they went to their hotel. People from all over the world became friends for life in Benny's. It was like Cheers for rock 'n' rollers. You didn't buy drugs there, but certainly you could consume them. Sometimes the queue for the toilets would be twenty-deep with people waiting to do a few lines.

When I first started going there, it had been open only a short time. After I split up with Lilo I moved into an apartment being rented by a friend, promoter Brian de Courcy, who at the time was up from Melbourne working on one of Harry M Miller's theatre productions. Lisa would come around and stay with me some nights. The flat was just around the corner from Benny's. I knew about the bar because the owner, Grant Hilton, was a tour manager and general hand for me then. Before he opened Benny's he was manager at another rock 'n' roll haven in the Cross, the Manzil Room. Because I didn't know many people around that neighbourhood, the bar seemed like my only choice in order to have a local social life.

If Grant wasn't on the road for me, he used to be a driver for bands who were staying in town for a few days and he'd take them wherever they wanted to go. At the end of the day, he would ask them to come and have a drink at Benny's. Through that it became known to a lot of people in the music fraternity.

Ray Evans, who was managing Renée Geyer, once hired the place to have a party for her, and from then on it became even more of a place to hang out if you were in the music business.

That early 80s period was fantastic for rock 'n' roll in Australia. The local touring scene was thriving and, as I had hoped when we started Frontier, more and more overseas new wave acts were coming to tour. Benny's was a symbol of those times. The fun of being on the road in Australia was captured, magnified and dissected within the four walls of Grant's hip drinking establishment.

On the next floor, above the bar, in one of the two office spaces, was where the promoters hammered out the fine details of Narara 83. We didn't always make it out of the building when the meetings ended.

Some months earlier a friend, New South Wales government adviser Greg Jones, had told me that the state government owned Old Sydney Town and some of the land around it. It's a beautiful spot about an hour's drive north of Sydney. I'd been there before when I took Nicholas on a trip. It had re-enactments of how life was in Sydney not long after settlement, with redcoats firing guns and having duels, and convicts doing it tough, a bit different from what was about to land on its doorstep in 1983, but with a few similarities.

I had suggested the idea of a gig there to my partners at Premier/Harbour and Frontier, but they weren't interested. My friend (although not for long) Eric Robinson liked the idea. He could do most of the production, so he decided to put together a consortium with other Australian promoters. In the end there were me, Eric, Zev Eizik, Michael Coppel, Harry Della, John Woodruff, Grant Thomas and Peter Rix.

We had discussions with the local council, the state government and the manager of Old Sydney Town. Michael Cleary, who was the New South Wales Minister of Sport, Recreation and Tourism, liked the proposal and was a big help in getting it approved, as was Greg Jones. After that, it was simply a matter of booking the acts. With a handful of the country's top promoters working together, that was never going to be a problem – unless we wanted Midnight Oil. They, for whatever reason, decided against appearing, something that really got my goat once I had a microphone in my hand after Chisel's performance.

The event didn't run as well as it should have, at least initially. Hundreds of people were getting off trains at Narara instead of Somersby and having to be directed to the proper location. There weren't enough people on staff, so for the first day Peter Rix and I were parking cars in the car park. Cocaine was running hot and cold, mind you. There wasn't a lot of sleep for many of the crew behind the scenes that weekend. Grant from Benny's had been hired to take care of the VIP alcohol requirements. He enlisted a bunch of local carpenters to build a proper bar backstage, which became known as the Narara Hilton.

I was doing my compere bit on stage whenever I got the chance and by the time Cold Chisel came on, late on Sunday, the second night, I was on a roll and flying. Nothing could stop me. Chisel finished to a rapturous reception, so I bounded on and started a huge rave about 'the best fucking rock 'n' roll band in the world' and words to the effect that 'we' have to get them to do an encore.

Cold Chisel didn't particularly want to do an encore, but I was oblivious to that. I just got more excited and descended into my begging routine with Barnesy. I kept it up for quite a while, to the point where the roadies were stripping the stage of Chisel's equipment around me. Quite a number of people were pissed off by my enthusiasm, I discovered later. My partners, first of all, were over my lengthy rants by then, even if all of them would have known what to expect. To round off my party piece, I turned my attention towards Midnight Oil, tearing them and their manager Gary Morris to shreds with a torrent of abuse, in absentia, for refusing to attend our fabulous event. None too happy either were Rose Tattoo, who were waiting to go on after Chisel, or, as it transpired, after me. Just to make it worse, Robbie Williams and Sam Righi, my colleagues at Harbour who looked after The Tatts, were also stageside and fuming. That was the beginning of their vendetta against me at Harbour and Frontier. When I finally got off the stage, I was hyperventilating, so I went and sat down by the lake at the back of the compound. Lisa came over and sat with me, then abused me relentlessly for my behaviour – a good day at the office all round.

All I can say in retrospect is that I was taken by the moment. The moment had serious repercussions, however. Eric Robinson, who had been a close friend, didn't speak to me for a couple of years after that night, because he thought I had been too out of control. He didn't want me to go on stage – on his stage. I thought that was unfair, because I thought I was the best at what I did. Nevertheless I was happy about the overall success of the festival. It made money, although not as much as we would have liked. It grossed around $1.5 million. The weather held out, there was no trouble and everyone went home happy. Almost everyone.

A few months after that, due to the success of the first one, it was agreed there should be a Narara 84. All of the usual suspects were enlisted, except me. The others had got together and decided they didn't want me involved because, in their view, I was too much of a liability. They didn't mind me having a financial interest; they just didn't want me around. I discovered this at a meeting at the Sebel Townhouse with my mate Peter Rix, who looked pretty uncomfortable having to tell me I wasn't wanted. They had issues apart from my swearing on stage. I brought in most of the crew for that gig and they weren't happy with some of them. That could have been due to certain extracurricular activities being conducted that would have come into conflict with the local police presence.

Rix says now that dumping me was one of the hardest things he has had to do, but he assures me it was a business decision, not a personal one. I considered suing, since it was partly through my efforts that Narara had happened in the first place. I took legal counsel and was advised against it.

Maybe I was too consumed by the idea of being Mr Personality at Narara. It wouldn't be the last time my antics got me into trouble. Years later, in 1995, Pearl Jam took offence at me for getting on the microphone to take care of a crowd problem in my own inimitable style. We had an incident in New Zealand at an all-ages show where two or three kids nearly got crushed to death. I went out on stage and tried to stop it. Eddie Vedder went berserk, saying how dare I go out and start talking to his audience. We lost the next Pearl Jam tour. For the past fifteen years, Gudinski has been blaming me for that because of all the on-stage stuff, but it wasn't just that; Gudinski's backstage behaviour also had something to do with it. They hated all that, really hated it. My reunion with Pearl Jam on tour in 2009 proves my point, I think. It was one of the most successful tours of their career and of mine.

Back in my state of exile, Narara 84 wasn't nearly as successful as the first one, not that I mean to gloat. I would have been happy if it had been a monster.

The line-up was a mix of Aussie and overseas acts, which to my mind didn't quite work. Talking Heads, The Pretenders, Eurythmics and Simple Minds were among the international acts, alongside locals such as Hoodoo Gurus, The Models and Mondo Rock. It rained heavily and there were only about half the numbers that attended the first festival. A young English tourist died, believed to have drowned in a local dam. It lost money, so it was agreed it would be the last.

I was having problems with Frontier around that time. I had taken a back seat from the international touring side of my work to some degree while I was working with The Church and Sunnyboys overseas. Robbie Williams ran a lot of the tours by international acts in my absence. One argument I had, with Philip in particular, was over my insistence that we bring out English band The Cure. We had toured them successfully in 1981; in fact, I like to think I was at least partly responsible for breaking them in Australia.

I wanted to do them again. They were much bigger in 1984 after the success of singles such as 'The Lovecats' and 'The Walk' internationally the year before. I thought it could be a huge tour, but Philip, the man holding the purse strings, was against it. He couldn't see them building on what they had done business-wise the first time. I fell out with the band's agent, Martin Hopewell from the Cowbell Agency in England, over that and Chris Parry, the owner of their label Friction Records, never spoke to me again. The Cure came out for another promoter and it was a monster.

Nevertheless, Frontier was in great shape. We hadn't lost money since we started and we made a profit every year in the 80s. Money was flooding in. Although the management side of my business was coming to an end and the Dainty relationship had long since dried up, I was doing well out of my partnerships in Frontier and Premier/Harbour. Also, I was still promoting some outdoor shows due to my relationship with Rod Muir at Triple M.

There were changes in my set-up at Michael Chugg Management. We moved from Alfred Street into an office in the Olivetti Building in William Street, Woolloomooloo. Harbour did likewise, setting up just across the hall from us. Lisa started working in the office, doing publicity. I took on a new receptionist, Tommasina Rasso, who had just finished school. Eventually she took over from Kathy, who left in 1985 and has had a successful career in management, marketing and radio since then.

Not long after Tommasina started, a seventeen-year-old schoolboy walked into our office and asked to see me. When Tommi asked if he had an appointment, he said, 'No, but he'll want to see me'. I saw him. The boy's name was Con Nellis. He was in year 12 and he had decided he was going to be a rock promoter. He wanted to come and work in the office, for nothing, to get some experience. I liked him. I liked his front in knowing what he wanted and for coming straight to someone like myself. I found out later he had gone to Peter Rix's office by mistake and been redirected.

Con started working for me after school, doing general errands, bits of paperwork, but mostly just hanging around soaking up whatever was going on, much in the way I had done many years before in Melbourne when Consolidated Rock was just beginning. He had some experience. Before coming to me, he had done some after-school work for promoter/impresario Michael Edgley, but this was his first taste of the rock 'n' roll lifestyle. He took to it pretty well. By 1985, Con was working with me full-time. He set up as a business and did design and printing of posters for tours, among other things. From then until 1998 he was my right-hand man. In those years, he got to know me better than I knew myself.

By 1985 I was having occasional doubts about who I was, but mostly I was having an amazing time being Chuggi. There was a lot of excessive behaviour going on in the 80s and music and entertainment were at the heart of it.

I'd known Rod Muir since we were both young Tasmanians starting out in the music business in the 60s, although by the time I started putting on shows and managing bands he was already a well-known radio DJ on the island. Even then he was a bit of a jack the lad, running around in flash cars with his flashy girlfriend. We had a falling out then. I had a band, The Thing, entered in a Tasmanian Hoadley's Battle of the Sounds contest in Launceston. Halfway through the show, I caught Rod trying to pull the plug to our amplifiers out of the wall. We had a big fight and we weren't friends again until years later on the mainland.

By the early 80s, Rod was incredibly wealthy from his ownership of Triple M in Sydney and from the money machine that was his consultancy company, Digamae. He liked to party. He was rich, successful and an adventurer, a bit like a Richard Branson but with more of a glint in his eye and tons more class. He was also very generous. The amount of French champagne and everything that went along with it that got consumed in his company was ridiculous. Those were crazy times.

Rod was a keen sailor. He had a succession of racing yachts and he liked to take his friends out on the water on weekends. I didn't do a lot of racing with him, because it wasn't my thing, so I'd be the land manager, which meant I'd be waiting at the quay with the French champagne and the other accessories. It was great, but it was all very macho, big boys and their toys kind of stuff.

In 1985 he asked me to join him on one of his international sojourns, to take part in the Transpacific race that sails from Los Angeles to Honolulu every two years. They call it the Transpac Slide. Rod had been around the world a few times racing by then. He had world-class crews on board, including America's Cup sailors. He was serious about it, as much as Rod could be serious about anything.

On this occasion he had a boat called *Doctor Dan*, which he had bought in New Zealand. The Triple M logo adorned the sails. We took it to America and spent a month in Los Angeles training for the race. Again I was the man on the ground with the party materials. Eric Robinson was on the crew and Richard Clapton was there as a kind of club mascot. Like me, he didn't get wet, but he certainly involved himself in the 'training' back at the hotel. Rod had asked Richard to write and record a song called 'The Transpac Slide', which he did, so that Rod could blast it from his massive speaker system on the front of the boat. He and his mates used to do that in Sydney Harbour, heading out to sea wearing ZZ Top wigs, beards and sunglasses and bopping round to 'Gimme All Your Lovin'', 'Sharp Dressed Man' and 'Legs'. 'The Transpac Slide' was released as a single a few months after the race on the Oz label, with 'Sail On *Dr Dan*' on the B side. Both songs were credited to Clapton/Muir.

I enjoyed the madness, the eccentricity and the indulgence of those times with Rod. That kind of lifestyle was becoming the norm for me. There were plenty of indulgences back home as well, with and without Rod, that would make most people's hair curl. The brotherhood of Frontier had card games going on every weekend that turned into wild nights. Racehorses were being bought and bet on. On tour, it wasn't unusual to stumble into the hotel room of someone on the team and find it full of girls, although that wasn't my scene. Copious amounts of alcohol and drugs were being consumed. If somebody had told me to give up that lifestyle, I would have laughed out loud, but within months that's exactly what I did.

10

Chasing the Magic Dragon

In February 1984, just prior to the Australasian leg of The Police's *Synchronicity* tour, I went to Hawaii for the first time. It was a business trip. The Police were playing there and I wanted to convince them, face to face, to do more promotion for the show Frontier was doing with them in Auckland. The gig was only four days away and wasn't selling particularly well.

On the day of the Honolulu show, I had a meeting with the Hawaiian promoter, Ken Rosene, along with some of his people. The vibe in the room was terrible. They made it very clear they didn't want some Aussie promoter treading on their turf. Then the door opened and in walked this guy. His name was Frankie Winston and since he seemed to be the only one interested in me, we got talking. Then we watched the show that night together from the press box and became friends.

Frankie had a colourful story. He had been part of a drug ring in California, run by Australians, working as their street organiser, but quit when he thought his time was running out on the streets of LA. He packed up and moved to the island of Kauai, opened a restaurant and began a new life. Frankie was a really friendly, fun-loving guy with great taste in music. I made a promise that the next time I was in Hawaii I would pay him a visit.

That opportunity came towards the end of the Transpac race. I wasn't on board *Doctor Dan* for the sail from LA to Honolulu. Instead I flew ahead five days before she was due to arrive, just to set up a welcome for the crew and to have some time to myself.

I phoned Frankie and arranged to fly into Kauai, the day after I arrived in Honolulu. He'd given me instructions to get to his restaurant. I drove for twenty minutes or so and then turned a sharp bend and suddenly there in front of me were these amazing waterfalls and a sign by the side of the road that said Hanalei. Immediately the song 'Puff the Magic Dragon' came into my head, particularly the line about 'frolics in the autumn mist, in a land called Honah Lee'. The Peter, Paul and Mary song was based on their experience in Hanalei. It was the most beautiful place I had ever seen. It was paradise.

I met Frankie and we drove to his place, down single-track roads, over old wooden bridges, until we came to the house. It wasn't much more than a little wooden beach hut, but it was surrounded by beautiful tropical flowers and sat in the shadow of Mount Makana, which is the mountain known as Bali H'ai in the movie *South Pacific*. Much of the film was shot in and around Hanalei.

That evening we sat on the beach with a few beers and watched the most spectacular sunset. I spent four more days on Kauai before I had to head back to Honolulu to meet Rod and his band of merry sailors. I fell in love with Kauai then. I wondered what Lisa would make of it.

After the Transpac race and the peaceful escape of Kauai, the rock 'n' roll culture I was caught up in started to lose its appeal. Lisa and I were going through a rough patch then. We were living in a house I had bought in Manly, but as usual I was away a lot and also, because Lisa was a young, assertive person, she didn't put up with my frequently wayward behaviour. By then, Lisa was working for Rod as his personal assistant, so she knew that when he was up to no good and I was with him, trouble was never far away.

Rod, amazingly, was feeling the same way as I was about the party lifestyle. One day he announced that he and his wife Kathy were taking a break, for three weeks, and heading off to a health retreat called Camp Eden, which is in the Currumbin Valley, smack in the middle of the Gold Coast hinterland in Queensland. I was surprised at this development, but curious. When Rod came back, the change in him was astounding. He had lost weight, had stopped smoking, looked much fitter and healthier, his diet had improved and mentally he was as sharp as a tack. I was impressed.

Rod had a farm near Peats Ridge, just north of Sydney. When he came back from Camp Eden, we went up to the farm for four or five days. The Rod Muir I saw there was the one I had known in Tasmania twenty years before. That's how radical the change in him was. We'd go for long walks and he'd tell me how great he was feeling after his long retreat. Conversely, I was depressed, overweight, eating badly, indulging in too many drugs, too many cigarettes and too much alcohol. I wasn't getting enough exercise, I was divorced, my relationship with Lisa was on and off and I was uneasy about my role in the rock world. I was close to hitting forty and feeling like it was all becoming the same. My life just seemed to be going around in circles. Rod's rejuvenation had a profound effect on me. Suddenly I realised you didn't need drugs or booze. You didn't need any of that.

I checked into Camp Eden a few weeks later for a month. I was at a really low point when I went there. It's in an idyllic spot, set in the lush, peaceful surroundings of the hinterland rainforest with pleasant accommodation and facilities, the kind of place where you wouldn't mind putting your feet up by the pool and settling down with a good book, a margarita and a big fat joint. I got a lot of reading done. I can't explain the exact feeling of arriving there, other than it being one of apprehension mounting on terror, mixed with a steely determination to go through with it. This was Chuggi, a rock pig of more than twenty years' standing, entering a new phase of his life. It was a revelation, an epiphany. I was thirty-eight.

The first few days were terrible. You've just come off everything and you're drinking water. And there are people there from all walks of life who have no real connection to you or what you do. That was the first eye-opener for me. I found I had nothing to say to them, because I was so totally wrapped up in what I did. Rock 'n' roll, that was my world and I stuck to it.

After a week or so, I changed. I started to talk to other people, began to communicate with them, even began to feel for them. I learned moderation and I learned how to interact with strangers. I had no communication skills with outsiders, just from being so immersed in the music business. This will sound utterly pretentious, I know, but I used to shun normal people. It wasn't just because of the drugs and booze, but also from being in that closeted music environment, whether it was in LA, London, Sydney, Darwin, or Hobart. That was my life.

This sudden change was difficult at first, but gradually I began to enjoy it. I wanted to have a conversation with men and women who hadn't spent most of their lives in dark, noisy rooms being naughty. At the same time, I was losing a lot of weight and getting really fit.

The regime at Camp Eden was completely new to me. I shared a room with three other guys. It seemed a bit like the army, although I was pretty sure soldiers were allowed to smoke. Here there were no cigarettes, no alcohol, no dairy and no meat. No phones. And you had to be up at 6 am, an hour in my schedule that was often considered time to call it a night.

On the first morning, before I was awake, I found myself standing in a field doing tai chi exercises. It was hell. For three days I hated being there. I had headaches. I was feeling like shit, because everything that was part of my life was gone.

After a few days, I started to realise I was still a young person. I met a guy called Pat Gay, who had a big effect on me. He'd had a triple bypass. His situation was completely different to mine and yet we got on really well. Our friendship took off the mask of what I had become.

A week into my stay, I began to feel so much better in every way. The tai chi teacher, an Englishman called Rob, was fantastic. He had done many amazing things in his life and lived for a while in a cave in Nepal, he told us. I didn't ask him why. He was an incredible teacher. After the classes, he would take us indoors and conduct forums. These discussions showed you the patterns that had developed in your life. For some, including myself, the sessions explained how you had come to hate yourself. Those forums really opened me up and woke me up as well. By the time I left, a month later, I was a different person, or so I thought.

Being there for that period did change my life. I realised that you could do anything you want in life no matter how old you were. In past generations, you were fucked by the time you were forty. I thought that was going to happen to me. The decision I made to go to Camp Eden has kept me alive. If I hadn't gone there, I wouldn't be around today. There's no doubt about it, because I wouldn't have worked out what I was doing, which was killing myself.

Certainly that first visit altered my lifestyle to a degree for the next two or three years. I gave up cigarettes, I cut out the drugs and I lost 11 kilograms. It was four weeks well spent, but it wasn't enough to convince me to change my habits altogether.

After the next few retreats, I'd come back to Sydney and still have a joint, but I wouldn't smoke the whole bag. I'd do the odd line, but I wouldn't make it a habit. I was rejuvenated without being totally converted. Over the next twenty years, I'd visit Camp Eden and other retreats many times. Instead of being a cure, health farms became a short-term solution to a long-term addiction to rock 'n' roll.

Mum and the Crying Machine in 1947.

My siblings: Julie, me, Paul and Christine at Lowhead Beach near Launceston in 1956.

Me: The La Trobe Christmas Cycling and Athletic carnival in 1961.

Mum and her number one son at Sydney Harbour in the late 80s.

Mum and me in Perth 2009.

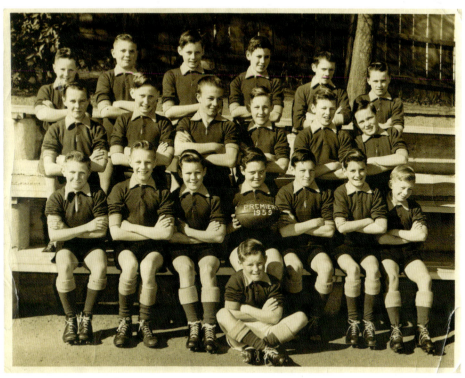

The winning team, Glen Dhu Primary, in 1959. I'm the one leaning at the end of the second row.

My father Victor, Nicholas, Lucas, my mum Lorna and Sophie at Nick's 21st in 1998.

Lilo, Nick and his dad at Nick's 21st in 1998.

With Nicholas, Lisa and Sophie. Getting ready for the Dial A Video launch in 1989.

Nick, Sophie, Fat Dad and Lucas. APRA Ted Albert Lifetime Achievement Award in 2005.

Three generations of Chuggs. Me, Nick and Harley in front of the stage at AC/DC in Sydney 2010.

With Ian Saxon and Jimmy Buffett on board the *Windward Passage* in Sydney Harbour in 1987.

With Doc McGee (Bon Jovi's manager) and publicist supreme Patti Mostyn in the late 80s in Sydney.

Me with John McVie and his girlfriend at *Rockarena* in 1977.

Speaking at the CMA Music Conference in Chicago in 1999 with my friend Trevor Smith.

Michael Gudinski, Frank Sinatra, Tony Cochrane and me at the Sydney Entertainment Centre in 1988.

On stage at the Guns N' Roses gig at Eastern Creek in 1993. This was the origin of my rant, 'Hey, you in the black T-shirt!'

Sue and Michael Gudinski, Philip Jacobsen, Lisa and me at Mushroom's 10th Anniversary at Luna Park Melbourne.

The late Wayne de Gruchy and me helping an overexcited punter at a 2SM concert in the mid 70s.

Me launching Dial A Video.

Backstage at the Pacific Circle Music Conference at Darling Harbour in 2001 with my tour manager Jon Pope. Everyone was pleased I lost my voice.

Me and Andrew Tatrai – security and logistics guru.

One of my longest associates, the mighty Scrooge Madigan, at Long Way to the Top in Perth, 2002.

My 50th with legendary tour manager, the late Wane 'Swampy' Jarvis.

Peter 'Sneaky' McFee – one of the best production men all round.

Two great mates: Billy Joel and Denis Handlin backstage in the early 90s.

Bill Silva, John O'Donnell, me and Ian Copeland at the launch of PCMC in Los Angeles in the late 90s. The late Ian Copeland was a huge inspiration for both me and Michael Gudinski. We stole the name Frontier from his agency Frontier Booking International.

Molly Meldrum and my future wife Lisa at Narara Festival in 1983. Molly living the dream of outing me ... never happened.

Shortly after Billy's amazing speech when presenting the Ted Albert Award to me in 2005.

Doing my quiz show at the International Live Music Conference in London in 2009. Johnny Rotten eat your heart out ...

If you promote Kiss you have to dress up. Backstage in Adelaide, 1999.

Performing during 'Love is in the Air' at Long Way to the Top in 2002.

My great friends Ted and Nikki Gardner in Los Angeles in 2001. They nursed me after the heart attack.

My business partner Matthew Lazarus-Hall and me.

Two great friends, Tommi Raso and Ian 'Saxby' Saxon backstage at Simon and Garfunkel in Auckland in 2009.

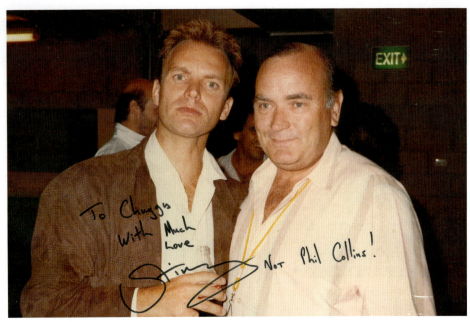

With Sting. He insisted on introducing me as Phil Collins.

Me and Elton jointly celebrating our 60th birthday at Acer Arena in 2007.

At the APRAs in 2007 with Peter Garrett and Rob Hirst of the Oils.

Launching Live Earth 2007 with Rob Hirst, Toni Collette, Neil Finn and Nick Seymour at the Sydney Football Stadium.

The cast and crew of the hugely successful Long Way to the Top. At front are me, Eric Robinson, Amanda Pelman, Ted Robinson, Amber Jacobsen and Kevin Jacobsen.

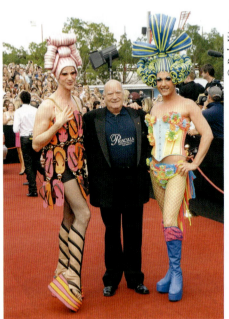

On the red carpet promoting Priscilla at the ARIA Awards in 2008.

Me and Jacqui Crouch from Moneypenny (my voice of reason) at the 2005 ARIA Awards.

Receiving the CMA Award for Contribution to Country Music Worldwide from a great Australian, Keith Urban.

Roger Daltrey, me and Pete Townsend backstage in Melbourne during The Who tour in 2004.

With Rod McSween, super agent, and Pearl Jam backstage in Sydney 2009.

Undoubtedly one of the world's greatest entertainers and a wonderful bloke, Robbie Williams, in Sydney 2003.

One of the great female rockers and a beautiful person, Gwen Stefani in 2007.

With the incredible Bette Midler, Garry Van Egmond and Dave Humphries at the end of the triumphant 2005 tour

Somewhere with my favourite Richard Clapton.

Me and Jack Thompson. A great Australian and very dear friend. At Long Way to the Top.

Backstage with Duran Duran during the second Robbie Williams tour in 2003.

Mark Pope, the legendary creator of *Rolling Stone* magazine Jan Wenner, me, Sophie Chugg, Chris Moss and Brian Cadd at the relaunch of *Rolling Stone* in Sydney 2009.

Me and Sophie in Paris in 2007. Sophie posted this on Facebook and 'Euro Chugg' was born.

My brother Paul living it up in Phuket at my 60th in 2007.

Chutimon (Maam) and me in Phuket in 2010.

One positive to come out of my rehabilitation at Camp Eden was that I got back together with Lisa, a few times as it turned out, but in 1987 we signed on for good. In March, we went on a holiday to Fiji. Frontier had just done incredibly well out of a ZZ Top tour, which went through the roof, so all of the partners were pretty flush. I met Lisa in Fiji after the last ZZ Top show in Auckland. Fiji was terrific, but I wanted Lisa to see Kauai. I told Frankie to expect us. We spent a few days in Honolulu and while we were there I asked Lisa to marry me. She said yes.

Then I took her to Kauai. Lisa fell in love with the place as instantly as I had done. We wanted to get married there. Immediately. Within a few days we had approval, with Frankie's help, to get married in the botanical gardens in Hanalei, which was a coup, because previously no white people had ever got married there.

I rang Australia and invited people to come the following week. Gudinski and his wife Sue said yes, as did Philip and Maxine, and Frank Stivala and his wife Sue. Gudinski would be my best man. Lisa rang her mother and father and they came over. Tommi from the office came as well and brought my son Nicholas, who was about to turn ten. There were a few other friends from New Zealand.

Ian Saxon, Frontier's occasional tour manager, also flew in from Las Vegas. I found out later he had been there raising money for a drugs run with one of the crime families. That also explained the strange coincidence of Ian and Frankie knowing each other, from having worked together in California years earlier.

The wedding was a great success, just perfect. We went to Honolulu and shopped for all of the wedding attire. We bought rings from Cartier and outfits from Chanel. That ZZ Top tour really came in handy. We arrived at the botanical gardens in a limousine. The minister from the local church conducted the ceremony. There were flowers everywhere. It was a magic day. Then afterwards we had a huge Thai feast. There was a band, featuring Coco Ho, brother of Hawaiian pop star Don Ho, and some great music Frankie had put together on compilation tapes.

Frankie found us a beautiful old house on the beach for our honeymoon. It was blissful. We moved in there with Nicholas before the wedding and then after it Lisa's parents looked after him before they took him home. Lisa and I stayed on for a few more weeks of wedded bliss in paradise.

That was my highlight from what became a big year for me, for Lisa and me and for Frontier. By then I had stopped doing some of the things that had got me into a cycle of despair in 1985. I quit going to the weekend card games Frontier personnel liked to indulge in. My drugs and alcohol intake was considerably less than it had been before Camp Eden, but there was one part of the culture at Frontier in the 80s that was harder than cocaine to give up and that was horses.

Racehorses and gambling were part of the fabric of Frontier from the beginning. As soon as we started making money in the early 80s, we were looking for ways to spend it and one way that didn't involve getting off our tits, with a few exceptions, was buying racehorses. Philip was into it long before anyone else, but by 1985 we all had a vested interest – Frank, Philip, Sam, Robbie, Gudinski and me. We bought a two-year-old filly we called Got the Vibe. That was an expression banded about in the Frontier offices, especially by me. The horse was the daughter of 1970 Caulfield Cup winner Beer Street. We put her with trainer Lance Smith.

She turned out to be a pretty decent horse and won a few races. She was winning good mile and a half races against quality colts and geldings and was shaping up to be a Caulfield Cup shot after winning three races in a row. We were having a lot of fun with her, so we started buying a few more horses. Sadly, during the lead-up to the Caulfield Cup, Got the Vibe broke down and had to be destroyed. Next we bought a black colt-gelding yearling and called him Dundas Lane. He didn't show much form in 1986. The following year, however, he began to hit his stride. We entered him in the Norman Robinson Stakes at Caulfield. Dundas Lane came out and won by a huge margin at very high odds. Not long after that, Robbie, radio identity Keith Williams, Ian Saxon and myself were at a midweek meeting at Canterbury. Dundas Lane was running in Melbourne that day. We cleaned out the bookies. They had to write cheques. We had a grand or two on it. Three weeks later, it backed up at another big race in Melbourne and won by ten lengths at 40/1. I had $5000 each way on him, so now we were winning stupid money. We bought two more horses out of the winnings. Three weeks before the Victoria Derby, Dundas Lane fronted up at Flemington in another three-year-old classic and won by a nose.

On the day of the Victoria Derby, we had Billy Joel in town, so we took him and a bunch of other people to the races. Dundas Lane was favourite. I knew he wasn't going to win because he had just got over the line in his previous race, but it was a great experience having a favourite in the Derby all the same.

My dad was a good punter. He could pick the first four of the Melbourne Cup with astonishing regularity. Two weeks before he died, we sat together and picked some horses. We backed the winner of the Adelaide Cup that day.

Another horse some of the partners were in that did well was called Frontier Boy. He was a great horse, but he couldn't run more than 3000 metres. He won the St Leger over that distance. The day he ran against Vintage Crop in the Melbourne Cup (3200 metres) I was in Mario's Restaurant in Sydney watching it on the big screen. Three lengths out he was still in contention and I was on the table screaming. He came fifth. The proudest moment for me, though, was when Frontier Boy won the Hobart Cup and we sent my dad down to collect the trophy. He loved that.

We won a lot of money on horses, but between gambling on them and buying them we spent more than we won. Fortunately, Frontier was going through a bumper phase. In the space of two years we had toured Neil Young and Crazy Horse, Bob Dylan, ZZ Top and Orchestral Manoeuvres in the Dark, among others. And in just a few months in 1987, Bon Jovi, Joel, Crowded House and Billy Idol all did great business. The Joel tour in October and November was tremendous fun. Billy was great to work with and he liked to have a good time on the road in more ways than his public image suggested. He was also an extremely good cook. Whenever he was staying in an apartment or villa rather than a hotel, he would invite around a bunch of people from the entourage, including myself, and cook up a storm.

If things were looking good in the office, they were even better at home. Lisa was pregnant. I was more prepared for it this time than I had been with Lilo and Nicholas ten years earlier. On 14 May 1988 my daughter Sophie Victoria Chugg was born at Manly Hospital. I was delighted.

I felt as if I had turned a corner after the turmoil and hedonism of the years just gone. I did lose touch there for a while. Now life was good.

11

For What is a Man?

I had many reasons to hate my old man – having the shit kicked out of me as a kid didn't fill me with gratitude or respect – but one thing I can appreciate about him is that he introduced me to the music and movies of Frank Sinatra. I could never have predicted that decades later these two grumpy old pricks would be in the same room together, or that I would be the person responsible for putting them there. It happened, though, and when it did, in 1989, it had a profound effect on me in my personal and professional life. To get to that point, you have to understand a few shenanigans that went on beforehand.

Dad served in the army during World War II. He was based in the Solomon Islands and in 1944 he got loaned out to the American forces there for a year. He was operating the landing barges and that kind of thing, but more important to me, or to my musical education, was that he struck up friendships with a lot of the GIs.

My nan, Dad's mother, was one of the greatest cooks. She would make these fabulous fruitcakes and send them over to my dad where he was stationed. Every time a care package turned up, there would be a couple of fruitcakes in there. The Yanks have never known how to make a fruitcake in their lives, so after a while they started asking him, 'What's that?' My dad was keen on what was arriving in their care packages as well, which, among other things, included 78s of the latest music coming out in the US. He struck up a deal with some of the GIs and they began swapping the contents of each other's parcels from the loved ones back home.

After the war, three or four of these guys remained friends with my dad, so every year he'd send them a fruitcake and we'd get a parcel containing a bunch of records. This is how I got hooked on music. All these great records would arrive at home – people like Fats Waller, Fats Domino, heaps of stuff. And Frank Sinatra. So, from the age of four, I was listening to a lot of this incredible music. Of course I wasn't allowed to touch any of the records, but when my parents were out, I did.

It got even better as I got older. In the 1950s and early 1960s, my dad had a gig as a bouncer at the movie theatres in Launceston. In those days, there were about seven cinemas in Launceston (now there's one little complex). So my friends, my sisters and I went to almost every movie released between about 1955 and the early 60s. We used to go to the movies four or five times a week. And I was seeing all these wonderful movies. Gene Kelly and Fred Astaire were my idols, and of course Sinatra fitted right into that scene. The image of him back then as the charming young movie star and pop singer was in sharp contrast to the reality when I met him thirty or so years later. My Way, I learned quickly, was the *only* fucking way with Frank.

In 1988, Frontier was on fire. Guns N' Roses and Sting did well for us at the end of the year and 1989 got off to a good start with tours by REM and Iggy Pop. The next one off the rank, however, was as far removed from Iggy and his leather pants and self-mutilation as you could get – and completely at odds with what Frontier had become at that point. We were rock promoters through and through, but in 1988 we were approached with an offer that, as some of Sinatra's Italian friends might have put it, we couldn't refuse. The proposed tour would feature Sinatra, Sammy Davis Jnr and Liza Minnelli and it came about like this.

Earlier that year, in January, a young promoter friend of mine, Tony Cochrane, now the head of the incredibly successful V8 Supercars series in Australia, pulled off an incredible coup by getting Sinatra, who at the time was enjoying a comeback as a live act in the US and Europe, to come to Australia for a one-off performance at a new resort, Sanctuary Cove, on the Queensland Gold Coast. Local property developer Mike Gore was the man behind Sanctuary Cove and he brought in Cochrane to arrange a concert spectacular to launch the place. Gore originally wanted Neil Diamond, who was hot in Australia, but Diamond didn't want to come all the way here for just one gig, no matter the fee. So Cochrane negotiated with Sinatra's people instead.

It was a bold move for a couple of reasons. First, Sinatra was still in dishonour in Australia for his behaviour during his previous visit in 1974, when he famously called female journalists at a press conference 'hookers' and then left the country vowing never to return. Second, even though he was being offered a fee of $US1 million, no one actually believed Sinatra would come back here. When they announced it, everybody thought, 'There is no fucking way Frank Sinatra is going to come and sing at Sanctuary Cove.' That was the attitude from the media, from everybody. Everybody just thought, 'This is a wank', a stunt by Gore and his white shoe brigade.

It was only when Mr S arrived in Sydney two days before the show that people started to believe he was playing. Cochrane had been to the States months before to discuss the idea with Sinatra and his manager Elliot Weisman, the man responsible for engineering Sinatra's return to the limelight after years of inactivity.

Weisman had enjoyed some years of inactivity as well. A player with underworld connections, he spent six years in jail for fraud involving a theatre development in New York before taking over Sinatra's affairs in the mid-80s. When Tony, Gudinski and I had dinner together with Weisman in Sydney in 1989, Weisman explained in great detail how he was picked up outside prison on the day of his release and driven to New York by some 'friends'. Once there, the Mafia Godfather informed him that he would now be looking after Frank Sinatra's career, as a reward for his loyalty (read silence) during and after his trial.

Cochrane got on well with Weisman and Sinatra at their meetings in New York to set up the Sanctuary Cove show. What clinched the deal, however, was that Cochrane promised he would be able to fix stroppy Sinatra's difficult relationship with the Australian media. Sydney publicist Patti Mostyn was the engineer of that. She announced at the Sydney press call just prior to the show that Sinatra would be happy to have his picture taken with any members of the press who were interested. Chairs and tables flew in the rush – and Sinatra the troublemaker was back onside.

At the time of the Sanctuary Cove concert, which also had Whitney Houston and Peter Allen on the bill, I was enjoying a little rest and recreation on Ian Saxon's boat *Rolling Thunder*, sailing up and down the Queensland coast, taking it easy, drinking Moët. A few other people came and went – Dicky Wilkins was one of them; Ricky May was another. I wasn't aware at the time that Ian was on his way to Hamilton Island to pick up ten tonnes of hash, although as it turned out it would take nearly a year for his consignment to arrive. At the time all we were concerned about was keeping ourselves amused. Ian suggested mooring the boat at Sanctuary Cove marina, so from there it wasn't a giant leap to suggest that we go and see Ol' Blue Eyes, so that is what we did.

Back then, development on the Gold Coast was nothing like it is now. Nowadays it's all virtually built up along the Gold Coast and Sanctuary Cove. Then it was just this weird spot in the middle of nowhere. They were still building the golf course.

Anyway, off we went to see Frank. It was a sold-out show, 16,000 people, and Sinatra was on form. In the second half, the hits fell over each other: 'All of Me', 'You Make Me Feel So Young', 'Come Fly With Me'. It was a great concert, but the venue was a shambles. It was on a swamp full of mosquitos. It was a fucking horror, sitting there getting eaten alive. Every chair sank into the ground up to the seat. But I thought: 'They've pulled it off.'

I'd known Cochrane since my early days as a promoter. He was a lighting guy/electrician in Adelaide who contracted to a lot of promoters in the late 70s and early 80s. He was just a kid starting out in those days. I thought Tony had done well to come from that to putting on one of the biggest stars on the planet, the chairman of the board, Mr S. I went backstage afterwards and said, 'Well done. Congratulations.' Everyone else in the business was there and nobody else said a word to him.

But there was nothing else on my mind. It was never in my head that Sinatra might come back to Australia after the Sanctuary Cove gig. I was just being nice to Tony, because I'd known the kid since he was a roadie in Adelaide, when he'd turn up with the follow spots. I just thought: 'Good on him.'

Then, about six months later, I got the call. Cochrane had scored those big three names for a short Australian tour – two shows in Melbourne, two in Sydney – but he needed a financial partner. Would Frontier be interested? I was blown away by the idea, but Frontier stayed away from that stuff because a lot of those older acts wouldn't pull shit. We'd steer clear of those kind of tours that other people would do.

I don't think Tony believed I'd call him back, knowing that we were mainly interested in rock 'n' roll, but I talked to Michael about it and we agreed we should do the tour. The prospect of getting those three was never about how much we were going to lose, it was a foregone conclusion we'd make money ... It was just about having three such huge stars in Australia at the same time.

Michael went over to the US to see the show. I didn't go because I was on the road with someone else. In those days, Michael was the face internationally. I knew a lot of people, certainly, but that was his gig. He was the international guy. My gig was to put it on the road and market and do all that. When he came back, Michael was convinced we had made the right move.

It was quite a funny tour. Tony and Michael had never really got on, mainly because of Michael's arrogance, but we put up a lot of the money because Tony was just a young guy making his way at that stage. We did all the production and took care of all the logistics.

The original tour had begun more than a year earlier in the US, as the return of the Rat Pack – Sinatra, Davis Jnr and Dean Martin – but Martin had pulled out after only a month. Some said it was the clash of personalities between him and the other two, others said he was ill, more still believed Martin hadn't got over the death of his son in a plane crash the year before. Whatever the reason, the Rat Pack reunion was over before it really started.

Cochrane had gone over to the States to try and convince Weisman, Sinatra, Davis Jnr and Martin that the show would work in Australia and that he, Cochrane, should promote it. They weren't keen. After Martin quit and was replaced by Minnelli, the project appeared to be doomed down here. It was Weisman, inadvertently, who turned it around. He called Cochrane, primarily to ask if he could use the title 'The Ultimate Event' – the one Cochrane and Gore had used for the Sanctuary Cove gig – for the Sinatra, Davis Jnr, Minnelli tour in the US. While answering that one, Cochrane made another bid to bring the unlikely trio to Australia. This time they agreed.

We started in Melbourne. Two shows at the National Tennis Centre on 28 February and 1 March, were followed by the Sydney Entertainment Centre on 3 and 4 March. Apart from dealing with three huge egos, their separate entourages of musicians, technicians and personal assistants and so on, it was an eye-opener to discover how important these people were, or at least thought they were. That became clear even before they arrived.

Management, shortly before their arrival in Melbourne, informed us that the talent and their crew didn't like going through Customs and Immigration. Basically what they were saying was: 'We are not going through Customs and Immigration. Fix it.'

So we fixed it. When they got to Melbourne Airport, the entire party was taken to a private room, where they had their passports stamped, and then they were quickly sent on their way. None of the party got searched. The entourage just walked through. It was a different time then, plus everybody in Australia wanted to go to the show, so it wasn't difficult to find people who were obliging, knowing that perhaps we might be able to find a ticket for him or her somewhere.

It was during those few days in Melbourne that I got to learn the ways of Francis Albert Sinatra at close quarters. I was a bit in awe of him, but he really *was* a grumpy old prick. We'd be having dinner in an Italian restaurant and Barbara, his missus, would say something wasn't right and he'd get the shits and walk out. His son, Frank Jnr, was the orchestra conductor and Frank treated Frank Jnr like shit. Of course, Frank had that reputation anyway, but that didn't make it right.

The whole tour was weird. The three stars travelled with their own people. You never saw the talent arrive together or travel together. And Liza was pissed much of the time. Frank would walk into the room backstage and look at all of us and he'd just grunt. Sammy would walk in and keep us all thrilled for twenty minutes. Frank was grumpy. You got nothin', plus it was hands on twenty-four hours a day.

We had the police looking after security for the tour, which made life a lot easier for everybody. It was like working with royalty. Tony Edwards, a lovely guy who is now security manager at Acer Arena in Sydney, was a police inspector back then, but he also used to do a bit of moonlighting as a security guru for us. He got busted a few years ago and resigned from the police force. He was doing all these high-profile tours.

Anyway, he was looking after the tour for us. The two guys he used as assistants on that one were actually federal police officers. It was great, because we'd get into Melbourne or wherever and having him involved would get rid of all the bullshit. He could talk to the Victorian police on their level. It was shocking, some of the shit that used to go on. He could stop traffic, stop traffic lights. It was all too easy.

When the tour entourage arrived at Mascot in Sydney, we all got into limousines. We left for the Intercontinental in the city at 5.30 pm in the middle of peak-hour traffic. We had two outriders and two back riders and one of them would shoot ahead and stop traffic, but every traffic light went to green just as we approached it. We were coming at a hundred kilometres an hour down the freeway. We got from the airport to the hotel in about nine minutes. They had it so down. Tony arranged all of that. The police commissioners had no idea that was going on.

When Sinatra got out of the car at the hotel, he turned round and said: 'Gee, the traffic really works well in this town.' That was about the nicest thing he said during the tour. Next night, with his temper in full flight, it wasn't so nice.

The day had been fine. Barbara had insisted that she wanted to see a kangaroo, but instead of going to a zoo or wildlife park, they had the parks and wildlife department bring a wallaby to the presidential suite of the hotel for her and Frank to have a look at.

The show went well, too. Some were saying Sinatra was passed it at seventy-three, but his voice held up well for all of the tour. It was that voice that could be heard screaming at the top of its lungs at 3 am after the performance – and it was not pretty. After the first Sydney show, the newspapers came out early in the morning with reviews and one of the headlines was 'Sammy Steals the Show'.

I had just got back from dinner at Darcy's with Weisman, tour director Gary Labriola, Michael Gudinski and Tony Cochrane, and I went to the hotel just to check on the security. While I was there, the papers arrived. I was sitting in the room where the security was, just shooting the shit, when I suddenly heard this bang, bang, bang on the door of the penthouse suite of the hotel.

Standing there was the old boy, Mr S, outside the door, banging and screaming: 'Get up! Get up! We're all going home *now*! I'm never going to sing with that little black cocksucker again.'

I grabbed the paper and there it was: 'Sammy Steals the Show'.

'Mr Sinatra, there are no planes at this time in Sydney,' I said. 'Why don't you go back to bed and we'll sort this thing out in the morning.'

'Fuck you,' was his response. Grumpy again. Anyway, after a nervous eleven hours, Sinatra awoke the next morning and decided to go on with the show.

Labriola told me later that Sinatra didn't speak to Sammy Davis Jnr after that. You didn't do that to Frank Sinatra. Frank was the boss. But Sammy loved it. He was going out of his way to shove it up Sinatra's arse. Poor Sammy died a year later from throat cancer.

A day after that escapade, I didn't have to worry about Sinatra's tantrums ever again. It had been a stressful time, but it had been a fantastic tour as well and it had raised the profile of Frontier. And we all did really well out of it. Everyone made money. We could have charged a thousand bucks for the front-row seats. And doing it in the round was a great idea too, which is what they had been doing in the States to maximise crowds. The only downside for the artists was that the stage didn't rotate, so the three of them had to really work the room.

There's no doubt about what the highlight was for me, though. I flew my mum and dad from Tasmania to Melbourne for the first-night performance. My Auntie Barbara and Uncle Brian came with them. I put them in the $125 seats, not the $250 seats. They were very excited, my dad especially, because he was such a big Sinatra fan. About five minutes before the show started, Labriola came up to me and said: 'Chuggi, I need two really trustworthy people. Barbara's friends haven't arrived and I need two cool people to sit next to her in the front row.'

'MUM! DAD!'

So Mum and Dad sat with Barbara, and Frank sang to her all night. Mum got the shits because Barbara hung on to Dad's hand for the whole show. But that night was when the penny finally dropped, when Dad *got* what I was about. He said fuck all, but I knew. From that day on, our relationship changed for the better.

12

`Are These Your Drugs, Sir?`

Ian Saxon was a tour manager on that Sinatra, Minnelli, Davis Jnr extravaganza. Although there were only four dates, it was a huge operation, with sixty-seven of their people on the road, including the musicians, crew, the assorted management personnel from each camp and the stars. On top of that, there were another seventy or so Aussie musicians, handpicked from the Melbourne and Sydney Symphony Orchestras. For that reason, we needed everyone on the Frontier roster working.

Ian's official title was Musicians' Liaison, but really he did whatever had to be done. One of his roles was to keep the Sinatras happy, not something I would have wished on my worst enemy, but he handled it with his usual professionalism and tact.

Sadly for Ian, that tour was one of the last jobs he did for Frontier. His lifestyle, in and outside the music business, was about to come crashing down on top of him. But for my powers of persuasion, he might have avoided the lengthy jail term that was to befall him. He wanted to move to Italy. I convinced him to stay in Australia to be tour manager for singer Tracy Chapman. He was arrested three days before the tour started.

I've never thought of Ian as a criminal, even though he ended up serving sixteen years in jail for drug smuggling and prompted headlines of 'Australia's most wanted man' when he escaped from Long Bay Jail in 1993 and went on the run for two years. He was and still is a good friend, a kind, smart man who paid a terrible price for his wrongdoing. He was a wonderful person when he worked for Frontier and everybody liked him. He drove the limo when Lisa and I got married on Kauai. He's my daughter Sophie's godfather and was very generous towards her when she was a baby. She grew up without seeing him.

In the 80s Ian was just part of the large roster of freelance crew who went on the road for Frontier, looking after international acts. Most of us who worked and played with him knew he had more going on than part-time tour managing. He always had money, he owned property in Sydney and elsewhere and he had a boat, *Rolling Thunder*, the one on which I had enjoyed a few weeks rest and recreation when Sinatra was at Sanctuary Cove.

It became clear after his trial that the boat and Hamilton Island, where he was headed on that trip in 1988, were both crucial to his drugs operation. He spent almost a year up there. He never mentioned his other activities to anyone at Frontier or in my office and we didn't ask any questions. We had an idea of what he was up to, but had no concept of its scale.

I've known Ian for forty-five years. He was a budding pop star in the 60s in his native Auckland. He released a single with his band the Creditors in 1965 called 'I'm Getting Better'. Then he moved to Sydney and formed Ian Saxon and the Sound with well-known singer Colleen Hewitt. After that, he had a brief stint with a group called Southern Contemporary Rock Assembly, who made a couple of albums and played at Sunbury 72.

I met him in Tasmania, on one of those early tours by Billy Thorpe and The Aztecs in the mid-60s. Ian was working for Billy's manager John Harrigan, so he did the tour as a kind of MC. He'd introduce the acts and do a few songs at the start. He did the same thing with Ray Brown and The Whispers across Victoria and Tassie. I saw him again at Sunbury with SCRA. After that, during the 70s, I'd see him occasionally at gigs or on the circuit, but we were more acquaintances than close friends.

I started working with him in the mid-80s. I didn't know it at the time, but when he arrived back in Sydney then he had just served six years in jail in Tahiti, his first prison term for drug-related activity.

Ian worked out of an office he rented from promoter Kevin Jacobsen in Glebe Point Road, Glebe. He had his own touring company, Jigsaw Productions, a partnership with Francie Rigg, doing club tours with American blues artists such as Elvin Bishop and Lonnie Mack. Then he started doing work for Frontier and for promoter Adrian Bohm. Gudinski would give him the tours that he himself didn't have much interest in, such as Suzanne Vega, Phoebe Snow and Herbie Hancock.

That was in the era when Frontier was frying much bigger fish, including Bon Jovi, Guns N' Roses and Billy Joel. Ian would help out on those ones as well, but more often than not he would be tour manager on the smaller ones. He probably did only about half a dozen as TM. When he was helping out, it would be as the go-to guy. Ian looked after the talent.

He was given the title 'special projects manager' when I asked him to look after jazz legend Dizzy Gillespie for ten days in Sydney before the start of his Australian tour. That was a labour of love for Ian, who was a big fan of Dizzy's. After the Bon Jovi tour in 87, the band flew up to Port Douglas in north Queensland for a week of R&R at the newly opened Mirage resort. Ian was sent up there with a blank cheque book. In his autobiography *Star Man: The Right Hand Man of Rock 'n' Roll*, Bon Jovi's minder Michael (Danny) Francis described that holiday as 'the lost week'.

Ian was a very good tour manager – efficient, friendly with the acts and hard-working. We went out on the road together. When American singer Jimmy Buffett came to Australia in 1987, Ian and I shared hotel rooms on the tour. I found out years later that the police recorded some of our conversations in a hotel room in Perth during that run. They were on to him even then. Unknown to me, or the police, there were blocks of hash underneath the bed in the room.

When Ian started on the Sinatra tour, he had just spent a couple of weeks on the road with Iggy Pop. Prior to that, Iggy had done support slots with Jimmy Barnes, one of Premier/Harbour's (and Mushroom's) biggest acts, in New Zealand. Jimmy was huge there, so we were doing outdoor shows to 20,000 or more, but we needed a strong support as insurance. Gudinski had also taken the precaution of getting a sponsor, Pepsi.

At the first show, in Wellington, Gudinski came up to me just before the start and said he was going to the dressing room to let Iggy know about the sponsorship deal, just to make sure he didn't say anything untoward on stage. This is Iggy Pop we're talking about. I told him not to do it, but he wasn't having it and off he went. The head of Pepsi Australia was there, along with some of the company's Kiwi and American heavyweights. Iggy's first song was called 'Fuck Pepsi' and included the endearing phrase 'my piss tastes better than Pepsi'.

Clearly Ian would have had his hands full with Iggy on that Australian tour. He and Swampy Jarvis were the only crew. But Ian had other concerns. Between the tour ending and the Sinatra circus beginning, he had to stash the 10 tonnes of hash he had just imported into Australia. I knew nothing about it.

After the Sinatra, Davis Jnr, Minnelli gigs in Melbourne, which went well and without much incident, everyone was primed for the mass departure to Sydney, 137 people in total. Ian was in charge of the ticketing. Commercial flights had been booked in the morning and afternoon for most of the entourage, while the talent and their teams had a private jet, which was also scheduled to fly in the afternoon. A police escort had been arranged from the hotel to the airport. We had been warned, however, that if Frank suddenly woke up a few hours early and decided to go, we'd have to go. Sure enough, Frank being Frank, he wanted to go early. There was no time to re-arrange a police escort. The limos were sent up from the bowels of the hotel and off they went.

Ian and Gudinski stayed to mop up, in other words to pay the bills and to make sure no one had been left behind. Everyone had gone, but some expensive-looking baggage had been left outside the hotel by mistake. Ian contacted Frank's manager, explained the situation and offered to bring the bags on the commercial flight he and Gudinski were catching in the evening. The order came back that these bags were way too important to travel on a commercial aircraft. They would have to come in a private jet, just like their owners.

So Ian had to book a private jet and he and Gudinski flew to Sydney, with a policeman on board, carrying the valuables of the Sinatras, Minnelli and Davis Jnr. The bags, we were told later, contained mainly jewellery, probably worth millions of dollars. Sammy liked a trinket or two and Barbara often wore diamonds. The stars didn't even know they had been missing.

Almost a year later, on Australia Day 1990, Ian's days of jetsetting were over. A birthday dinner had been organised for him at Sabatini's restaurant in Surry Hills. Lots of people turned up – roadies, managers, agents, people from all parts of the business, even a few who were involved in his clandestine operations, I discovered later – everyone except Ian. It was a surprise party and he wasn't there to enjoy it. His birthday had been the week before, but we'd had to change the date because he and a few other potential guests had been in Adelaide at the wedding of another Frontier tour manager, Mick Mazzone.

There were thirty or forty friends waiting for him in the restaurant. Time went on and there was no sign of him. A couple of hours went past. By 10 pm, by which time everyone was a little the worse for wear, we were starting to worry that something had happened to him. We tried calling him, to no avail. Then all of us went home. At midnight I got a phone call from Chris Watson, who was a lawyer who specialised in drug cases. He told me the National Crime Authority had arrested Ian. Watson was heading down to their headquarters in Sussex Street in the CBD. I got him to pick me up on the way. It had been a big night, even without Ian, so I was flying by that stage. It had never occurred to me in the restaurant that he could have been arrested.

When we got to the NCA, we were escorted in to see the officer in charge of the case. He was sitting behind a desk and in front of him was Ian's Samsonite briefcase. I knew that all the documentation, float money, itineraries and backstage passes for the Chapman tour would be in that briefcase. In my bolshie, drunken state I told the officer that the contents of the case were mine and that I wanted it back, because the tour was only a couple of days away.

He opened the case and showed me the ounce of cocaine sitting there next to a pile of cash. 'Is this yours too?' He wasn't smiling. He told me angrily to go outside and wait in the street until he was ready to talk to me. I didn't argue. I was out there on the footpath for a couple of hours.

None of us really had any idea how big this bust was. We knew Ian sold hash. We used to get it from him, wrapped in a beautiful gold seal. Ian was charged with smuggling 10 tonnes of cannabis resin into Australia and with laundering money.

As soon as his arrest and the charges were made public, all hell broke loose. Most of the daily newspapers did a terrible beat-up on the story, at least from our perspective, calling Ian a big-time Frontier rock promoter who had brought everyone from Sinatra to Bon Jovi to Australia. As soon as one of the papers went with that line, everyone, including radio and television, ran with it. Ian was an impresario one day, a drug baron the next. Gudinski hated it. Every time an artist such as Bon Jovi was mentioned in an article, Frontier had to protect itself by issuing lawyers' letters to the media organisation in question, asking for it to be made clear that no one, whether it be Bon Jovi, John Mellencamp, Frank Sinatra or any of the other artists Ian had worked with, were involved in either drug smuggling or money laundering.

Ian's ties to Frontier, although not on the level stated by the media, put serious pressure on the company. Somewhere along the line, Ian had told an associate that the money he was laundering came from rock 'n' roll, not from drugs. If you read between the lines of the newspaper reports the suggestion was that, if money was being laundered, then there was a good chance Frontier was involved. We were starting to look like big-time drug-dealers. Big time drug-takers some of us may have been, but not dealers.

We had nothing to do with money laundering, but the media didn't want to believe that and the NCA really thought they were on to something. Within days of Ian's arrest, the NCA issued search warrants on a wide range of properties associated with Frontier, including my office, the Harbour office, Frontier's office in Melbourne, my home, Tommasina's home and her parents' shop in Bondi. They raided Ian's property in Noosa, where Mick Mazzone was spending his honeymoon. Later they did Mick's home as well. They raided Philip's farm in Queensland and set up camp there for weeks digging up parts of it looking for stashed booty. It was a hard time.

On the day my house in Manly was raided, I was in Brisbane with tour manager Nick Pitts prior to the opening night of the Kylie Minogue *Enjoy Yourself* tour. Lisa rang in a state to tell me there were two carloads of coppers outside the front door and two more at the back. They went through everything and took away papers, tapes and other property. Fortunately, they didn't find the block of hash with Ian's gold seal on it I had hidden in a jewellery box in the garage.

The biggest upheaval of all was having Frontier's books seized and scrutinised. At least when that was over and they had found nothing, we could move on, but for a while the scandal surrounding the case put a cloud over the company.

Ian's situation got steadily worse. As the investigation went on, a scrunched up receipt found in a drawer at his brother Lloyd's house led the police to a garage in Coogee, where they found gold bars, gold krugerrands, black pearls, slabs of hash and about $5 million in cash. Lloyd was sentenced to nine years for his part in the operation.

The NCA also had all of Ian's paperwork, including some from previous Frontier tours, such as receipts, diaries and notes. I had to identify Ian's handwriting. In fact, I had to make a statement to the NCA concerning my relationship with Ian. He understood all that. I couldn't very well say, 'No, it's not his handwriting'. Later on, I had to appear in court to testify in the case. None of us knew enough about the drugs or the money for it to be used against Ian.

My guess is that Ian had been under surveillance from the moment he got out of jail in Tahiti. The copper who interrogated me told me months later that they had been called in on the day before the arrest and told they either busted him or they would have to pull the operation, because it was getting too expensive. They pulled him over for speeding the next day, found the coke in the briefcase and they had him.

It was all pretty heavy, but if he hadn't had that coke in the car that day the whole thing would probably have gone away. If I hadn't persuaded him not to go to Italy, none of it would have happened. When he escaped and fled to America, that destroyed the career of one of the top NCA guys, so they were determined that when they caught him he wasn't getting out for a long time. They wanted to throw away the key. He was in jail for sixteen years. That doesn't seem right when you compare it to the sentences handed out to murderers and the like.

I've seen Ian a few times since his release in 2008 and he is in a good place, physically and mentally. He's not allowed to enter Australia.

13

'Hey, You in the Black T-shirt!'

God or the devil played a cruel trick on me in 1993. I was named Australia's Father of the Year. The award was given to me for a number of reasons, but it's unlikely that textbook parenting was one of them. Certainly my wife Lisa wouldn't have seen it that way. On the morning I was due to accept the accolade at a ceremony in the ballroom of the Sebel Townhouse in Sydney, she was in a room upstairs with our divorce papers. We'd had a huge fight the night before. I'd been thrown out of the house weeks before that. There are no photographs of us together from that day, even although our children and my son Nicholas were in attendance. The circumstances leading to that sorry scenario take a lot of explaining.

Not long after our daughter Sophie's birth, my relationship with Lisa deteriorated – pretty much for the same reasons my first marriage collapsed. Chief among them was that I was away from home a lot. I was going overseas on business and I was on the road in Australia and New Zealand on a regular basis. The late 80s and early 90s was an incredibly busy and profitable time for Frontier. Guns N' Roses, Sting, Neil Young, Bon Jovi, Crowded House, John Cougar Mellencamp, Aerosmith, Kylie and Mötley Crüe were just some of the big tours. I did all of them.

During that period, Lisa, Sophie and I moved from our house in Manly to a new place nearby, at Seaforth, still in the northern beaches area of Sydney. It was a lovely house, but it became a problem for a while because it needed work. We couldn't have people around until it was finished. We went through good and bad patches in our marriage in the first couple of years there. During a period when we were getting along, in the winter of 1990, Lisa fell pregnant again. This time we had a son, Lucas Alexander Chugg, who was born on 5 April 1991. By then, however, Lisa and I were starting to grow apart.

A pattern was emerging. One day in early 1992 I walked into Harbour and there was a little Chinese girl I'd never seen before sitting in one of the back offices. The sun was shining through the window onto her and she looked like an angel. She was working for Con Nellis, I discovered, who by then worked out of Harbour or my office at least some of the time. I was just blown away by this woman. She was so exotic. Her name was Mayling Ko.

Mayling was a Chinese–Canadian. She was born in Newfoundland to a Chinese father and a Canadian mother. She was smart. When I met her, she was doing part-time work for Con as well as studying geology at Macquarie University. After a few months of seeing each other around the office, we would go and have coffee together. I had never met anybody like her. I was nearly twice her age, so she wasn't that interested in me. I had to work at it.

I discovered that her father's mother had a property in Elizabeth Bay and that there had been a big family dispute between the grandmother and her father when he married a Canadian rather than a woman of Chinese origin. Her parents, cut off from her grandmother's wealth, now lived in a modest apartment in Epping. She had attended the private girls' school SCEGGS. One of her friends there was a girl called Sally McPherson, who would become my general manager when I set up Michael Chugg Entertainment in 2000.

Early in 1993, I took Lisa and the kids and Lisa's mother on a holiday to Disneyland in California and to Frankie's in Kauai. It was a disaster. Sophie and Lisa's mum got sick and Lisa ended up looking after both of them for most of the trip. By the time we got home, we weren't talking, then we started fighting and that's when I left.

The first Australian Father of the Year award was presented in 1957 to Sir Edward Hallstrom, the Sydney philanthropist who donated much of his fortune to the setting up of the city's Taronga Zoo. He was a trustee and later chairman of the zoo. Other notable winners included prime ministers Sir Robert Menzies, Sir William McMahon and Malcolm Fraser, artist Ken Done and restaurateur Peter Doyle. Then I came along.

The Australian Fathers' Council was set up by the chairman of David Jones to promote Fathers Day and the award was designed to recognise a father who had displayed a dedication to helping children, not necessarily his own. By 1993, I had been involved with children's charities for many years, most successfully through a music industry charity the Golden Stave Foundation, of which I was a trustee. In the ten years I had been involved with Golden Stave, we had raised hundreds of thousands of dollars for various organisations, including the Shepherd Centre in Sydney, which pioneered the practice in Australia of teaching deaf children to speak.

My belief is that when they approached me to be Father of the Year it was partly to do with their wish to raise the profile of the award with the media, which had diminished in recent years, but it was also an acknowledgement of my charitable deeds. Perhaps it was significant that the recipient of the award two years earlier was Dr Bruce Shepherd, the founder of the Shepherd Centre.

It put me in an awkward situation. I couldn't decide whether I wanted to go through with it, what with Lisa and I being in the middle of a messy split. The timing wasn't the best, but then it was for a good cause. The award lunch raised thousands of dollars for charity and I knew I could invite people along who would dig deep. I agreed to do it. Lisa couldn't believe I was going through with it.

I rang Peter Rix and lots of other friends from the industry and invited them to the lunch. There was irony in this worthy, honourable function being held in the Sebel, the holy temple of rock 'n' roll debauchery in years gone by. I knew a lot of my friends would see the funny side of it, considering some of the scenes they would have witnessed within the same four walls. If they had known about the tragedy I was about to play out, they might have laughed even more.

Everyone was seated in the ballroom just before the ceremony began. It was a full house, made up of music industry people, some of my family and assorted dignitaries. It was the biggest lunch they had had at the Father of the Year to that point. I think some of the previous recipients who were there were horrified by it all. The Reverend Bill Crewes, from the Wayside Chapel in Kings Cross, was the incumbent who would hand over the mantle to me.

While everyone was waiting in the ballroom, I was pacing up and down in the hotel room upstairs, smoking and wondering how I was going to convince Lisa to come down and sit with me through the presentation at least, if not the whole lunch. She was horrified that I had been asked to be there, never mind her as well. In my heart, I knew there was no way it was going to happen. Meanwhile Nicholas, who was sixteen, was taking care of Sophie and Luke, who were five and two respectively. He knew what was going on and seemed to be taking some kind of pleasure in it. Perhaps, drawing from experience, he could see my chickens coming home to roost. I asked him to go downstairs and fetch Peter Rix. I went to meet Peter in the lobby.

I explained to Peter that my wife was refusing to come downstairs and sit with me unless I agreed on the divorce settlement that she had presented to me. Peter, an experienced lawyer, had nothing to offer me, other than a look of bewilderment and pity. The ceremony went ahead, with Peter sitting next to me where Lisa should have been. I made a speech, during which I acknowledged the love for and from my wife and children. Lisa and I split up three months later. As with Nicholas and Lilo, I have been able to maintain a strong, loving relationship with Lisa and our children Sophie and Lucas since then.

If trauma was uppermost in my personal life, earlier that year it had a dramatic effect on my professional one as well. Guns N' Roses had been to Australia once before, in 1988, and the tour had gone off without too much stress attached, even if dealing with guitarist Slash and singer Axl Rose could be a test of patience at times. Rose's behaviour prior to his arrival for the Guns N' Roses *Use Your Illusion* tour in 93 had everyone running scared.

That was mainly because on the preceding leg of the band's world tour, in South America, he was out of control. I'd get up every morning and pick up the paper or switch on the TV to see what mess the band had got themselves into next. Usually, Rose was at the centre of it. In Buenos Aires, he walked naked through a hotel lobby. In Chile, 178 fans were arrested after the band turned up three hours late for the gig and Rose kept walking off, threatening to end the show. He was charged with endangering human lives a few days later in São Paulo, Brazil, when he threw a chair at a bunch of people.

They were supposed to go to Asia before Australia. I tried to convince their English agent not to let them go, because if Axl had carried on the way he was doing in South America I feared he could get himself shot. They did three shows in Tokyo.

There were only two gigs in Australia, one at Eastern Creek Raceway in Sydney on 30 January and the other at Calder Park Raceway in Melbourne on 1 February. Their reputation preceded them, however, and by the time they were supposed to arrive even the police were nervous. I worked hand in glove with Blacktown police to get that Sydney show happening at Eastern Creek. Apparently they even had a plain-clothes guy following the tour in South America just to see what was going on before they got here.

When they landed in Australia from Tokyo, there was a two-week gap before the first show, so Axl – being Axl – went home to America. The rest of the band went to Port Douglas for ten days to relax, much like Bon Jovi had done at the end of their tour a few years before. I went up there for a couple of days, but I left tour manager Jon Pope in charge for the rest of the time, along with Robbie Williams.

I also left my son Nick up there. He loved it, of course, hanging out with a famous band and their gorgeous girlfriends, some of whom weren't much older than he was. He would stay in the house they had rented and hang out with the girls while the band went off and played golf, although one day he went with them. Slash hooked a drive and it went straight through someone's lounge-room window. The irate owner came out in a fury. It was John Farnham. Nick knew John, introduced him to Slash and all was well.

All the time they were up there everyone, including Guns N' Roses' management, the band and all of my colleagues, was convinced that Axl wasn't coming back. I started to believe them. All of the papers had picked up on it, predicting mayhem and disasters. Meanwhile, the remaining band members were going down to the local pub in Port Douglas at night and doing a few songs for the stunned locals.

By the time the shows happened, Axl had returned, but the media were still in a frenzy. These were the two biggest rock shows of the year. For the Eastern Creek gig, which attracted 75,000 fans, the crew built Nick a little nest up on one of the lighting rigs, where he had the perfect view. I grabbed a bit of posterity for myself, unwittingly, when some of the fans started running towards the stage and I did my bit at the microphone. 'Hey! You in the black T-shirt, slow down!' Hundreds stopped in their tracks.

Of course, all of the press the next day described it as a boring event because no one got killed, no matter that all 75,000 punters were having the time of their lives. Calder Park wasn't quite so successful, but only because it rained. Overall, it was a fantastic couple of days. Nevertheless, when it was over, it came as a relief.

It was a successful tour, but that didn't stop me from passing on the next one and handing it to Paul Dainty, who landed a $1 million profit. I just couldn't be bothered after that one, going through all that pain, all the aggravation Axl caused. I just couldn't do it again. On reflection, I'm an idiot, but sometimes you get to the point where you just can't face the hassle.

Mayling worked with me on that tour and over the next couple of years we spent a lot of time together, personally and professionally. We did all sorts of things together. I took her to Camp Eden. A lot of people said I was stupid. She didn't have a lot of time for Gudinski or Jacobsen or any of those people in the office. At various times while I was going out with her, they all tried to get on to her. Lisa and I had split up, even though we were still married, when Mayling and I started a relationship.

When I moved out of Seaforth, I got an apartment in Naremburn, still on the northern side of the city but a bit closer to the CBD. Mayling moved in for a while and then moved out again. She was like that. She was always straight up with me, but she was still young and wasn't sure what she wanted. My age was a bit of a problem for her.

As Christmas approached, I could at least console myself with the knowledge that Frontier had just had one of the most successful tours in its thirteen-year existence. Madonna's *Girlie Show* tour in November went off. We did eight stadium shows, three in Sydney, three in Melbourne and one each in Adelaide and Brisbane. It was a monster and it was a great show. There are moments as a promoter when you look out at the crowd and just marvel at the spectacle. Gudinski and I walked up to the back of the MCG at the first Melbourne show and did just that. We even took a few young fans from the back row and put them in whatever seats were available in section A. Those are the days you live for as a promoter, when the fans, the talent and the organisation combine to create something greater than the sum of its parts.

Early in 1994, I heard that a Woodstock twenty-fifth anniversary concert was going to be held in August near the site of the original festival in upstate New York. I was planning to go over there around that time anyway to see The Eagles, because we were bringing them out to Australia the following year. I thought I should go check out Woodstock. Then I decided I should take a lot of people with me.

I rang Jon Pope and told him to organise a tour bus over there, one that would sleep about sixteen people. Then I started organising a tour party. Eric Robinson came for a few days. Molly Meldrum and his broken leg joined us to do interviews with the artists. Trevor Smith was there with his wife Jan. Journalist Toby Creswell and his partner. Con Nellis. Denise De Silva from Mushroom. Rebecca Battles, an Aussie woman who was a major player at MTV in New York. Mayling. And a few others I've forgotten.

The festival line-up was a great mix of old and new, including some of the acts, such as Santana, Country Joe McDonald, Joe Cocker and John Sebastian, who had appeared at the original concert twenty-five years earlier. Also on the bill were acts that I had toured in Australia in recent years, such as Peter Gabriel, Bob Dylan and Aerosmith. It was a great weekend. I ended up working there in artists' liaison, just because I knew some of the crew and because I could. I volunteered and they paid me a dollar a day. Shit money, great time and great networking for future tours.

One of the other bands on that bill, Red Hot Chili Peppers, would cause me untold grief a year later.

Early in 1995, a group of people, including me, came up with the idea of staging an outdoor festival called Alternative Nation. Its primary purpose was to rub the Big Day Out off the face of the earth. BDO promoters Ken West and Vivian Lees had succeeded in turning a Sydney one-day event into an annual, national touring rock carnival in the space of two years. What a nerve!

Alternative Nation was a collaboration between Frontier and Michael Coppel. I was in on it, but the real driving forces were Coppel and Gudinski. Gudinski had a thing about Lees and West, but Coppel was worse. Their only intention was to blow the BDO out of the water.

We got together. Coppel booked some acts. We booked some acts. It sounded like a great idea. Three back-to-back shows over Easter. We booked the Chili Peppers, who were one of our clients at the time, to be headline. I had started working with Ted Gardner, my old mate from Men at Work days, who was managing Tool, so they were on the bill as well. It was a fairly strong line-up. We booked the Institute of Sport Centre in Brisbane, Eastern Creek – scene of one of my greatest triumphs with Guns N' Roses – in Sydney, and Olympic Park in Melbourne.

We announced the tour. Tickets went on sale. First-morning sales went really well. At 2 pm that afternoon, Red Hot Chili Peppers' management rang to say they weren't coming. One of them had a drugs problem, had gone into rehab and all touring had been cancelled. Sorry.

We were fucked from that day on. Stone Temple Pilots pulled out as well. We started looking for replacement acts and found them in Lou Reed and Faith No More, but we had to pay them a fortune to come out at such short notice.

This was the first time Frontier and Coppel had done anything together. There was bitter rivalry between Gudinski and Coppel that had existed since Coppel was running A.C.E. with Zev Eizik. You weren't allowed to start anything in Melbourne with Gudinski around. He'd do what he could to shut you down. That was what it was like in Gudinski's Melbourne then. The reason I lived in Sydney and stayed in Sydney was because in Sydney you could co-exist. There was nothing about wiping everybody else out. That's the reason I never went back to Melbourne. I was glad I didn't have to get involved in that shit.

I went to all three shows on the Alternative Nation tour. In my role as advance man, checking the sites, I left the Brisbane show, just as the rain was setting in halfway through, to fly to Sydney. By the time I got to the airport, the cabbie couldn't see where he was going. Out at Eastern Creek the following afternoon, it was beautiful. By late afternoon it was a mudbath. A hail storm arrived at Olympic Park in Melbourne minutes before the show started.

Everything about Alternative Nation was a disaster, not least having to lick our wounds and admit defeat to our BDO rivals without them having to lift a finger, although they might have done that. Mudstock, as it came to be known, lost us $3 million. And we weren't done.

A few months later, we toured Mighty Morphin Power Rangers. You don't hear that mentioned often in Frontier circles. It's not listed on the company's tour history (last time I looked).

In 1994, Mighty Morphin Power Rangers was one of the most popular kids' shows on television worldwide. They followed that success with a movie in 1995, which also did well. Gudinski went to see the stage version in the US. He wasn't totally convinced. We were all a bit nervous about doing it, but I figured it was worth a gamble, so off we went. The problem was that by the time it got to Australia kids had moved on to something else. It stiffed. Another couple of million down the tubes. We had never made a loss in any one year since we started.

The finger of blame veered in my direction. That was just another nail in my coffin at Frontier. I was responsible for the Mighty fuck-up because I drove the whole thing and talked everybody else into it. I took the rap for most things, but that's when the resentment really started to creep in. If they hated me then, a year later they were going to be falling over each other to be first to kick my arse.

14

Six Days in the Jailhouse

Los Angeles County Jail smacks you in the mouth like a giant fist when you enter it. It's one of the biggest prisons in the world. In 1996, when I found myself locked up there with 22,000 other criminals, it was *the* biggest. The place was intimidating, scary beyond belief, full of noise, fear and bravado and reeking of authority and disinfectant.

I deserved to be there, although I wasn't looking at it from that perspective at the time. I had nearly killed someone. I couldn't deny it. Now I was paying the price, behind bars, dressed in an orange jumpsuit and wondering which of my 250 dorm buddies was most likely to slit my throat.

You can get tickets on yourself living the rock 'n' roll lifestyle, jetting around the world, hanging out with the rich, famous and beautiful. I was guilty of that, just as I was guilty of driving home drunk in the middle of the night and crashing into someone.

The law got the better of me that night, and I'm glad it did. The events that followed were wake-up calls that changed my attitude to life and made me think twice about my reckless behaviour. Not only that, jail marked the beginning of the end for me as a director of Frontier Touring, although it would be three years before I took that leap. After prison, even just a week of it, nothing was quite the same.

Gudinski was with me on the fateful day. It was March 29, 1996. I'd been doing business in LA for about three weeks, seeing shows and having meetings. It wasn't our busiest year at Frontier. We'd done Jeff Buckley, Chris Isaak and Jimmy Page and Robert Plant in the first quarter, which went well, and we had Red Hot Chili Peppers coming up in April, but most of our efforts were being directed at the second half of the year, with tours by Sting, Sex Pistols, Bush, No Doubt and Garbage. Justified or not, I was in celebratory mood. It was a Friday and we were supposed to fly back to Australia that night, but I had another plan. We had lunch at Mr Chow's in Beverly Hills, one of Michael's favourite restaurants, with an agent friend and his wife. I was staying at the Hotel Nikko nearby.

After lunch, I drove Michael back to Santa Monica in my rental car. He had to attend a meeting with Neil Young's manager Elliot Roberts. My driving wasn't the best. I bumped a few kerbs. I was so tired. I wasn't keeping it together. I had told Michael by then that, instead of flying home, I was going to Billy Thorpe's birthday party out at his house in Studio City in the San Fernando Valley. He wasn't happy and started giving me a lecture about drinking and driving. Michael would always leave his car somewhere if he had been drinking. He begged me not to go and to come to the airport with him. As usual, I did my arrogant 'I'll be right mate' routine and off I went.

Then I drove to see my good friend Ted Gardner and his wife Nikki, who lived at North Curson Avenue near Beverly Center. Ted's the guy who gave me grief years earlier when I wouldn't let the band he was tour managing in Australia – Men at Work – do an encore. He had stayed in LA when Men at Work found success in the US in the early 80s. Now he was managing American band Jane's Addiction and running the festival he and the band's singer, Perry Farrell, had founded, Lollapalooza. I made a point of catching up with Ted and Nikki every time I was in LA. On this occasion, however, they could see that I wasn't in the best condition and warned me to be careful, not to do anything stupid. They knew the cops in LA were everywhere. I said I'd be fine.

The party at Thorpie's was great fun. A lot of people from the music industry were there. I'd been to plenty of parties at Billy's before, when the likes of Olivia Newton John and Tina Turner and Mick Fleetwood would show up. Billy had a lot of friends through the many different facets of the music business he had pursued during his time in LA, so he had no shortage of takers when invites were sent out.

At around 1 am, I decided to leave. I wanted to meet up with a few people the next day, Saturday, and so I thought I should get some sleep. I'd had a lot to drink, mainly vodka, and probably a few other things besides. I can't remember, but I was in no state to tackle the road through Laurel Canyon that is difficult enough to negotiate during the day, never mind at night, pissed. Billy tried to get me to stay the night, which I could have done easily, but instead I told him I had work to do and so I wanted to get back.

I got up to the top of Laurel Canyon and I was coming down the other side. It's quite bendy. I was cruising along the road, just near the Houdini castle. I was feeling quite happy that I had one more day of meetings and then I was going home. Suddenly this little red car came around the corner and it was moving really fast. Maybe I panicked, but for whatever reason I crossed the centre of the road and smacked into it. If I had been sober, I would have reacted more quickly and avoided the collision.

I wasn't hurt, apart from a couple of bruises, but the young guy in the other car, who was with his girlfriend, was pretty knocked about. I got out of my car and walked over to see if the kids were okay and then made sure that one of the people in the nearby houses had rung the police. Then I thought: 'Fuck me, I'm in deep shit.' I should never have taken that road in the first place. It's the worst over-the-mountains road of the lot. I was just full of myself thinking I could get away with it.

I had a few joints in the back of the car, so I dumped them in somebody's garden about a hundred metres up the road. Then I waited for the police and the ambulance to arrive. I sat on the side of the road thinking about what was going to happen. I saw myself losing the ability to come into America, all that sort of stuff. That was a real worry, although only one among many.

When the police came, I was still sitting by the roadside and I must have appeared pretty dishevelled. They were okay. I think because I was looking forlorn they weren't too aggressive, but they put handcuffs on me and bundled me into the back of their car anyway.' They took me to a nearby hospital to have me checked out then took me down to the Van Nuys lock-up, which was – and is – a notorious jail. Van Nuys is in the middle of the Barrio district of LA, so it's pretty tough. It must have been about 3 am by the time we got there. They took my photo, fingerprinted me and put me in the lock-up with six or seven guys.

My only other experience of a jail cell had been in New Zealand twenty-one years earlier, when I got put in the Auckland lock-up for a few hours for saying 'fuck' on stage while I was trying to stop some people at the front of the audience, particularly a young woman, from spitting at the stage during a Fairport Convention concert.

Saying 'fuck' on stage in New Zealand then was a pretty big deal. It was the second of the Fairport Convention tours I had done as tour manager, and this time singer Sandy Denny was with them. We were playing in Hamilton and halfway through the show a woman down at the front started abusing Denny quite severely and spat on her. I walked out on stage, grabbed the microphone and told the woman she was a fucking disgrace and to get out. The crowd cheered. Three nights later, when they were playing at Auckland YMCA, I saw the police come into the building followed by the same woman I'd shouted at in Hamilton. I thought: 'Here we fucking go.'

So they arrested me, because I had verbally assaulted her. Then they took me down to the lock-up because I wouldn't admit I had said fuck. In the cell with me were two 25-stone Islander gay guys. They were obviously tripping. One of them was getting a bit tetchy. I was having terrible visions of what they might do to me. Eventually I couldn't stand it any longer, so I looked up at the camera in the cell and said: 'Yes I did say fuck. Now, can you let me out?'

I went to court two days later, where the judge told me it was disappointing that someone in my position would use such profanity in a public place – no mention of the fact that the woman I had said it to was spitting at the star. I got fined $100. The band thought it was hilarious. I met one of the arresting officers about a year later when I was back in New Zealand on another tour. He was arresting one of the members of English band Wishbone Ash, drummer Steve Upton, for doing the same thing I had done. One of their songs is called 'FUBB (Fucked Up Beyond Belief)' and when he introduced it at an outdoor festival a woman in her garden heard him say it and complained to the mayor. The copper told me later that, after locking me up, the duty officers had been taking bets about how long I'd last in the cell with the two gay giants.

The Van Nuys lock-up didn't pose any obvious, immediate threat like I had experienced in Auckland, but it was distressing nonetheless. It was the middle of the night and I was the only foreigner in there. There was a phone in the cell, but it was only national so I couldn't reach anyone in Australia, not that it would have been much help in the circumstances. My most urgent need was to make bail, which had been set at $US30,000. That seemed crazy to me, but I had been charged with drunken driving. That's a felony rather than a misdemeanour. How on earth I was going to get that kind of money on a Saturday morning (even worse, Sunday in Australia) was beyond me. You had to post bail before 4 pm, otherwise you were there for another night; but on Saturday, if you didn't come up with the money it meant being locked up until Monday. Thank God that when I called Ted Gardner he was at home.

Ted came down to the jail. He could see that I was distressed. All I could say to him was, 'Get me out of here.' Ted got me a lawyer, but, just as important, he had a platinum American Express card. He called AE and explained the situation. They said he could pick up the $30,000 from a Western Union office in the Valley. What they didn't tell him was that Western Union only issued money orders to the value of $500 maximum. So he arrived early in the afternoon with sixty money orders and bailed me out.

We went back to my hotel and it was then I realised I had left my passport in the rental car, which was now probably impounded somewhere and being searched for illegal substances. Ted took me to the police pound the next day and they let me go through the car, which was severely damaged, and I retrieved my passport. That was one problem solved, but more rude shocks were to follow.

The first of these came from my mates, my fellow directors, at Frontier. They did everything they could to distance themselves and the company from the incident. Rightly so, you might think, given that I was in the wrong and that my trip to Thorpie's was in my own time and on my own budget. I guess I expected more support from a bunch of men I had been working with shoulder to shoulder for fifteen years, longer than that in some cases. Philip Jacobsen didn't give me any support at all. I got a very hard time from all of them in the months ahead.

I flew home soon after my release and tried to work as normal, but I knew I had to go back for my trial a few weeks later, so that was always on my mind, that and the lack of support I was getting from my colleagues. Gudinski had got a call from Thorpie at 4 am in Australia on the Sunday, to tell him what had happened. His wife had to answer it because Gudinski still hadn't arrived from LA. He had to call Thorpie back when he got home. Michael was furious.

Fortunately for me, when I did go to court, in April, the lawyer Ted had hired for me, Steve Cron, had done a plea bargain and had the charge reduced from a felony to a misdemeanour, which meant there was little chance of having to do serious jail time, but I wasn't out of danger. The judge sentenced me to twenty days in the County Jail, plus he ordered two hundred hours of community service, which I could perform in Australia. On top of that the crash victim sued me for loss of earnings. That dragged on for about six months until eventually we agreed on a financial settlement. It was almost six figures. I would have paid the same again not to do my time at the LA fun palace.

I didn't have to do my time straight away. The court ruled that I had to return there on 21 June, whereupon I would be transferred to the County Jail. Again I went back to Australia and back to work. On 17 June, Con came with me to LA and we stayed at the Sunset Marquis the night before I was due to hand myself in.

I was at the court for a few hours, then the police took me out to the back of the building and at 5 pm the prison bus pulled up outside. I got on the bus in cuffs. It was full of new inductees and prisoners who had been to court that day. We got to the jail and buses were coming from all over the place. At this point I was finding it hard to accept that all of this was actually happening.

I was put in a holding cell with hundreds of others. Every now and then, the guards came and picked someone out and took him away. I was standing at the back thinking that sooner or later they were going to realise I shouldn't be there and let me go home. That was all I could think about. It was all a big mistake, a dream.

Eventually I got taken out and put in a big room where they gave me the orange jumpsuit and sandals. Then I handed over all of my clothes and had a shower. Then I was off to my cell. It was one big communal hall, like a barracks, with bunks running along the walls on two sides. There was no privacy. In my block there were about twenty white guys, seventy or eighty Mexicans, thirty or so black guys and the same of Koreans. Of course, they were all hanging around in their respective racial groups, so the black guys were over one side and the white guys on the other.

It was pretty scary. A couple of the white guys took me under their wing, but there were a lot of heavy-duty criminals in there. Some of them couldn't have been more than seventeen. What was clear was that all of the factions hated each other, but there was particular tension between the blacks and the Koreans.

I wasn't too concerned by this. My lawyer had told me that despite my sentence of twenty days there was every chance that they would let me out after a five or six days, due to the regular intake of more serious offenders at the jail. A couple of the white prisoners I befriended, who knew the drill, backed him up. I figured I'd be long gone before any trouble erupted, but I was wrong.

I'd been there for a couple of days and I was counting the hours in the hope that my lawyer was right. I'd had a one-on-one with the prison psychiatrist. I had eaten some disgusting food. I had made a few friends. In fact, once it got around that I was Australian, inmates from all backgrounds seemed eager to talk to me, more out of curiosity than anything else. Australia was a big mystery to most of them, so I drew a map of Australia on the wall and gave some of them, the Mexicans and the white guys mainly, a geography lesson.

Then one man, an arsehole who had been on my bus on the way in, became the bane of my existence while I was locked up and jeopardised any hope I had of an early release. He thought he was Mr Big. This idiot said something back to one of the guards – I don't know what it was about – and before we knew it everyone in the cell, hundreds of us, were herded down to another part of the prison in the basement. Down in the bowels of the prison was where all the really bad fuckers were. Day three and there I was banged up with murderers, rapists and drug-dealers.

This basement area was filthy. There was water everywhere, with faeces and bits of stale food floating around in it. I could see that the guards had thought: 'Okay, we'll fix these bastards', all because of what the little upstart had said to one of them. I hated him and I hated being there. As you walked along the corridors, you had to be careful because if you got too close to one of the cells the occupant would try to pull you up against the bars, just to scare you.

The tension got much worse in this new environment, to the point where the Koreans and the black dudes were ready to rumble. It was about to boil over into a bloodbath. That's when I had my James Cagney/Mother Teresa moment. I don't know what possessed me, other than that I thought I was back with

Fairport Convention in New Zealand or mouthing off into the mic at a Guns N' Roses gig, but I leapt onto a table, stood up, raised my arms and started yelling at the top of my voice:

'Listen, you fucking idiots. We're down here because that fucking arsehole [pointing at Mr Big] wouldn't shut his fucking mouth. Now, if you all start fighting, we are going to be down here for another fucking week. If you want to give the coppers a hard time, this is what we do. We clean up the fucking cell.' And so we did. We all got together and cleaned the place up. A few hours later, the area was spick and span.

It was one of my greatest performances, though I say so myself. If I hadn't defused that situation, we would all have suffered.

Next day, we were moved back up to where we had been initially and suddenly I was a bit of a celebrity. I had them all laughing. On the sixth day, the guards summoned me. They were letting me go. I was ecstatic. I couldn't get out quickly enough. As I was leaving, one of the guards said to me: 'Go back to your own country and fuck up over there, you old bastard.' He wasn't laughing. I didn't respond.

When I got out, Mayling and Con were waiting for me and we went straight to the Sunset Marquis hotel in West Hollywood to celebrate. By the time I got back to Australia, however, any notion of celebrating my freedom had evaporated.

The whole terrible, shameful affair shook me up. It took me a long time to get over it. I had nearly killed an innocent kid, after all. I felt pretty guilty about it, plus with all the flak I was copping from my so-called friends and partners, I wasn't in the best frame of mind. To top it off, Mayling left me not long after that. It wasn't a good time.

That I had put someone's life in danger was bad enough, but I was pissed off at how my arrogance had got me into that situation in the first place. Living the crazy rock 'n' roll lifestyle I was living, you start to think you're infallible. You blame everyone else except yourself.

What was amazing was that the story didn't make it into the newspapers or any of the media. Frontier didn't do anything to try and hide it, but it didn't come out. If it had, there would have been even more resentment within the company towards me, I suspect, especially if business suffered as a result.

Jacobsen turned against me because of the accident and Gudinski wanted nothing to do with me. It irritated him that he had told me not to drive to Thorpie's and I had gone ahead anyway. He kept telling me afterwards it was my fault and that I should have come home that night. It didn't make me feel any better that he was right. The accident caused a lot of irritation within the organisation. It wasn't their fault that I was driving while I was drunk. It started to affect things at work, because the incident put me under intense pressure.

Maybe I was on a bit of an ego trip then, but I didn't really believe that at the time. Thorpie didn't think so and Ted Gardner didn't think so. Sam Righi thought so, but he had been trying to undermine me for years anyway. He had been hoping to get rid of me since 1983.

After the accident was also around the time Gudinski started losing interest in the touring arm of his business. From 1996 onwards, he wasn't making regular trips around the world any more. That's when I started getting back into it and travelling a lot and doing all the things that Gudinski used to do, but over the next three years that just got harder and harder for me, because the acts I wanted to promote weren't always big names; I just thought they could be. The question kept getting asked as to why we were touring these little bands hardly anybody knew about.

Jacobsen, who held the purse strings, went from being a very important part of my life and a big adviser over many years to being my worst nightmare. The objectives I had were beginning to clash with Michael's and Philip's. I was obsessed about promoting in Asia. Gudinski didn't see it. I wanted to set up Frontier in America. Gudinski wasn't opposed to the idea, but I really wanted to set up there and perhaps move there, so his lack of urgency on the matter frustrated me.

All of this was nothing compared to my state of mind after the trial and prison. That was the first and most important thing I had to address. I spent four of my first six months back in Australia at the Golden Door health retreat just north of Surfers Paradise in the Gold Coast hinterland in Queensland.

Some of that time was due to my legal obligation to treat my drinking problem. Aside from my rehabilitation at Golden Door, I went to Alcoholics Anonymous meetings in Surfers every morning at 6 am. All of this contributed to my community service and had to be signed off by a Justice of the Peace and presented to the court in LA. Eventually I completed the two hundred hours demanded of me.

What Golden Door really did for me was something just as valuable as paying off my debt to society. I was well screwed up then, but looking back I can see I was more damaged than I believed I was. I went to the health farm for a variety of reasons, as penance, to think, to get healthy. In the years ahead I started going there as often as I could. I figured it was the best way to get myself properly focused. I was going to need a clear head if the next phase of my life was going to be as successful as the one I was beginning to have doubts about.

15

A Power for Good

The second half of 1996, including my stints at Golden Door, was no less eventful and traumatic than the first half. During my enforced visit to Los Angeles, while having a drink with friends at the Sunset Marquis, I bumped into Neil Finn and Crowded House's manager Grant Thomas. I knew Neil and Grant very well. Frontier had done all of the Crowded House tours in Australia, but no more, it appeared. The band was splitting up.

I was shocked to hear that, especially since it seemed to me they were on the verge of being huge in America. It would come out eventually that Neil was tired of touring and needed a break from the commitment and responsibility, as the band's chief songwriter and front man, of keeping Crowded House a going concern. Grant said they wanted to go out with a bang, however, and our discussion in that bar that night led to the biggest show of my career, Crowded House's Farewell to the World concert on the forecourt of Sydney Opera House on 24 November 1996.

Before we got to the Opera House steps, I had a painful as well as exhilarating few months ahead of me. When I got out of jail and met up with Mayling, I could sense something wasn't right with her, but I was already traumatised by what had just happened to me, so I let it pass. A few weeks later I learned what was going on. She was about to leave me. I think she felt I had been using her, rather than the other way around, as some of my friends saw the situation. She wanted to get even.

On the trips we did to LA, it wasn't unusual for Mayling to stay on for a few days to do other work of her own after I had gone back to Sydney. That's exactly what she did when I left prison and went home. While she was there, she met someone at the Sunset Marquis, a guy from the film industry. She started seeing him.

We weren't living together at that point. Mayling had moved into Colleen Ironside's Sydney apartment after Colleen got a job in Hong Kong. When Mayling got back, I went around there to see her. It was her birthday and I wanted to take her out. There was a bouquet of flowers on the doorstep when I got there. They were from the guy in LA. A week later, he turned up in Sydney and she told me she was going back to LA with him – to live.

I was freaked out, really upset by it. She came around to pick up the rest of her stuff from my place and ripped up a few photos of the two of us together while she was there. It ripped me apart. I was a disaster area. I was obsessed with her and she had hung me out to dry. After the hell of prison life, albeit for only a week, and the cold shoulder I was getting around Frontier and Harbour, this stab in the heart didn't come at the best possible time.

I couldn't let her departure become an obsession, however. I had my job to think about. In August, I was taking Aboriginal band Yothu Yindi to America to perform during the flag handover ceremony at the Paralympics in Atlanta. I'd become friends, even a kind of mascot, to Yothu Yindi over the previous few years. They were on Gudinski's Mushroom label and Premier/Harbour had toured them in 1994. During that period, I become their unofficial adviser. The band's song 'Treaty', released in 1991, was recognised as a landmark in Australia's pop and cultural history by then. They seemed the perfect choice for Atlanta. It was unfortunate that they weren't shown the respect they deserved when they got there.

I used the trip to Atlanta as an excuse to see Mayling, if she would see me. I called her and she agreed to meet me in LA on my way through to Georgia. I wasn't handling the situation very well at all. I was still a wreck. We went shopping in LA and spent half a day together. I wasn't allowed to go to the apartment she was sharing with her new man. She seemed to be terrified of him. We didn't resolve anything. Then I set off for Atlanta. It was a thrill going there, to be part of something important outside my normal sphere of interest. Nick Pitts, Frontier's production manager, was with me, along with Mandawuy Yunupingu and his Yothu Yindi band mates.

Nick was a really good friend. He was an English guy I met when he was doing monitors for ABBA on their Australian tour in 1977. Then he did the 84 *Synchronicity* tour with The Police and moved to Australia to run Frontier's production set-up. The night before the handover ceremony, we sat in a bar somewhere for hours and the poor guy got an earful of my misery rather than being able to soak up the significance of what we were doing in Atlanta. I was pouring my heart out and crying over Mayling and just being horrible.

Next day, with me slightly the worse for wear, the anticipation and excitement of taking part in the momentous Olympic event turned quickly to disappointment when we got to the stadium. That was due to the American production people who were in charge of the closing ceremony. We turned up and were guided past all these beautiful flowers and lavish dressing rooms, then we were put in a room not much bigger than a cupboard, with nothing in it but stale bread and shit floating on the floor. I was not impressed. Yothu Yindi did themselves and Australia proud, though, singing 'Treaty', and would do so again when they took part in the closing ceremony of the Sydney Olympic Games and the opening ceremony of the Sydney Paralympics in 2000. I was co-producer of that opening ceremony and of the closing ceremony at the Paralympics. That was quite an honour.

Watching that ceremony in Atlanta made me wake up to myself about what I had been going through with Mayling. The courage, strength and good humour of thousands of disabled athletes put my pathetic behaviour into perspective. I got over it, or at least I got the hard part out of the way.

Mayling came back to Australia a few months after that. She was very upset because her brother had just died. I tried to stop her going back to LA, but to no avail. She ditched the guy eventually, not surprisingly. She found out that he was married with kids in Boston, so she went to Canada.

I saw her again, much later, around the end of 1999, when I was setting up my own business. I met her in London and in Los Angeles. When I left Frontier, she was one of the people I went to see. I valued her judgement and she has done great work for me over the years. After that, she came back to Sydney for a while and I started courting her again, slowly, but it didn't last long.

I never really got over her. She continued to do work for my businesses even though I didn't see her regularly. We spent some time together in Europe in 2000. We were going to get married at one point. We were in Germany, going to a friend's fiftieth birthday, when the subject came up. It didn't happen. I was in a bit of a mess around that time. I was taking a lot of drugs. I was hanging out with an English agent friend of mine in London, and we were doing bad things. We encouraged each other to do bad things. That was the peak of our craziness. We'd sit up for two days drinking, smoking and doing drugs.

Sometime in that period, Mayling and I were staying at the Royal Garden Hotel in Kensington in London and I said something that upset her and she moved out. After that, I didn't see her again for years. She moved back to Canada, met someone else and had two kids with him. Strangely, some would say, we're still close. I talk to her regularly and whenever I'm in Canada on business we catch up for dinner.

I continued my treatment and rehabilitation at Golden Door, but in between time I had to start work on the Farewell to the World extravaganza. Through discussions with Grant and the band, we reached agreement on the venue and the fact that it would be a free concert. We had agreed also that any proceeds from the event, even though there was no admission charge, would be given to the Sydney Children's Hospital Foundation. I had been involved in that charity, which raises funds for the children's hospital in Randwick, New South Wales, since the 1980s. I'd run benefit concerts, music industry lunches, that kind of thing. I'm immensely proud of what I helped to achieve there. The kids' cancer facility at Randwick is second to none and was funded partly by the foundation. To see the bravery on kids' faces in that unit is awe-inspiring. That environment helps children stay alive. Through my involvement with Golden Stave, we raised money for rebuilding, for vital new equipment in the wards, and for other essential new technology at the hospital.

Since that first fundraiser I did back in Launceston for the bike club in the 60s, I've helped raise more than $20 million for a variety of causes, whether through benefit concerts, lunches, being actively involved at board level of charity organisations or simply by making a donation where I think it's warranted. I realised a long time ago that you only get what you give. It's all about karma. So it felt natural for me to get involved with as many of those charities as I could, time permitting. You always feel good about it and I do honestly believe that giving in that sense comes back to you in other ways. I think I am a generous person, with my time and my money. Making money for myself or for my businesses has never been the driving force in my life. If that's a failing, as some of my former business partners would attest, then so be it. I've always approached business from the perspective that if you do the job properly, the money will follow.

I've given generously to charity myself, but the greatest reward for me has come from working to that end in conjunction with like-minded people in the music industry. It's not an industry with a great reputation in the general public's eyes. I don't pretend to be a great walking advert for it in some respects, but over the past thirty years, when disaster has struck at home or in our international neighbourhood, the Australian music industry in all its many forms – management, acts, venues, agents, promoters, record companies, publishers, publicists and the music media – has capitalised on its power as a popular form of entertainment to raise millions of dollars in emergency aid or as financial support for a worthy cause.

The first big ones I was involved in were the Ash Wednesday Bushfire Appeal and the Rock the Way to LA Olympic Appeal in 1983. That was around the same time I became involved in the Golden Stave Foundation in Sydney. That body was set up by a few people in the industry; Polygram chief executive Ross Barlow, publishers Peter Hebbes and Jack Argent, and my colleague from the Stevie Wright and The Church phases of my career, Chris Gilbey. Gilbey and Hebbes, being English, had got the idea of an annual fundraising lunch from a similar charity lunch they had attended in the UK called the Silver Clef.

In 1982, I went to the Golden Stave event at the Sebel Townhouse and thought it was fabulous. It was just a bunch of music industry people having a great time raising money. It starts at noon and finishes when everyone falls over. I got involved because there didn't seem to be anyone else there representing the touring side of the business. In the early days, the lunch would bring in around $3000. Nowadays it's more like $500,000.

I gained a reputation, another outlet for my love of the microphone, as the MC at the Golden Stave lunch for many years, conducting the lottery and abusing people into spending more money. It was great fun, but I've given up that part of it now. You can't run a lottery when your memory's going and you can't remember who to give the prizes to.

In 1985, I was coordinator for the Australian arm of Live Aid and helped stage the Newcastle Earthquake Appeal concert in 1990. Close to 45,000 turned up for that one, an amazing figure in Newcastle. It featured Midnight Oil, Jimmy Barnes, Split Enz, and the Angels, among others. The concert raised almost $1 million. Unfortunately, that money sat in the lord mayor's trust account in Newcastle for years.

With actors Bryan Brown and his wife Rachel Ward and DJ Doug Mulray, I co-organised the Bush Bash that raised $500,000 for Sydney City Mission in 1992 and in 1994 I coordinated the New South Wales Bushfire concert at Sydney Football Stadium. That was a wonderful show. We had 25,000 at the SFS to see Sting, Bryan Adams, Jimmy Barnes, Paul Kelly, Hunters and Collectors, Daryl Braithwaite, Diesel and Deborah Conway, who gave their time and talent at short notice for a great cause. That concert raised close to $700,000 for environmental bodies such as Ian Kiernan's Clean Up Australia, which used some of the money to have wrecked cars pulled out of Bangalow State Forest in New South Wales. The National Parks and Wildlife Foundation benefited also, as did the New South Wales Community Disaster Relief Fund.

So, by the time Farewell to the World came around, I knew what needed to be done to make a big-time charity event work. This one was slightly different, however. We wouldn't be raising money from punters directly, since the concert was free. That meant the money would have to come from sponsorship and public donations, which didn't involve too much co-ordination. The real challenge came in staging an event for an undetermined number of people at a venue not designed for large crowds.

Securing Sydney Opera House as the venue was a simple task. I had plenty of ties there, stretching back to when it opened and Stevie Wright was strutting his drug-addled stuff in the concert hall. I was involved in 2SM's outdoor Concert of the Decade there in late 1979, which had Stevie, Richard Clapton and my acts Stars and Kevin Borich on the bill. That was the biggest free concert in that neighbourhood before Crowded House. Also, Peter Rix and I ran the first ten years of Sydney Festival's New Year concerts at the Opera House.

We had a false start. The concert was scheduled to happen on 23 November, a Saturday, but was postponed for 24 hours because of rain. There was another factor, however. US President Bill Clinton was in Sydney that Saturday and had elected to have a guided tour of the Opera House, which meant closing down the area for several hours, so our job would have been made ten times harder if the show had gone ahead. Later, we got a cheque for $3000 from the White House as compensation for the inconvenience the presidential party had caused.

Although we anticipated large numbers on the Sunday, we weren't expecting any trouble. Crowded House was (and still is, I imagine) a band you could take home to meet your mum. They were never going to incite a riot or anything. They did, however, pull 250,000 people to Circular Quay and beyond. There wasn't a single vantage point for kilometres in any direction hours before the show started. It turned out to be one of the most magnificent concerts I have been involved in.

I could tell early on that the numbers were going to be phenomenal. The whole forecourt was full by the time the first band, You Am I, went on. When Powderfinger played after them, there was a sea of people in every direction, even on the other side of the harbour. Macquarie Street leading back into the CBD was packed with people.

The police, naturally, were freaking out. No one had ever seen so many people gathered together in that spot before. You couldn't move at the gig, but we felt we had it under control. I had to work with a loudhailer for about an hour at the entrance before Crowded House came on to keep the crowd calm, but we were never worried. The night, as it turned out, was a wonderful celebration of a band Australia holds close to its heart.

That was the end of big concerts outside the Opera House. It was deemed too dangerous. Now you're not allowed to have more than 6000 people on the forecourt. The 90s introduced tougher health and safety demands on concert promoters. When you look back on a lot of the shows we did in the early days, I suppose we were pushing the envelope. But we had this idea, this belief, that we had a relationship with the kids and that because of that nothing bad would happen.

We raised $500,000 for the Sydney Children's Hospital Foundation that day. More important was that, through Crowded House's patronage, the organisation boosted its profile considerably. The impetus from Farewell to the World helped the foundation to raise $20 million over the next few years, money badly needed for a large rebuilding program at the hospital.

Despite their farewell to the world, that wasn't my last fundraising night out with Crowded House. After they reformed in 2006, they seemed the natural choice to headline the Sydney Live Earth concert in 2007, especially since it coincided with the release of their comeback album, *Time On Earth*.

The concert at Sydney Football Stadium, one of twelve held around the world on 7 July 2007 to raise awareness of climate change, made $1 million. After the trust fund experience in Newcastle seventeen years earlier, it became an unwritten rule among those of us who staged large-scale benefit concerts that we should maintain some control over how the proceeds are used. With that in mind, we didn't want the whole $1 million going to Live Earth co-founder Al Gore's war chest. We kept 50 per cent and distributed the money to worthy Australian ecological and environmental projects, such as Greening Australia.

My enduring memory of Crowded House's closing performance that night is of the stage lights going off during their encore. I think half of the crowd thought it was some kind of statement on the band's part about saving energy. In truth, our generator ran out of fuel. I was furious — and not a little stoned. English promoter Harvey Goldsmith, who was coordinating the English event at London's Wembley Stadium and watching the live telecast of the Sydney show, called me on my mobile to say how much he liked the lights-off gesture. Only then did I see the funny side of it. It was only in April 2010, at a dinner saluting Harvey Goldsmith at the

Musexpo in Los Angeles, that I finally told him the truth, that we'd run out of bio-diesel.

The two other major benefit concerts of that decade were Wave Aid in January 2005 and Sound Relief in March 2009. Both of those were coordinated by me, Joe Segreto from Homebake Festival and events producer Mark Pope and Amanda Pelman, with the addition of Gudinski and Tom Lang for Sound Relief. These were fantastic events. Wave Aid raised $2.3 million and Sound Relief close to $8 million.

What made these concerts so successful were the collaborative efforts of hundreds of people in the Australian music industry, as well as some outstanding contributions in various ways by overseas performers. Leonard Cohen, for instance, who wasn't directly involved but who was touring Australia at the time, donated $200,000 to the Victorian Bushfires Appeal after Sound Relief. No one who was there or watched it on television will ever forget John Farnham's heroic performance of 'You're the Voice' with Coldplay at the Sydney leg of that event.

These concerts showed the power of the Australian music industry to do good – and not just at home. With Wave Aid, we held back money raised from the sale of concert DVDs to donate to worthy projects in parts of the region that were devastated by the Boxing Day tsunami in 2004. In Phuket, for example, one of the worst-hit areas, which relies heavily on tourism for its survival, we used some of the funds to supply English teachers in local schools. Since I have a home there, I have seen first-hand the benefits this program has brought to communities who suffered terribly after the tsunami.

I believe in the Australian music industry. Like any business, it has its faults, but I honestly think the majority of people who work in the local music business do it for the love of it and from that we produce excellent results. The collaboration that forms when disasters such as floods, tsunamis and bushfires demand our help is just one illustration of that.

16

TCB

Just because the industry comes together in times of crisis doesn't mean that it's squeaky clean, far from it. For all that we like to bask in the glory of our charitable gestures, there are those among us who would rob you blind, given the opportunity. I could name at least twenty ways to rip off bands, singers, managers and even promoters. Equally, I know people in those professions who have been the perpetrators of scams. I'm familiar with these methods of stealing because I have been around them for most of my working life. They are less prevalent today than they were in the pioneering days of Oz rock, but they are still around. Some agents I know stole systematically from their artist clients. I was never actively involved in the practice myself, but I was close to it, so close, in some cases, that I was obliged to turn a blind eye rather than do anything about it.

If you are an agent, there are a number of options open to you if you want to skim cash from the bands you're supposed to be looking after. You can rig the system. In the 60s and 70s this was easier to get away with than it is now, simply because there was less accountability around in the fledgling days of rock 'n' roll. Back then, every second person walking into town looking for a piece of the action was carrying a Colt 45 and wearing a ten-gallon hat, but even in the more sophisticated 80s exploiting the system was still rampant among some of the leading agencies in the country.

The most common way for an agent to steal from an act is in the setting up of one of its shows, but more effectively in the organisation of a tour. This practice is known commonly as skimming, but rigging would be another suitable name for it. Kickbacks are at the heart of it. This is how it works. If you are an agent, you deal with all manner of operators and businesses, from tradespeople to stage-builders, PA and lighting companies, transport companies, caterers, travel agents, venue owners and promoters. In putting a show together for one of your acts, you may have to deal with one or all of these other businesses to make it work. Often you are working with these same people every day on different deals for any number of your clients performing in different parts of the country.

In the days before Dirty Pool came along and changed the system, you could do a deal with the club owner or the promoter to sell your act to them for $1500 and then tell your act they were getting $1200. You could do a deal where the promoter got $3 a head from the band's fee and gave back to you, the agent, a dollar, or two dollars in some cases. This is before you get to what was then considered legitimate, where a monster band in its heyday could play multiple nights at a venue in Sydney that had sold 1200 tickets for $6 each and at the end of it their agent handed them $2,000. The bulk of the remainder was going to the agent.

Kickbacks from venues in Sydney and Melbourne in particular, but in other cities as well, were commonplace for leading agents in Australia in the 70s and 80s. A few agents I worked with had things going on other than what went through the books. Some of them had serious gambling habits that had to be financed. Venues were giving kickbacks to the agencies systematically. An agency might send someone once a week to pick up the money from all the venues that were on the plan.

There was another way of ripping off the artist. You could build excess charges into tour budgets by producing false receipts. There were plenty of ways to do that. You could get a company to give you a bill for $50,000 when the cost was only $35,000 or $40,000 and split the difference. Following that same principle, you could get the venue to charge 15 per cent of the gig fee for the hire of the room, chargeable, of course, to your act, and then give you back 5 per cent. You could get the booking agent to put an extra $2 into the service charge for tickets and give it back to you. All of that money came out of the band's budget.

After you, as an agent, had built these kinds of relationships with all of the other businesses needed to make shows happen, it wasn't too difficult to rip off bands as a matter of course, until it became normal practice.

Dirty Pool started because John Woodruff and his colleagues knew that systematic stealing from their acts was going on and they were determined to stop it; that's apart from their main objective, which was to completely overhaul the way bands made their money. They didn't put an end completely to the kickbacks that were going on. That illegal behaviour stemmed largely from an arrogance and greed among some of the people who got into the music business early and who believed, for that reason, that they were a law unto themselves. For as long as they got away with it, they were. Lots of people were really cocky in the 70s. It was still all up for grabs. There were plenty of cowboys out there, making up the rules as they went along. People got ripped off but, if that happened, you made sure it didn't happen to you again.

Skimming still goes on in some areas of the industry, but it's not nearly as endemic this century as it was in the last one. Did I personally instigate or take part in any of those scams? No. I looked the other way, but I know I got money from them. The corruption caught up with the person I witnessed doing it the most, right in front of my nose for many years. By then his reckless behaviour, his gambling debts and the way he used company money to pay them off made him a marked man. That cost him his career. I couldn't have been happier.

International tour accountants are wise to all that kind of unscrupulous behaviour nowadays, or at least some of them are. They're the ones like a dog with a bone, who just won't let go of a budget spreadsheet until they know every last cent is accounted for. Others are pretty slack.

There are lots of other practices in the touring business that fall into the dodgy basket, although not all of them are illegal. With all that money floating round, kickbacks in the right places can boost considerably any of the ancillary businesses' income.

For example, when Frontier first toured The Eagles, they brought out staging from Europe. The cost seemed to us ridiculously excessive. We challenged the band's manager, Irving Azoff, and he reimbursed us to the tune of $200,000. Chances are someone down the line was getting a kickback. You come across that kind of behaviour all the time. It's something I've had to be vigilant about just as much since I set up on my own as I did when I was at Frontier.

There are instances where my company today, Chugg Entertainment, will pick up the accommodation bill for a tour by a big overseas act, but the American or European tour manager will say he or she is going to book the accommodation through his or her own travel agent. You know immediately that the tour manager is getting kickbacks from the hotels, or somewhere down the track they are going to get free rooms. If I'm providing the accommodation at, say, The Four Seasons, and I can book it for $180 a night, why would a tour manager want to book it at $340 a night? Have a guess.

Those are some of the scams you have to be aware of continually in the touring business. There are many dangers when you are dealing with companies spread around the world. We are continually protecting what we have worked hard to establish. Some overseas managers and agents try it on all the time. It's intricate and so dodgy that if you take your eye off the ball for a moment you lose the game. Not that I am blameless. I've made some mistakes in structuring deals with overseas acts and I've had the odd tour accountant throw furniture at me in arguments over fees structured into the band's deal. I've seen Gudinski having some amazing arguments with overseas agents and managers and it has become really personal.

I try not to get on the phone and start screaming at agents and managers, but sometimes that's what you have to do. My bark tends to be worse than my bite, but I'll use it if I think it will give me some sort of advantage. At Frontier, we would use that kind of bluster tactic a lot. We'd even stage arguments between ourselves —Gudinski, Jacobsen and me — just to get bands or managers off our backs. If you can't beat them, confuse them.

It's a hard, often ruthless business. If anyone ever comes to me and says they want to be a promoter — and they do — I tell them the last thing you want to do is become a promoter. They think I'm doing that to keep them out of my business, but really I'm telling them they're going to get fucked over if they do it. There's a degree of exploitation rather than outright thievery that is common in the industry, particularly if you're new to it, which makes it harder for up and coming promoters to establish themselves.

Every now and then you'll see some new guy come along who wants to be a rock promoter. You'll read a few articles about how he's going to change the industry. I've seen a few of those over the past couple of years. All that happens is that the trucking companies, the sound companies, the lighting companies, the advertising manager of the local radio station . . . all of them just put up their rates and rip the guts out of these people. I've seen guys come into this business and lose a couple of million dollars in the space of a few months. Everyone rips into them, takes advantage. If I'm paying $20,000 for sound and lights and some guy comes along and the sound and lights company think they can charge him $30,000, they will. I see it all the time. These guys come into the touring game and they think they know it all, but they don't know the right tour directors or the right production managers, so they just get scammed.

It has always surprised me that an industry that had so much cash flying around in those early days didn't attract the attention of organised crime; by that, I mean gangsters. Certainly in the 50s and 60s there was a bit of overlap in that some of the clubs where bands played were owned by colourful racing identities, but none of them wanted a bar of the live music business. That's just as true today. Why gamble on a business where you can drop half a million dollars in minutes when you have a steady income from clubs, drugs and hookers? Nowadays, since GST was introduced in 2000 and with electronic ticketing the norm, there isn't nearly as much cash around, which makes it much harder to rort the system.

Crooks are around on the fringes and I've met plenty of them. Hanging out with criminals is a bit like hanging out with musos; they're weird but they can also be funny and nice people; it's just that their business is being a criminal. None of them has ever tried to infiltrate the business. All that *Underbelly* stuff, there's no real music involvement in any of that.

There was at least one exception, in my experience, and that was in 1970, when notorious Sydney villain Stan 'the Man' Smith pulled a gun on me. Smith, who died in January 2010, was a notorious racketeer and standover man in the 60s and 70s. For whatever reason, in 1970 he decided to get into rock promotion and brought out a few bands from overseas, including a bikie blues band from Canada called McKenna Mendelson Mainline, to tour. They were a fairly well respected band in North America and Europe, very much immersed in that heavy blues sound that was around in the late 60s.

While they were in Australia, a couple of them got busted for drugs. Somehow word got back to Smith that I had dobbed them in. I wasn't even in the country when they were here. I was in America. I had nothing to do with it. A few months later, I was at a gig at Bondi Lifesaver and my friend Lee Dillow introduced me to Stan Smith. Smith was almost frothing at the mouth and started laying into me for ruining his tour. We were sitting at a table and he pulled out a gun and held it under the table pointing at me. He was flying, completely off his face, which made it even scarier. I was stoned, so I got increasingly paranoid with every passing second. *Tripping standover man slays stoned, innocent rock promoter*. It wasn't looking good. I just kept talking to him and eventually managed to calm him down, but it was pretty out there. I did what I do best and talked my way out of it. He could see I was telling the truth. That's the only time I've ever had anything like that happen to me. I found out later it was my old mate Ray Arnold who had been big-noting to the gangster and somehow put me in the running to have my nuts blown off.

An even bigger villain than Smith, the dreaded Mr Sin, Abe Saffron, once called me to a meeting (I felt I should go) to see if I was interested in helping him put together a package tour of American acts he wanted to bring out to Australia. Chicago and The Beach Boys were two of them. I can't remember the others. It was going to be a stadium tour. He paid airfares to go out to America and have meetings with the relevant agents and managers, but nothing ever came of it. Saffron did back a few tours, but I think he, like other high-end crims, realised that you can lose money too easily.

One of the many reasons I wanted to get away from Frontier and Premier/Harbour in the late 90s was because of personal issues I had with one of the partners, Sam Righi, with whom I'd had running battles for the eighteen years he had been fronting the Harbour Agency. I'd had enough of him. I'd had enough of Philip Jacobsen. I'd had enough of not being able to do all of the tours that I thought we should be doing, of getting shouted down. At the age of fifty-two, I was just a little bit over other people telling me what I could and couldn't do.

17

A Break With Convention

Philip Jacobsen, financial whiz that he is, once did an exercise for Gudinski and me showing that the three of us would be better off financially if we left our money in the bank and didn't do any tours. From a rigidly anal accountancy perspective, he could have been right, but he might as well have been speaking Swahili for all that we were going to take any notice of him.

Philip is a seasoned gambler and horse breeder, but he's not a gambler in the same sense that Gudinski and I are gamblers. Philip likes to bet on sure things. It's in his DNA. Gudinski, on the other hand, will talk you into believing he's on a sure thing, whether or not it's true. Mostly, his record proves that he can back up the talk. He's a powerful, experienced player who can turn things around. I'm more of an impulse gambler. I won't back something just because the figures tell me it should work, although obviously that is a consideration. I have to have a gut instinct about a tour, about an act. I get a vibe about something and that's what drives me to take the risk. That has been my undoing a few times, once or twice to the point where I thought I was going under for good, but I didn't. Something has always come along to get me through to the next phase.

Taking risks is an integral part of being a promoter. We all live by our wits to some degree. In 1999, after twenty years in the evil empire, I took a punt and left Frontier Touring, albeit with a little prompting from a multinational corporation, Kerry Packer's Consolidated Press Entertainment. It wasn't an impulse, out-of-the-blue decision. It was something that had been building up in me for several years, but when the time came it was still a gamble. In the eleven years since then, I've had incredible highs and almost career-destroying lows. In either instance, you have to move on to the next thing, or at least I do. If you sit around worrying or gloating, opportunities will pass you by.

The idea of breaking away from Frontier festered in my gut for a few years, but by early 1997 I was sure opportunities were being lost. I started to feel trapped within the organisation.

To try and fight my way out of that claustrophobic situation, I came up with the idea of running an international music industry conference in Sydney. More than any other Australian promoter, I had been attending overseas conferences for years by then and always found them extremely useful in building relationships with managers, agents and promoters from the US and Europe. I figured that if I could get an annual large-scale event of that kind on the Australian music industry calendar it could do great things for Aussie artists and companies, especially if we could convince some of the main players from LA, New York and London to attend. It would be a great way to showcase Australian talent and to network with the big guns.

In 1995 and 1996, Frontier had done tours with the great American singer and songwriter Jeff Buckley. The other partners weren't terribly interested because Buckley wasn't a big money-earner for us, but he was another act I thought we should be doing to build him up in the long term. I got friendly with his manager David Lory on both of those tours and knew that he had been one of the organisers of the successful New Music Seminar in New York, which ran annually from 1980 until 1995. I explained my conference idea to him and he offered his assistance with presenting it to people in the US.

I called it the Pacific Circle Music Convention. Kathy Howard came in on it with me. Together we started planning it for October 1997, just around the time of the ARIA Awards. We found a venue, the newly developed Australian Technology Park in Redfern. That wasn't our first choice, but none of the more established conference venues were available. We approached the New South Wales government and Premier Bob Carr's office was helpful with funding. Then we drew up a wish list of local and international music industry figures to speak and take part in forums, workshops and the like over the five days of the conference. We began searching for bands and performers to play at showcase concerts all over the inner city during the five days. It fell into place quite quickly. We got leading names such as English promoter Harvey Goldsmith, probably the most famous promoter in the world, as a keynote speaker, along with Dr Larry Livingston, a music director and speaker on the circuit from the University of Southern California, and Mandawuy Yunupingu from Yothu Yindi. Through some of the connections I had made at conferences in other parts of the world and from my general networking overseas we had a really impressive line-up. On paper it looked sensational.

We chased sponsorship. We talked to the record companies and got their support. My partners didn't want to know. They were totally against it. To be fair, Gudinski sat on the fence because he didn't know what it was all about. He didn't attend those conferences as regularly as I did. His Mushroom Records didn't put much into PCMC, but his publishing arm, Mushroom Publishing, did, through its boss Ian James.

All of the major record labels supported it really well and a few brought out some of their overseas acts to do showcases. Matchbox 20, then pretty new, played to about 100 people at the Globe in Newtown. Six months later Coppel brought them back to Australia and made $250,000 profit.

I needed the conference to be a success, not least because I was pouring my company's money into it. Also, I was getting blocked at every turn at Frontier. They didn't want to do the tours I wanted to do. They were being slow to pay dividends on our earnings, I suspect because they knew I was short of cash. It was getting nasty. I was on my arse, but Frontier was doing all right. They just weren't making it easy for me at all.

My personal life wasn't doing any favours for my bank balance. In my divorce from Lisa, she had taken just about everything, so I was trying to fight my way out of that problem. I'd just had the drama with Mayling. Ironically, when Con Nellis set up an office in Los Angeles to promote Pacific Circle Music Convention, she was his employee.

We went all out in promoting PCMC. Aside from the LA office, we had former Double J and Triple J host Rusty Nails helping us in London and David Lory in New York. In the weeks leading up to the event, we had launch parties in all of those cities. London-based Aussie DJ Jonathan Coleman helped us with the London one. I had a lot of support, but a few people were against me, not just my buddies at Frontier.

Phil Tripp, self-appointed Australian music industry analyst and all-round loose cannon, seemed to do his best to undermine PCMC. He had his own industry conference developing in Sydney and it seemed he didn't think there was room for another one. Tripp moved to Australia from America after a career as a production manager. I always felt that he was quick to shoot down the Australian industry. At PCMC, waiting outside the front door of the convention on the opening day, I thought he was out to get me.

Ironically, when Tripp first arrived in Australia, Gudinski and I were about the only two people who would give him the time of day. He let that be known for a few years. I used to get angry with what I saw as him pulling down our industry in the media rather than building it up.

The convention stiffed badly, for a variety of reasons. Before that happened, Kathy pulled out. My company took over her share of the debts.

In hindsight we, or at least I, got it wrong in several ways. I shouldn't have held it at the same time as the ARIAs, the biggest night on the Australian music calendar. We thought a lot of people would come from the industry in and outside of Sydney and embrace the convention and then go to the ARIAs, but they just went to the ARIAs. A lot of the acts performing at the

ARIAs were rehearsing for two or three days beforehand and some of the industry people we needed to be at the convention were too caught up in that, so relying on them was a mistake.

We needed to attract large numbers from the general public and that just didn't happen. The weather didn't help. It was cold and wet for most of the five-day period. Hardly anyone knew where the Technology Park was back then, because it had only just opened. We had bands playing all over the place. We needed to get 10,000 people a day at the park. We didn't get remotely close to that number.

Looking at it now, the event was too big. Instead of walking before I ran, I ran. I wanted to make a bold statement at the start. My bank statement said I lost around $750,000 of my own money.

But I persevered. The following year, I trimmed it down, but it still lost money. Over the two events, I was down more than $1 million. In the third year, I brought in Daryl Herbert from Definitive Events in Melbourne to run it with me and it picked up. We changed the name to Australian Music Week, because there was a feeling among some people in the industry that Pacific Circle wasn't Aussie enough.

The failure of the conference was a great disappointment to me. It put a lot of pressure on me, because I had financed it largely by myself. I realise now the industry wasn't ready for it. I was fifteen years too early, but at the time I believed in it. I needed to believe in it, given the predicament I was in with my partners at Frontier. That's why, when the Packers came along, I didn't need to think twice about getting the hell out of the evil empire. Actually, the Packers were keen on buying Frontier before they came to me, but Philip was having none of that.

There were so many reasons to leave Frontier and yet I had stalled on it for a long time. Aside from my dissatisfaction with some of my partners, specifically Jacobsen and Righi, I'd had a feeling for years that Gudinski just wasn't interested in Frontier. He no longer travelled as much as he used to, plus he had just sold Mushroom Records to the Murdoch empire for $40 million. He didn't appear to have the hunger any more. What was worse was that it appeared the partners had a vendetta against me. It was getting personal.

The beginning of the end came when Gudinski, Philip and I went to New York to have a meeting with US media and broadcasting conglomerate Clear Channel. They had flagged their interest in buying Frontier. Gudinski said he was in favour of the idea because it would give the rest of us a payout, maybe not as big as the one he had got from Murdoch for Mushroom, but big all the same.

It was an important meeting. All the Clear Channel heavyweights were there. We'd had a document made up at Frontier listing the attributes and achievements of the company. All of the partners had a hand in putting it together. When I sat down in that meeting and read it, every mention of my name had been removed. The impression that was left was that Michael and Philip ran Frontier. That was it. I couldn't believe it. I read the document again and I didn't exist. I thought, 'If that's all you think of me, why am I even here?'

My chief frustration was that I was meeting with constant resistance to suggestions I had for tours. Frontier was becoming too conservative, too complacent. They couldn't understand the value in losing $40,000 on Radiohead, as we did on their first tour, in order to get their next one and the one after that;

to back ourselves in picking bands that would start small and go on to be huge. 'Speculate to accumulate' never entered their heads. It was a daily battle. That was the same thing I was about to run into with the Packers. Why lose money? The ideal for Frontier was to do three or four tours a year for big money and forget the rest; to rest on our laurels. But we wouldn't have got the three or four big tours a year if we hadn't done the smaller tours. If you're not in the game, you're not in the game. If you're not going to do the up and coming acts, eventually you're going to run out of acts altogether.

Some of my friends had been urging me to get out and start on my own. One of them was Thorpie, who had been spending a fair bit of time with me after he moved back to Sydney from Los Angeles in 1996. He had been pushing me to get away. He could see I was unhappy and doing things I didn't want to do. My mate and fellow promoter Peter Korda was of the same mind. Mayling had been saying it to me forever, but then she had no time for Gudinski and the others; a mutual loathing, I'm pretty sure.

When I did get out, late in 1999, the manoeuvre was quite dramatic. I had planned a trip – a run as we called it – with Gudinski, to go and meet some of our regular contacts overseas. Over the years, we did scores of those trips, to London, New York, Los Angeles and quite often several places in between, but they had become rare for him in the latter half of the 90s.

A few days before we were scheduled to go, I set off on my own. We had arranged to meet up in LA. I went to visit five or six agents I knew in LA, in New York and London, to tell them I was jumping ship and setting up on my own. I wanted to get their support. When I had done that, I flew back to Sydney, went to Peter Korda's office and wrote a letter of resignation to Frontier. I called Gudinski's office just to make sure he was there. By rights, he should have been flying to LA the next day to meet me, but I had suspected he had no intention of going. When I found out he was in Melbourne, I knew I was right.

I flew to Melbourne, went to the office and threw the letter down on Gudinski's desk. I don't think he believed I could do something like that. Just quit. Even after I'd done it, I don't think he believed it. Gudinski had lent me money for PCMC. In hindsight, that was a set-up. He had me sign an agreement where defaulting on the loan triggered the sale of my share in Frontier, Harbour and Premier – all in all, a cheap buyout for them.

I did my first gig outside of Frontier at Christmas 1999, presenting Channel 7's Christmas concert at Darling Harbour, which went out live nationally. I launched my new company, Michael Chugg Entertainment, in January 2000 and I was able to convince a few people I had worked with in the Frontier empire to come and join me, among them Caroline Tully, who became general manager, Renee Rudolf and Scott Leighton. Barbara Dennis, who had been running my office in Sydney, didn't come with me. Susan Heymann came on board through work experience and today runs the business and does marketing. We moved into an office in William Street, next to the old Double J building.

Michael Karagiannis was Packer's man at Consolidated Press Entertainment. My deal with them was that they would partner Michael Chugg Entertainment on tours they thought worthwhile and would back me financially up to $500,000. I needed something that gave me a bit of safety to bail from Frontier, so that was it. Again, on paper, it looked like a solid proposal, but it didn't take long for it to unravel. Pretty quickly I realised I had another Philip on my hands. Karagiannis wasn't interested in bands such as Gomez and No Doubt, who weren't pulling in big bucks. Consolidated Press Entertainment loved the big wins, but they couldn't understand why you would do those smaller acts.

He wanted to know why I was even considering doing tours like that. I had to explain to him, as I did with mind-numbing regularity to Philip, that investing in small tours by up and coming bands is a way of securing your future. You build relationships with acts as their careers progress and when they get huge, as at least some of them do, you get the big payout. He didn't get it. It was too long-term and too high-risk.

I've always been about building acts. You pick up acts that are happening as well, but a lot of the acts I've promoted and toured since leaving Frontier – Coldplay, No Doubt, John Mayer, Dixie Chicks, Newton Faulkner, Rodrigo and Gabriela – started off almost unknown, playing in 300-capacity clubs. Then the next time you bring the Dixie Chicks out they're playing to 80,000 or 100,000 people. John Mayer does 40,000–50,000 when he comes to Australia.

To compound my frustration, Karagiannis then accused me of only bringing my mates' bands to Australia, as if that would make any sense. Worse still, when overseas bands weren't selling particularly well, he wanted me to pay them out before they got to Australia and to cancel the tour. I didn't work that way, so to keep the tour going I ended up paying a few bands out of my own pocket. Once again, pressure was starting to build on me.

It got messier when my old adversary Paul Dainty entered the picture. Karagiannis had done a deal with him as well. There was a suggestion that a partnership involving me, Dainty and CPE would form into one big happy family, but that was never going to happen. Dainty claims that his end of the three-way deal was that he would take care of the $1-million-plus guarantee tours while I would look after all of the smaller tours, but I never had that discussion with Karagiannis or anyone else at Packers, so that's why I was a little surprised to find out, an hour after we'd had a three-way meeting to discuss working together, that Dainty was on the phone trying to secure a tour with Bon Jovi, a band I had been working with for most of their career.

The straw that broke this camel's back was Bob Dylan. In that first year on my own, I did fourteen tours. Not all of them made money. Eels was a poor seller and I dropped about $200,000 on Status Quo, but overall I was happy that I was out on my own and surviving. I was also convinced that Dylan, who was available early in 2001, would be a monster. I'd worked with him three times at Frontier. He was unpredictable, but I had that vibe again. I'd been watching reaction to his performances overseas and he was going off. He was still getting traction out of his 1997 Grammy-winning album *Time Out of Mind* and there was a highly anticipated new one due in 2001. It felt right.

Karagiannis said no. I could not believe it. He didn't think it would make money. I knew he was wrong. I didn't have the money to do the tour on my own. That was the closing chapter in my relationship with the Packers. Despite our differences, Michael was a decent person and my exit from the partnership was made easier by his understanding.

There was a stroke of luck involved in getting me to the next stage. I've known Brian Taranto since he was a sixteen-year-old kid selling T-shirts on big tours around Australia. Since then, he has gone on to great success with his merchandising company and record label Love Police. I met Brian a few weeks after Karagiannis had turned me down on Dylan and I told him the story. I explained to him that I had that gut feeling that a Dylan tour would be huge. He asked me how much I needed. I said $200,000. He said okay.

I left my deal with Packer and got myself organised. Dylan, as I had predicted, was a monster.

18

This Young Heart of Mine

The money I made from that Bob Dylan tour kept me going for the rest of the year and cemented my place as Bob's Australian promoter to this day. I could breathe a little easier, pleased with myself for turning around the potential disaster of the first twelve months operating under my own name, albeit with Brian Taranto's help. I had booked up-and-coming, hot acts such as Unwritten Law, Pennywise and A Perfect Circle to help establish the Chugg name as a promoter divorced from and more innovative than Frontier. I had staples on the books from the Frontier days in Sting and Bon Jovi to keep me afloat in 2001. I was starting to feel good about the new enterprise.

Also in March, just a few weeks prior to the Dylan tour, I went to London for the International Live Music Conference, an annual event I've attended regularly since its inception in 1989. It's a great way to interact with promoters, managers and agents from all over the world, professionally and socially. One of the agents I had planned to meet while I was in London was Ian Huffam from Xray Touring. I'd met Ian on the back of a boat on Sydney Harbour when he was touring Australia with English band Blur in 1997. At the time, Huffam was very excited about a new singer he had on his books, Robbie Williams, who he predicted would be a world phenomenon within a couple of years. 'You mean the little fat chap from Take That?' was my only response. I couldn't share his enthusiasm.

By 2001, Huffam was proved right. I'd seen Williams play by then, but only at a club showcase at the South By South West conference in Austin and it hadn't made much of an impression on me. Now Williams was a monster at home and had scored top-ten successes in Australia with the single 'Rock DJ' and the album *Sing When You're Winning*. I wanted him to tour for me. I could sense a little reluctance on Huffam's part to have me involved in an Australian tour, which he was hoping to slot in at the end of 2001. I found out later that a couple of my former colleagues at Frontier had been in the UK and Europe just before me and had been doing their best to convince anyone who would listen that I was washed up as a promoter – broke, going into bankruptcy, a liability.

I believe that's why, when Huffam offered me the Williams tour, it was conditional on me placing $1 million in the agency's bank account as a deposit within a couple of weeks. At that point I still couldn't be certain that some disaster might not befall the Dylan tour, even if tickets had sold incredibly well. I couldn't spare the kind of money Huffam was asking.

A few days later at the conference, I was in the coffee shop and I noticed Jack Utsick sitting there. Jack was an American entrepreneur who liked investing in rock 'n' roll, I think partly because he enjoyed the reflected glory of hanging out with famous people. He had his own company, Worldwide Entertainment Group, based in Florida, but he had just entered the Australian industry by partnering promoter Kevin Jacobsen in a few big events. I met Utsick for the first time in Sydney when the two of them brought the Bee Gees to Australia to perform at the official opening of the Olympic Stadium in Sydney in 1999. I walked up to him in the coffee shop at ILMC and told him I was going to tour Robbie Williams and I needed $1 million in a hurry. That, in a matter of minutes, brought about my first joint venture with Utsick.

When tickets went on sale for the Williams tour a few months later, we knew we were on a winner. Sadly for me, I was about to get a painful reminder that there is more to life than sold-out arenas.

In August, I set off on one of my runs, starting in London, to meet up with agents and managers and generally to put my solo face on the map with all of the people who knew me already from my Frontier days. While I was in London, I began to get twitches in my shoulder; not painful exactly, but it was uncomfortable. I didn't think much of it, although I mentioned it to both Con and Ted Gardner, when I spoke to them on the phone about my arrival in LA the following week. Although Con was no longer working for me, we still kept in touch and I knew he was going to be staying with Ted in LA while he was there doing business.

Con picked me up from LAX when I was passing through on that trip. I had to fly on to New York on business, but I made a plan to meet up with Ted, Con and some business contacts on my way back through LA to Australia a week later.

By the time I left New York, the pains in my shoulder were slightly worse. I thought I must have twisted something carrying bags.

One of Utsick's suggestions for an Australian tour was that we take a sidestep from the music field and invest in Monster Trucks, which at the time was doing big business in the US. Some of these truck events could attract as many as 50,000 people. He reckoned it would be huge in Australia. I didn't have the vibe at all, but I thought I should at least check it out. So I flew from New York to St Louis, Missouri, to see a Monster Trucks show. It was over 45 degrees centigrade in St Louis, which added to the discomfort I was feeling in my shoulder. I'd never felt heat quite like it before. It was fiercer and drier than anything I had experienced at home.

I met up with some of the promoters from the Monster Trucks circuit, but they couldn't get me as excited about it as they were. The ghosts of previous tour disasters hovered over the track as I watched the trucks scream past me.

Next day, as I was about to fly out of St Louis to LA, the pain in my shoulder got much worse. I rang Ted and asked him if he could arrange for me to see his doctor in Los Angeles while I was there. He said it wouldn't be a problem. We'd take care of it when I got there. Con picked me up again at the airport.

Next morning, I went out walking in the park near my hotel in West Hollywood. For years I had made a brisk walk part of my morning routine. After a while I started getting the pain again, but I still didn't think too much about it. I went to a chemist and bought some painkillers and it improved. It hadn't clicked with me at all that I was having a heart attack.

At the time, I had no blood pressure problems. I wasn't too much overweight. My last check-up had been good. I was just my normal self. The only other time in my life when I'd had some kind of worry about my heart was during the *Rockarena* Fleetwood Mac tour in 1977, when I suddenly got severe chest pains while I was talking to Paul Dainty in his hotel suite. I'd like to think that was an allergic reaction, but the doctor said it was a muscle spasm brought on by stress, nothing to do with my heart, at least.

If I had stuck to my original schedule on that American trip, I would be dead now. My plan was to fly home the night I arrived in LA on a connecting flight to Sydney, but a friend at the William Morris Agency, Akiko Rogers, one of the biggest music agencies in America, had asked me if I would give a talk to some of the young agents and interns at their office, so I opted to stay on an extra day and I did the talk the day after I got in from St Louis. Had I chosen to get on a flight across the Pacific instead, and the heart attack had come on mid-flight, there would have been little hope for me. Unlike when I stayed in LA for Thorpie's birthday, this time I made the right call.

After the William Morris gig, which went down incredibly well, Con and I went to Ian Copeland's Backstage Café in Beverly Hills. We had a few drinks, nothing outrageous. Ian was a good friend of mine. We had many big nights in there that stretched into the wee small hours, but that night wasn't one of them.

I woke up the next morning and I had severe pains down one side of my body. I had a shower. I took painkillers. I had a joint. Nothing helped. At 7 am, I rang Ted and told him I wasn't feeling well. He said he'd send Con to get me and take me to Cedars-Sinai Medical Center to get checked out. That wasn't far from where I was staying. It was only about a thirty-minute drive from Ted's place in Lake Hollywood to the hotel, but by 8 am Con still hadn't arrived. I called again and Ted's wife Nikki told me he was on his way. The pain was worse. I headed down to the lobby and then out into the car park of the hotel to wait for him. Another half an hour passed and I was in agony and fearing the worst.

I moved over to a park bench at the front of the hotel to sit down, or rather to slump down. Then I saw Con drive in. I couldn't understand why it had taken him so long, but I soon found out. On the dashboard of the car, I could see a McDonald's bag. Con loves McDonald's. He likes to start the day with a sausage McMuffin. So on his way to take me to hospital, he stopped at the drive-thru to pick up some breakfast, while I sat close to death outside the hotel.

Con, quite reasonably, didn't realise how ill I was when Ted asked him to come and get me. He went back to sleep initially. He figured that if I had been really bad I would have gone to hospital by myself, especially since Cedars-Sinai was only a few blocks away. I didn't know it was that close.

When Con got out of the car, he could see straight away that I was having a heart attack. By then my face had puffed up and I was a terrible colour and the pain was excruciating. He got me into the car and ten minutes later we pulled up outside the accident and emergency unit. Con was running, screaming, 'Heart attack, heart attack' at the waiting nurses and orderlies.

In seconds, they had a CPR machine on me and told me I was having a heart infarction. They put me straight onto a trolley, stuck nitroglycerine tablets under my tongue and rushed me into the hospital. Then they gave me a shot of something and wheeled me to an operating room.

It happened so quickly. I'd only been there for about ten minutes. I still didn't know for sure what was going on, because I didn't know what infarction meant. Then, when I realised it really was a heart attack, I started shouting at Con to call Ted and to make sure no one found out about me being in hospital. Con told me later that, when he left me as I was being taken to the operating theatre, he asked a nurse if I was going to be okay and she said: 'Brace yourself.' Con went into shock. When he phoned Ted, he was sobbing uncontrollably. All he could say was: 'I've killed him. McDonald's. I've killed him.'

I thought I was going under the knife, but then someone explained the new procedure where they put a device inside you and clean out the artery that way. I could actually watch it happening on the screen beside me. It was amazing.

While I was lying waiting for the procedure, two doctors walked in and started talking to me. One was Indian and the other one was Pakistani, they explained. They were very friendly. They kept talking as they examined me and it turned out they had both trained in Melbourne. Discovering I was Australian was enough for them to start telling bad Australian jokes in truly awful Australian accents while they were moving this thing around inside my body. I looked at the screen. I tried to laugh at another crap joke. I looked at the screen again. It was surreal. Finally they put in a stent and it was over in about an hour. Then I spent two days in hospital recovering.

The doctor in charge told me next day that there was a bit of damage to the heart but that I was lucky the blockage had been in only one artery. It would have killed me eventually, though. I was lucky that I was only ten minutes away from the hospital.

I'd question the wisdom of presenting a bill for $US107,000 to someone lying in a hospital bed after a heart attack, but that's what happened to me. Maybe the hospital management had a sense of humour more macabre than the ones I was subjected to while I was having my artery cleaned out. One of those guys wasn't finished with me, it turned out. The day I left hospital, the Indian doctor came in and said: 'I hear you're in the entertainment business. I have to go back to Melbourne to do a speech in a few months. Is there any chance you could hook me up with some cheap air fares?' I laughed at that one, which seemed to confuse him.

I spent those few days in hospital coming to grips with what had happened. My main concern, apart from my health, was that word would get out I'd had a heart attack. I was still feeling vulnerable after hearing the rumours that were being spread about my ability to compete as a solo promoter. It didn't help that I had been in hospital only several hours when a doctor called to ask how I was. He was the doctor of a close friend, Rob Light, the head of Creative Artists Agency's music division, based in LA. I figured if he knew I was in there, half of America knew. I couldn't afford to appear weak at this point in my career, in Australia or overseas.

Ted, Nikki and Con came to visit me a few hours after the stent was put in and again each day until I left. Ted and Nikki invited me to come and convalesce at their place. I was there for a couple of weeks. From the moment I got there, I was keen to get back into work, but they wouldn't let me. They put me in an upstairs bedroom and took away the phone and cigarettes. They had two pit bull terriers. Ted warned me that if I tried to get downstairs to a phone they'd rip my legs off.

As I got better, I began calling the office in Sydney. A few people there knew what was going on, but I wanted the heart attack to be kept as quiet as possible. Ted was right, though. Calling the office wasn't good for me. I was getting upset and stressed on the phone. That's when Nikki showed me how to use the internet and I started emailing instead of phoning. From then on, I embraced the internet as part of my business.

Just before I set off on that round-the-world trip, I had been seeing a woman from Sydney, Christie Robbins. I rang her from Ted's place and asked her to come out to California for a holiday. I'm a friend of guitarist Jeff 'Skunk' Baxter, once of Steely Dan and the Doobie Brothers and now, strangely, a defence consultant to the US government. Occasionally when I'm in LA, I'll go and spend a few days at his place in Beverly Glen. It's handy for where all the agents are in LA, cheaper than staying in a hotel and you can enjoy more of a home environment. Christie came over and we spent a couple of weeks together at Skunk's place before returning to Sydney. I felt well rested when I got back.

We were able to keep the heart attack pretty quiet. That was so important to me. At that point, if it had got out that I'd had a heart attack, the business would not have survived. I'm sure of that. It was the early days of having my own company and a lot of people would have used it against me, particularly as a sign of weakness. He's finished, they would have said.

Why wouldn't they use it against me? That was around the same time that a few people who were close to me at Frontier were going around the world telling everybody I had no money. I was already under the gun from them from the day I left. You don't walk out of the evil empire. You either get kicked out or you're there forever.

An insurance investigator turned up at the office a few months after the heart attack. I was covered for travel insurance, but clearly they felt $US107,000 worth of treatment deserved investigating. Over a period of a few weeks, he started asking friends and work colleagues questions about me. It was uncomfortable, but eventually they paid out.

I'm still not certain why I had a heart attack. I wasn't misbehaving at that point in my life and my doctor in Sydney, Dr Chung, was reasonably happy with me. I can only put it down to a combination of the heat in St Louis and the stress of travelling so much in a short period.

Doctor Chung put me on Lipitor and Cartia aspirin to keep the blood thin. I started looking after myself a bit more. I cut back on drinking. The only thing I didn't stop doing was smoking cigarettes. I still get checked out every year. You can only do that. These days I still take the Lipitor, plus I take a lot of vitamins, vitamin E and fish oil and that kind of thing. If you take enough of that shit, everything's cool.

Three months after my Cedars-Sinai adventure, I was in New Zealand for the first date of my Robbie Williams tour, at Auckland's Ericsson Stadium. There were 43,000 people at that show and every one of the eight gigs – three in New Zealand and one each in Brisbane, Sydney, Melbourne, Adelaide and Perth – sold out. It was fantastic.

Just as my Dylan tour at the beginning of the year had cemented a relationship with a world-renowned artist, so too that first tour with Robbie led to two more tours, in 2003 and 2006, both of which were staged in stadiums rather than the arenas that formed the bulk of the first one. Robbie and I get on really well. He calls me Choogs.

With two hugely successful tours by big names in the bag and with my health back to normal, Christmas 2001 was one of the best I'd had in a long time, but I wasn't out of the woods by any means. Promoting is always a gamble, as any of the main players will tell you. It can leave you flat on your arse quicker than you can say Mighty Morphin Power Rangers.

19

Another Day Older and Deeper in Debt

I'm not the best businessman in the world. Paperwork has never been my strong suit. The Packers didn't like my accounting style, or lack of it, nor did Peter Rix on some of the occasions we worked together. I'm more a doer, a motivator and an ideas person than an office guy. I get excited about shows, about putting them on, about the prospect of putting them on and about standing in the middle, basking in the magic. It sounds corny, but it's true. I'm addicted to that moment when the lights go down and thousands of people are pumped and ready for action.

Admittedly I picked a few tours that I got too excited about and then suffered the financial consequences. I thought I was invincible at one stage. Maybe if I saw the job more from a hands-off, business perspective I might be richer than I am, but

I wouldn't be happy. I wouldn't be motivated if it was all about the bottom line. Where's the fun in that?

I don't profess to be God's gift to accounting, but no one in my position would survive without knowing at least the basic principles. You need to know the touring business intimately if you're going to be able to adapt to the myriad problems that can befall a tour – and that's before we get to the occasionally testing antics of the musicians. Few people outside the industry are aware of how much work goes into putting on an Australian music tour or how many people are involved in making it happen. Nor do they have any idea of how much it costs. It costs a lot. Just competing for the tours before you even start spending money on the ground – bidding wars as they are called – can be a nightmare.

My view about winning tours from other promoters is that being a Johnny on the spot is essential. In the past thirty years, it would be rare if I left a gap of more than two or three months without visiting agents in LA, New York and London. Giving the impression in those cities that you live there, walking into someone's office every eight weeks or so, has been crucial to my business and crucial to Frontier, although not every Australian promoter operates that way. To me, if you work like that, making regular overseas visits to the big agencies, they perceive you as being around the corner. It puts you in their heads when they're thinking about selling one of their acts to Australia. If you don't do that, someone else is going to be there at the right moment. Most of the tours I do now come from relationships I built that way, simply by walking into those agents' offices as if I were just passing by.

The amount of fine-tuning that goes into a tour nowadays is so much more intense than it used to be when I started out.

It has got harder. And I'm getting older. In the 70s or 80s, you could look at the history of someone like, for instance, Canadian rock legend Neil Young, who had never been to Australia, and know it was going to work. You looked at record sales and you knew you were going to do the business, so you'd put a tour together. Record sales were a much more significant factor in touring an act then than they are today. From the number of singles or albums a band sold and how many times they appeared on Countdown, you could calculate how many bums you were going to put on seats at a show. Now, with traditional sales of CDs dwindling and the digital era running riot, it's harder to gauge who wants to see a band or singer perform live. You're left to rely on the vibe, your experience and how an artist is being received in other territories.

Australia has always been in a rare position in terms of touring. In America, if a band goes on tour, their agent books sixty cities and usually there will be a different promoter in each city. Sometimes there will be one promoter who has maybe Kansas City, Austin, two or three shows, but in the main it's a different promoter each time.

When touring started in Australia someone, whether it was Kenn Brodziak, Harry M Miller or Paul Dainty, would bring the act from overseas and promote shows all over the country. That was partly to do with the tyranny of distance and also simply because, as soon as one person had done it that way, it became the norm. So from the moment the act landed in the country until the moment they left they were with *you*. It's the same today. They aren't rolling into your town on the tour bus, doing the show and then your responsibility is passed on to someone else. You have to take that into account when you're doing the deal on an Australian tour.

The way deals worked originally in the late 60s and early 70s, a promoter would go to America or England and do a deal with the agent and buy the act; offer them a flat fee. In those days, the promoter would cover accommodation and airfares. Record sales played a big part. Nobody toured Australia unless they had hit records. So you'd work out how many people you thought you could get at each show. You'd work out how much money you would charge for a ticket.

Those promoters had a big chance of making a lot of money, because they were paying the artist a flat fee. If you budgeted to get a crowd of 3000 in Perth and 6000 turned up, you made a huge profit. There weren't a lot of promoters in those early days of touring. Dainty started national touring in Australia, as we know it today. There were a few others who did some of the stadiums and a few theatres in various cities in the late 50s and early 60s, bringing out Little Richard and Johnny Ray and that kind of act, mainly the package tours of early rock 'n' roll. Dainty was the first to get national touring by individual acts going. He made a lot of money. Sometimes the tours didn't work, but when they did the upside could be enormous.

As the business matured in America and England and as managers got smarter, the balance began to shift more towards the artist. That was particularly so in the second half of the 70s when acts such as The Clash, The Police and The Stranglers began to emerge internationally. That's when the percentage deals started. When Dainty did David Bowie, Fleetwood Mac, and Linda Ronstadt in the late 70s they were all flat deals. When Fleetwood Mac came back in 1979 and The Police toured at the same time, they were percentage deals. Just before Frontier, Evans/Gudinski started doing percentage deals with acts such as Blondie and Lou Reed. A lot of the tours they got in that period happened because they were offering the percentage deal and not the flat fee. That's how it stands now.

Some of the huge acts, like Elton John, Dire Straits or Billy Joel, would get a guaranteed fee set against 90 per cent of the door money, whichever was greater. Out of that 90 per cent they would deliver themselves to Australia and pick up their own internal travel and accommodation and production costs. It wasn't a bad deal for them, at 90/10.

When touring by overseas acts began in Australia, there was one stadium or one hall in each city. That was your choice of venues. In some cases, there were no indoor venues that could hold more than 2000, so a lot of shows were outdoors. Today it's pretty easy. In each city you have a choice of two or three venues. You have different-sized venues. With more venues of different sizes, you have more room to manoeuvre with small- and medium-appeal acts. You can't rely on just record sales anymore. There are so many other factors – the internet, marketing, branding. Street talk goes into how you evaluate a potential tour. Also, an act that is huge overseas but that doesn't appeal in Australia can bury you. That can work the other way. There are acts from overseas that do great business here but can't get arrested at home.

Overseas agents are the gateway to big international acts for Australian promoters. They can be your best friends or your worst enemies. They have business methods that can test your patience. Those runs I've been making for years to LA, New York and London have strengthened my relationships with agents, but that doesn't guarantee anything. They employ the same tactics with me as they do with everyone else. You have to be on the ball.

Politics comes into those relationships as well. For example, you could be in a situation where you're buying Bon Jovi from an agent and while he's selling you Bon Jovi he might get you to take Megadeth to do a tour. 'To get that act, you're going to have to take this act.' Sometimes that's what you have to do. Then you'll get an agent who has just sold you a tour that made you $3 million, but then he gets the shits because you won't buy another act because you know it's going to lose money. He *expects* you to buy the act *knowing* you're going to lose money.

With American agents, you'll get a situation of an act that has had one big hit; Macy Gray, for example. Before her Australian tour, she'd had one big hit and one strong album. She should have been playing theatre shows in Australia and maybe a few smaller ones, setting herself up. Instead, the agent insisted she play arenas. She did 15,000-capacity venues that were half-empty and there was no vibe. She was history.

There are times when, if I want to bring an act to Australia, I'll ring an agent and say, 'This is what I think you should do. I'll pay them $20,000 and they can do the Basement in Sydney and the Hi Fi Bar in Melbourne'. They'll look at it and realise that's the right thing to be doing to build the artist's career.

Rodrigo and Gabriela is a good example of that. You get agents who want to build careers and you get others who just want to take the money and run. There are American agents who have destroyed careers by selling them for stupid money. There are acts around now, such as Snow Patrol, who were really hot for a moment. Suddenly they were getting paid twice what they were worth. The Killers were another example. They'd get $200,000 a show and, sure, they'd sell out in Melbourne and Sydney, but they'd lose it all in Perth, Brisbane and Adelaide. That kills those acts. With an English agent, you're more able to build slowly and that way the artist gets a longer run.

The worst situation is when you've toured an act three or four times and you have a good relationship with them. The next tour comes up and they might have a new manager or someone new to the structure and suddenly you find the agent has gone to your two or three rivals and offered them the act that you've been working with for ten or twelve years. That happens to Gudinski, to Coppel, to all of us. It really pisses me off.

The overheads involved in putting together tours just get higher and higher. The Pearl Jam tour I did in 2009 is one example. People would look at that tour and see 40,000 punters at Etihad Stadium in Melbourne and think it must have made a huge profit, but the ticket-buyers don't know about APRA, the Australasian Performing Right Association, for example, which takes 1.5 per cent of every ticket sold to redistribute to its clients, songwriters. We, as promoters, have to supply a list of every song that is played at a concert. If there are three acts on the bill and one does seven songs, one does ten and the other does fourteen, the first one gets 7 points of the 1.5 per cent and so on. It gets split up. That money goes back to the writers and it can be a lot of money. In the 70s and 80s, a lot of local acts sponsored overseas tours with the money they got from APRA, which serves songwriters and the Australian industry as a whole very well.

Public risk insurance works out at roughly the same as 1.5 per cent. If it's a huge superstar act and you're doing an outdoor gig in the wrong month of the year, you need what's called non-appearance insurance, which used to be called rain insurance. That was like backing a 100/1 shot in the Melbourne Cup, because you had to name the period in the day it was going to rain. Sometimes the period would have expired and it would immediately piss down. So they changed it to non-appearance. You can pay up to 4.5 per cent for that.

A big point of dissension in the ranks in Australia now is credit card charges, which are billed back to the promoter. Ten to fifteen years ago 0.5 per cent of your gross might have been eaten up by credit card charges. Today, if you're putting on a show that appeals to a certain demographic, you can pay as much as 6 per cent of the total in credit card fees. So, taking all of those things into account on a Robbie Williams or a Billy Joel/Elton John outdoors show or a Pearl Jam outdoors show, you've immediately lost roughly 10 per cent of your gross. That's a big piece of what you have going on.

At the other end of the scale, you have the venues. When there was only one big venue in each city, arena or entertainment centre, it was costing 15 per cent of the gross, with power, security and security staff taking it up to around 20 per cent. These days, even being able to bargain, venue rental and the extra costs can end up costing 25 per cent of your gross.

For outdoor shows in the 80s we could put up a stage for $80,000. Now it can cost you $300,000 to build a stage. Then you have to transport it. Sometimes you'll have two stages, each one jumping ahead of the other on the tour schedule. If, at a stadium, there is a cricket or football match on there a week after the show, you have a bill of $80,000 to $100,000 putting the Terraplas – protective flooring – on the grass. For the last Robbie Williams tour in 2006, the flooring bill was $2.1 million for eight shows. Pearl Jam in 2009 was $700,000. Catering for the crew and artists at those large-sale events can cost $50,000–$60,000 per show.

There's a range of ticket prices these days because you have white-collar workers, blue-collar workers and people who aren't working. Let's say a ticket is $100. You have GST. That ticket is now $110. Next come the ticket agents. In the old days, you'd put tickets in as many outlets as you could. Then computers came along. Now a ticketing company will approach a venue and say they want exclusive rights to sell tickets for their venue and offer them a huge sum and demand a contract for five years or more – and get it. You have a situation now where the ticket companies can tell you, the promoter, how much your tickets are going to cost. They and the credit card companies are the bane of our industry. We are in a situation with computers where I could have a better ticket-selling system with better back-up on my website with a booking fee of two or three dollars and be making a lot of money and saving people $8 a ticket.

The 2010 AC/DC tour of Australia and New Zealand, in which I was a 30 per cent partner with Garry Van Egmond, had tickets at $149. Before add-ons, they were $122. That makes it hard for punters, because they are picking up the difference. With the ticket companies, there's a booking fee and there's a service fee, which gets split between the venue and the agent. The bullshit we go through over the ticketing charges are terrible. The reason you'll see some acts playing at a mansion or a winery is that those venues are what are known in the industry as green fields. Green fields means there is no booking agency involvement. So we can go in there and sell our tickets any way we want to.

The acts overseas can't believe the booking fees we have in Australia. Nowhere else in the world does the promoter pick up the credit card charges. So, when you're sitting down with an act after the tour and going through the figures on an 85/15 deal, they are trying to make me wear the credit card charges. In the past few years, that has become a real problem. I've had stand-up wars with some tour accountants because of that. Their argument is: 'Why should my band be paying this?' Before computers, these ticket companies would make a charge and if they were selling through, say, a newsagent there would be a service charge as well. But now that it's all on computers there aren't any outlets. It's all computerised, but the service charge is still there.

My company has a database now, which is a huge help in selling a tour. We get the record companies' databases. We send out e-cards, which are virtually TV ads. They have buyer buttons on them and that will get the e-card recipient through to the ticketing agency.

Promoting in the twenty-first century is a minefield. Gone are the days when you booked the local church hall for £5, drew up twenty posters, charged five shillings and got 300 people through the door and your old man did the security.

Frontier began just at the time when those radical changes in the way deals were structured with artists were introduced. That was coincidence. What isn't coincidence is that we started at the right time, when the new wave of artists coming from overseas drove the industry forward and propelled us, Frontier, into the big league.

No matter what I may have thought of them personally, I can't deny that for the most part the partners at Frontier, including myself, worked in tandem really well for the bulk of those twenty years we were together. We were a good team. Everyone had his role and did it to the best of his abilities. My gig, as general manager, was to get the shows on the road and to make sure everything worked like clockwork for the tour's duration. The problem I had starting out on my own after Frontier was that after so many years of working as a collaborative unit, suddenly I was having to be me, Philip Jacobsen and Gudinski all rolled into one – the Frankenstein's monster of rock. It was a steep curve. By the end of 2003, I was millions of dollars in debt. Something had to change.

Two years earlier, I was coasting. That first Robbie Williams tour was incredibly successful and got me some way out of the financial hole I had dug for myself with the Pacific Circle Music Convention. I took on a lot of tours, twenty-six altogether in 2002 and forty in 2003, to help cement my position in the market. Most of them made money, including some big ones, such as Elton John, Bon Jovi and Ray Charles, but by the time the Bon Jovi gig came around in December 2002, I was already back in the shit.

I'd had one good experience with Red Hot Chili Peppers, when they toured for Frontier in 1992, and one bad one, when they pulled out of Alternative Nation at the last minute in 1995. Seven years later, with their album *By the Way* riding high in the charts worldwide – and given that they have always been a quite extraordinary live band – I felt sure I was on to a winner when I booked them for a handful of stadium shows in Australia and New Zealand in November 2002. The tour lost $2 million.

Several months later Santana, riding a multi-platinum album, *Shaman*, and a greatest hits album, also stiffed. Another $1 million down the tubes. It was beyond me. I had two superstar acts that should have made money but which lost a fortune. We were doing shows in Asia that got caught up in the SARS epidemic and that didn't help. It was a tough period.

I've always done the right thing by the industry and I've always tried to pay my bills on time, no matter how bad things got. Because of that, a lot of people carried me for a while after those huge losses. I'm very lucky that a lot of people in the industry, such as suppliers and other affiliated businesses, had faith in me and liked me enough to wait to get paid. I owed money all over the place, but mostly people were cool about it. Without that kind of understanding, I would have gone under. In the end, albeit a long way down the track in some cases, everybody got their money.

I had then, and still have, a business manager and accountant, Jacqui Crouch from Moneypenny Services, looking after my affairs. Jacqui realised I couldn't go on running my business in the way I had been doing it. I needed help. She suggested that Matthew Lazarus-Hall should come into the company. Matthew was general manager at Ticketek. He was a spokesman for the company and also an earpiece, so he used to cop an earful of abuse from me on occasion when I got on my high horse about ticketing issues. It took me nine months to decide to do it, but then we brought him in and he very quickly became my right-hand man and later business partner and managing director. It wasn't easy for him initially, because he inherited a disaster area. I was sloppy. The business was a mess. Everything was complicated.

In 2007, we hired Renee Bryant, who had been working at BHP in Newcastle as financial controller, to run the financial side of the business. Then very quickly I had a finance department with five people in it. Over the next year or so, we moulded a really good team. Now the operation runs smoothly and I don't have to be totally immersed in the running of it.

The accounts department sorts out the contracts and the necessary deposits. I oversee the marketing and make sure that the right deals are done and make a few calls if I have to. I need to do what I do best, which is meeting people and setting up relationships. We're dealing with a lot of the agents today who are twenty to thirty years old. I'm lucky that I can have a relationship with those people.

In 2005, I began co-promoting shows with a young promoter, AJ Maddah, who did alternative and heavy rock acts such as Mudvayne, Yellowcard and Megadeth. That was a successful partnership, but after four years we went our separate ways. We had opposing views about how tours and the business should be run. AJ now runs the successful Soundwave Festival around Australia. He has a good thing going.

If you can find your mark with a festival, you're laughing. Lees and West could have been competition for the big promoters in Australia, but they're quite happy doing the Big Day Out and the odd tour here and there. Joe Segreto could have been competition, but he's happy doing Homebake. A lot of the potential rival promoters are happy to get a winning formula and do that. If you can get that, it's a great thing. AJ was doing as many as sixty tours a year at one point. Now he might do six. But if you can come up with a touring festival that can make you $6 million or $7 million in three or four weeks, why bother pouring it all back into the business?

I have publicist Gaynor Crawford, who co-promotes with me on the more roots-oriented tours, people like Martha Wainwright, and Rodrigo and Gabriela. She handpicks her acts. All I do is back her up and make sure the marketing and production is together. Renee Rudolf promotes all of our smaller acts such as The Kooks, Mystery Jets and Cold War Kids. I sign off on the deals, along with Matthew.

I employ good people and I try to stay out of their way, to let them get on with their job. You have to let go. You can't put someone in the position of running an entire tour and liaising with the acts and their people and then walk in and get in the middle of that.

Business is good. It's incredible the number of people who are going to shows nowadays. The baby boomers are going out more, which helps. They're going to see young acts that their kids are turned on to and vice-versa. The kids are going to see the older acts. We're starting to see whole families at shows.

My feeling today is that I have to expand the company, not to do more tours, which would be virtually impossible, but to incorporate new media, such as internet broadcasting. With Susan Heymann, I created a Pearl Jam TV on our website before their Australian tour in 2009 and it worked really well in getting fans involved and in creating a vibe long before the tour started. There will be a lot more of that kind of thing in the years to come. I also released a few albums under the Chugg umbrella in Australia, including Echo and the Bunnymen's 2009 album *The Fountain*. That's another avenue I'd like to explore further.

I know where my real strength lies and that's in live music. The world touring circuit has never been healthier than it is now. We've been through a recession or two, an Australian dollar slump and much else besides to get to this point. I might as well ride it out for a while and see what happens.

20

A Symphony for Billy

On the morning of 30 August 2001, after seven weeks of doing business in various parts of the world, I arrived at Sydney Airport and was on my way through passport control. The officer behind the counter looked at my passport, then at me, then at the passport and said: 'Gee, you were great on Billy killed the fish last night.' In my exhausted, grumpy, slightly inebriated state, I tried as best I could to form the words he had just said into a sentence I could understand, but to no avail. 'Oh, thanks,' I responded graciously, figuring it was the easiest and quickest way to get past him and his ridiculous observation.

Half an hour later, in a taxi heading for home, the driver looked at me inquisitively for a few minutes and then said excitedly: 'That show you and Billy Thorpe were on last night was fantastic.' That's when I figured out what the passport guy was on about – the television show 'Long Way to the Top'. Over the coming weeks, I'd get many more such comments from people around the office, in shops, at gigs, everywhere I went, about the show that was causing such a stir on the ABC, the six-part documentary on the history of Australian rock 'n' roll.

I knew about the show, since I was in it, but because I'd been out of the country for almost two months I'd forgotten about it and about when it was going to air. The third episode, 'Billy Killed the Fish', featured Thorpie, Lobby Loyde and me reminiscing about the good old days, such as the gig by Billy and The Aztecs at Bondi Lifesaver in 1974, at which the band's volume was typically obscene. The noise caused a school of tropical fish, housed in a large tank at the back of the dancefloor, to become the first known aquatic casualties of blues–rock. Hopefully those fish up in heaven can take comfort from the fact that the retelling on television of their demise inspired the most rewarding rock 'n' roll tour of my career.

Poor Billy. He had big plans for his sixties. The *Tangier* album that he sweated over for five years, his obsession, would have marked the beginning of a new and successful phase of his career, I feel certain about that. He'd had plenty of phases before then over his five decades in the music business – and made a success of all of them – partly because he was talented and partly because he was so driven to perform and to produce new music, to be out there doing it, no matter what was thrown in his path. He was very close to completing *Tangier* when the heart attack took him on 28 February 2007. No one who knew him could believe that the fittest-looking sixty-year-old in the country was gone.

My career is inexorably linked with Billy's. I saw him play at every level, starting out at the halls in Tasmania where I first went to see bands. I saw Billy and the original Aztecs – drummer Tony Barber, bass player John Bluey Watson and guitarists Valentine Jones and Vince Maloney – at the Albert Hall in Launceston. It was the first real rock show I'd seen. They were touring with English rock eccentric Screaming Lord Sutch. Billy blew me away. The energy of the band was unbelievable. And they were all dressed up in sharp suits. I liked that. When they came back about eight months later, along with Ray Brown and the Whispers, to the National Theatre in Launceston, I was there. Somehow I was able to find out which hotel they were staying in. I got to meet him and to talk to him and he was really nice to me. He was the same age as me roughly, but he was the star so he seemed older.

When he came back a year later, he had the new Aztecs, which was guitarists Col Risby and Mike Downes, drummer Johnny Dick, Teddy Toi on bass and piano player Jimmy Taylor. It was still a pop thing and it wasn't as hot, to my mind, as the previous line-up. In 1966, he hosted a TV show called 'It's All Happening' on Channel Seven, with the Aztecs as the house band. I followed his career through that and whatever else I could pick up. He was living the life then, with the flash cars and all the rest. He was a star of stage, screen and recording, yet he would come out of that era broke.

I maintained my friendship with Billy from the day we reconnected at the Consolidated Rock office in St Kilda in 1970 right through to the end. During his twenty years in California, I'd visit at least once a year, plus I looked after a lot of the shows he did when he came back to tour. When I took on Thorpie's management, it was based as much on our friendship as it was on business. He knew he could trust me. He asked me to do it just around the time he came back to Australia in 1994 to promote the *Lock Up Your Mothers* CD collection, a compilation of his best work. The album and the tour did well, but both Billy and I were concerned that he was being promoted as a retro act rather than a current one. His ego really couldn't handle that. He had more to offer. As the 90s progressed, Billy began to make his mark on Australia once again, but his past did play a significant part in that.

The first sign of Thorpie coming back to live in Australia was the Oz tour he did with The Billy Thorpe Band in 1996, just a few weeks after I got out of jail in LA. That was a busy time for Billy. By then he had written the first of his two autobiographies, *Sex and Thugs and Rock 'n' Roll: a year in Kings Cross 1963–1964*. He would call me in the middle of the night from LA to read passages of it to me, to get my opinion. I thought it was hilarious and soon I wasn't the only one. When it came out in November 1996 it was an immediate bestseller and went on to be a massive success. It helped that Billy knew how to sell himself. That's one thing he was always good at. The media loved him again.

It took him a couple of years and another book, *Most People I Know (think that I'm crazy)*, to realise that there was no point coming and going from LA when his future looked more secure in Australia, so he and his wife Lynn and daughter Rusty came back to Sydney. (His daughter Lauren stayed in New York.) With the release of the second book, and a show-stopping appearance at the Mushroom Records twenty-fifth anniversary concert at the Melbourne Cricket Ground in 1998, his profile was sky high. Suddenly he had the respect and admiration of a new generation. He was the revered elder statesman of Oz rock, not a title he warmed to particularly, but it was true. He was still pissed off after all those years about how his star had waned in the 70s, to the point where he had to leave the country to be heard. He wanted to prove himself again in Australia.

In his favour, by the end of the 90s there was less of a stigma about older musicians maintaining or even reviving their careers. At the top end, The Stones were still doing it, but other, less successful bands and artists, whose heyday was the 70s, were coming back because those baby boomers that loved them first time around were starting to go out again. Among them were The Who's Roger Daltrey, Peter Frampton, Alice Cooper, Procol Harum's Gary Brooker, Jack Bruce and Free and Bad Company's front man Paul Rodgers, who came together in February 2000 for an Australian tour called the *Ultimate Rock Symphony*. Billy was the token Aussie on the bill and he blew them away. At the second show, in Adelaide, after he had received a standing ovation for his early performance, Alice Cooper came up to him and me backstage and said to Billy: 'Who the fuck ARE you?'

As well as renewing their popularity with their original audiences, these and many other older artists were finding new fans as well and discovering younger musicians who admired their work. Many young Australian musicians looked up to Billy for what he had done in his career, for the foundations he laid in the early 70s at Sunbury and at the forefront of pub rock. I could see him being big again in Australia, not just as a nostalgia act but also as a legitimate older singer and songwriter. Then nostalgia came along and took everyone by surprise.

Paul Clarke, a producer from ABC television, rang me early in 2001 and told me that he and renowned music journalist and author Clinton Walker were putting together a one-hour documentary on Oz rock called 'Long Way to the Top'. They both wanted to know if Thorpe and I would be interested in being interviewed for it. We agreed to do it. Billy and I had no shortage of yarns to give them after thirty-five years in the business, so the interviews went way over time. There was just so much to the story, so much material, that it would have been impossible to do it in a day — never mind the hour they had scheduled for each of us. They must have had several hours of footage.

When they started out, I don't think Clarke and Walker knew quite what they were getting themselves into. During our interviews, we were throwing names at them that they didn't know and even by the time we stopped they had hardly scratched the surface. That's why the show stretched from one episode to six. It could have been twenty. They missed stuff, inevitably, including my mate Richard Clapton, but it was well put together. The show had the public and the industry buzzing. It travelled from the early days of rock 'n' roll with Johnny O'Keefe to the present and had plenty of footage from the ABC vaults and elsewhere, alongside some great interview material.

Not long after it screened, Billy and I were sitting in a restaurant and started talking about the idea of taking a show on the road under the *Long Way to the Top* banner. It was a good idea, but we were still concerned that the old-fart syndrome might get in the way of its success. I was thinking: 'Will they come to the show?' I discussed it further with Eric Robinson and he liked the idea. Amanda Pelman, who had worked at Mushroom Records for eleven years and discovered Kylie

Minogue, had just started working with me at MCE. She had experience in theatre and casting as well as music, so I valued her judgement. She became co-producer.

We went to the ABC to get them involved so that they would promote it. We had to pay them a licence fee because of the name and we had to pay Alberts, who owned the rights to the AC/DC song that the title came from. We approached the Jacobsen family, since their role in the early days of Aussie rock 'n' roll was crucial to its success. Kevin Jacobsen became co-producer and his brother Col Joye, one of the biggest stars of the 60s, agreed to open the show. Col's daughter Amber Jacobsen joined the team, as did manager and agent Brian de Courcy. Bruce Pollack took on the publicity.

The next step was to come up with a roster of acts. Billy, who also became a financial partner in the production, was always looking at the grand statement. Everything had to be bigger than Ben Hur with Billy, with him in the lead chariot. We had to keep it from becoming the Billy Thorpe Show, especially in the eyes of the other entertainers. We put together a wish list and worked our way through the names. It wasn't a hard sell. We wanted to concentrate on the early era of Oz rock and pop, so we restricted ourselves to the period from the late 50s to the early 70s. We also had to work out how many, or rather how few acts we would need to fit into a maximum three-and-a-half-hour performance. We ended up with a stellar cast that included Col, Little Pattie, Stevie Wright, The Masters' Apprentices, Normie Rowe, Kevin Borich, Axiom's Brian Cadd and Glenn Shorrock, Marcia Hines, John Paul Young and a dozen more. Billy performed with the original Aztecs and the Sunbury-era Aztecs.

We enlisted Bandstand host Brian Henderson to record an audio-visual segment for the show.

The budget was set at $4.5 million and the plan was to do six arena-size shows around the country. Tickets would go for between $80 and $135. When it went on sale, we couldn't believe the reaction. It kept selling out. We had to add shows in every city. In the end, we sold out eighteen shows across Australia.

It helped that we launched the tour with a special segment on 'A Current Affair' on television. Presenter Mike Munro came out to the rehearsal space we had at a factory in Alexandria and did the report from there. The ABC also promoted it really well.

Not surprisingly, given the number of egos vying for position, it wasn't long into rehearsals before clashes emerged about who was going on in which spot and for how long, with how many songs. Most of it was good-natured and often hilarious, but now and again it got heated. Rowe and Thorpe were always winding each other up, so if either of them got a few seconds more stage time than the other there was a debate about it. The original show we had outlined was so over time it wasn't funny. We'd still be doing it now if we hadn't chopped significantly from it.

When the show went on the road, on 24 August 2002 in Perth, any tensions that had developed at rehearsals in Alexandria quickly evaporated. The good feeling the show engendered among the participants and the audience was almost tangible. It was fantastic. The more we travelled, the better it got. Not only were these musicians, some of whom hadn't played professionally for years, enjoying being back on stage in front of 10,000 people a night, but they were enjoying being together, being backstage with their peers sharing road stories and reliving the great moments in their careers. Now and again someone would get the shits with Billy, doing his best to be in charge, but it never lasted for long. Stevie Wright was in poor health and needed assistance a lot of the time, but the rest of the cast were terrific with him. He was a real trouper.

The funniest parts of the tour were the parties. Taking over the bar after the show some nights, there would be 300 people getting it on until 3 am, with one of the musos at the piano and all of these old pros around it acting like they were twenty. Even some of the old groupies were there – and some new ones as well. It was like the old days.

That was the beauty of it, the very thing that we had worried ourselves about before we took it on. It was an exercise in nostalgia with a bunch of old farts, but it worked for that reason. It was like something that doesn't exist anymore. There is nowhere you can go in Australia where you can walk into a room and meet so many of your peers. This was it. Young rockers were coming along to the show and hanging out afterwards, bands such as You Am I and Jet, showing their respect and their love for the music. And the audiences just went crazy. I've never seen anything like it or felt so good about being on the road and doing what I do. It was simply amazing.

We grossed $10 million from that tour. We did incredibly well out of it. The acts did well also. Apart from their fees, which ranged from $2500 to $10,000 a show, many of the acts suddenly thrust into the spotlight after a long lay-off went back on the road under their own steam. For the ones who still had thriving careers, *Long Way to the Top* was the best advertising they could get. Everyone was a winner.

There was a down side. Buoyed by the tour's success in the cities, we decided to take it to regional Australia early in 2003 and that didn't work. For whatever reason, demand for those acts in the country wasn't as strong as it had been in Sydney, Perth, Melbourne, Adelaide, Wollongong, Newcastle and Brisbane. Due to the sizes of venues we played in the country we had to cut down the production, which meant losing songs and some of the acts from the original line-up. There was simply no other way of making it work. Consequently some of the acts, including Borich, Wright and Warren 'Pig' Morgan, sued us for loss of earnings. We settled with each of the acts we couldn't accommodate on the regional run.

We had a loose plan to do another version of *Long Way to the Top* later, with some of the artists from the next era. We looked at picking up a few of the 70s icons we had used on the first one and adding other acts from the 70s and 80s, but we worried about its depth and credibility. We weren't sure about the audience for it. Then of course Gudinski had to shove it up our arse a few years later by doing the *Countdown* tour and *Countdown 2*, so *LWTTT2* is still on the back burner.

One day in 2000, just a few weeks after the *Ultimate Rock Symphony* tour, Billy rang me and I could tell he was excited. He and Lynn were good friends with writer Vitek Czernuszyn and his wife Deborah Thomas, who at that time was editor in chief of the *Australian Women's Weekly*. The four of them had made a plan to go for a holiday in Morocco. Would I like to come? Vitek had friends there who could provide a place to stay. I wasn't keen. Morocco wasn't top of my holiday destination list, but I had planned a business trip to attend some of the European and American summer rock festivals around the same time, so I agreed.

My trip started in Germany, where I met up with Mayling, who flew in from Canada for a holiday. We went to a fiftieth birthday party for a good friend of mine, German promoter Ossy Hoppe, in Hamburg. From there we travelled to London, met up with Thorpie and the others and then travelled together to Morocco. Vitek's friend provided us with an amazing old house in Tangier.

We got in to Tangier late in the evening. Mayling and I were in our room when I heard music coming from downstairs. I went down to find out what it was and there was Thorpie in the middle of the room, with a guitar, playing the same riff over and over; just the one riff, hundreds of times. That was the riff that formed the foundation of *Tangier*. You can hear it on the title track of the album.

For the remainder of the holiday, if we were walking through a market or street and Moroccan musicians were playing, Billy would be over at them straight away, watching, listening, and asking questions to which he didn't always get answers. He would spend an age speaking to them, trying to pick their brains about the music they were playing.

Vitek's friend lived in an old palace in the heart of the Tangier Kasbah. The Rolling Stones had done some recording there. On our second night, we had the most magnificent feast there. Late in the evening, some musicians turned up to play for us. They were among the musicians we had seen performing earlier in the street. One of them was a member of the Moroccan Symphony Orchestra. It became Billy's obsession to record in Morocco using the orchestra, but it didn't happen.

The remainder of the holiday was spent travelling around to different parts of Morocco in a Kombi van. The more we travelled, the more ideas Billy got for his album. I slept in the back next to the luggage most of the time. It was Lynn's fiftieth birthday while we were in Rabat and Billy planned a surprise party at another old, fabulous palace there, again through Vitek's friend. Standing on the roof of that palace with the others that night was magical. We went to Fez as well, where Billy wrote a song, 'Since You've Been Gone', for his mother, the song that was played at his memorial service. After the holiday, I flew to a festival in Switzerland and the Thorpes went off into the desert for five days.

When we were both back in Sydney, we talked a lot about Tangier, or about Morocco at least, as the idea of a concept album began to take shape. When at last he knew what he wanted to do, his perfectionism dragged the process from weeks to months to years. There was no point in trying to hurry him along. He had a clear vision of *Tangier*, more than on any other record he'd made. It had to be perfect.

After *Long Way to the Top* ended, Billy had to move from the Mountain Street studio he had rented for years, the place where he spent long days working on new songs, including some of the material for *Tangier*. He transferred all of the equipment into another studio in Surry Hills, where he became even more ensconced. He shut himself up in the studio for the rest of his life. He was pretty close to getting the album finished, but it was killing him. He was obsessed. He just would not give up on it. By then, we had been trying for a couple of years to get a record deal. That was frustrating for him. After he died, it took forever to go through all the tapes of what he had done over several years. Not all of them were marked, which made it so much harder and time-consuming.

Billy died of a heart attack completely out of the blue and he had looked a picture of health, but I'm convinced that the way he punished himself working on that album was a contributing factor to what happened.

He'd had a scare before the big one. They were up at actor Jack Thompson's beach place at Coffs Harbour. Billy and Lynn were staying in the caravan on the property. Lynn came running in one day and said Billy was having some kind of attack. Jack got a bottle and filled it up with as much soluble aspirin as he could find and poured it down Billy's throat, to thin his blood. Billy underplayed that afterwards. Stories went around that doctors had told him he had problems and that he never filled out prescriptions given to him. When he died, there were similar stories about soluble aspirin wrappers being found all over the studio, but I never saw them.

Whatever brought about his death, it was a death too soon. When I got the call early that morning, I'd been having a big night. I wasn't at my best. After publicist Rina Ferris had called and woken me up to tell me the news, I noticed there were twenty-seven calls unanswered on my machine. All of them were from the media. I had to pull myself together. I ended up doing TV interviews in the park opposite my house in Neutral Bay, looking awful. I was in shock. I felt terrible. Eventually I had to go and see a doctor I felt so bad, but there was nothing seriously wrong with me physically. That was one of the worst days of my life.

Billy kept everything to himself, so we'll never know for sure if he was sick before the attack or not. That habit of keeping his life private extended to his business affairs, which meant that when he died his finances were in disarray. In short, he didn't have any money, despite the fact that he had been a rock star for most of his life.

He had vowed, after coming out of his first career as a pop star with no money, that it would never happen to him again, which is perhaps why he never allowed anyone to look after his money for him properly. But the simple truth is that a lot of the time Billy lived above his means until there was nothing left. He had no concept of how to look after money. He had royalty cheques from America that weren't deposited, other assets in the US that were frozen due to tax demands. I don't know what exactly happened in America, but he wasn't paying his tax from his royalties there, which would have been considerable given that his album *Children of the Sun* went top twenty.

Lynn, Rusty and Lauren had no idea about any of that. They were his princesses, but they didn't know what went on in his business life. It was a mess. I used to get calls from Greg Clarke at the studio saying the owner was demanding the three months rent Thorpie owed him. That kind of thing was common. He ended up working alone in the Surry Hills studio because he couldn't afford an engineer. He had no money. He always said he wasn't going to get fucked over after it happened to him as a pop star, but he fucked himself over by not taking care of business.

The biggest bugger is that the little sod had to go and have a heart attack before he could release his masterwork. We were just getting to the next step of his career. We were only getting started. I miss him like a brother.

21

Great Escape

I was seriously in debt even before the Santana tour in March–April 2003. That's when I decided to buy myself a villa in Phuket, in Thailand. Retail therapy has never been my thing and certainly not when I owe large amounts of money. This was another kind of therapy, one I wasn't able to explain even to myself. I just got a feeling that it was the right thing to do, so I did it.

I'd been to Phuket several times. I first went there on my way back from a European business trip in 1989, just to break up the journey. I did that occasionally when I started to do a lot of travelling for Frontier and during my management phase in the 80s. In the 90s I took Mayling there a few times. I went to other parts of Thailand. Lilo and I had a holiday at Pattaya Beach in the 70s along with Philip Jacobsen and his partner Maxine and I'd stopped over in Bangkok occasionally, although it's not my favourite city. I'd had holidays in Indonesia, in Bali, and I loved that too, but there was something about Phuket that affected me in a way none of those other places did. There was a feeling of tranquillity, of calm about it. It had such a soothing effect, a tonic for someone like me who was on the move constantly. Today it gives me a similar feeling to the one I get in Kauai; inner peace, or as close to that as I'm ever going to get.

Early in March that year, I was in London at the International Live Music Conference. I'd had a busy few months in the lead-up to that, so I decided I'd have a week at the Chedi Hotel at Surin Beach in Phuket on the way home. While I was in London I ran into an old friend, Michael Hosking, an English promoter I'd known in Hong Kong but who was now running a business with another promoter, Nigel Peters, in Phuket. Michael had moved primarily because he had kids and wanted them to go to the international school there. We arranged to have dinner in Phuket during my holiday.

As soon as I arrived in Phuket, something felt different. I checked into the hotel. I had this overwhelming feeling of well-being and not because I had been doing anything illegal. The feeling got stronger. I was mildly euphoric. As the days went by, it just felt great being there. I was so at peace with myself.

I had dinner with my friends and afterwards Michael said he wanted to show me something. We drove to an office in Cherngtalay and he showed me a model of the villa complex he and Peters were going to build. I really couldn't afford to do anything, considering the financial mess I was in, but the more I looked at these villas — there were ten of them — and in the natural state of euphoria I was floating around in, it just felt so right that I should have one of them.

Something clicked inside my head that day and I could see a whole new world opening up before me. At the time, I was finding that I wasn't enjoying Sydney as much as I used to. I'd been thinking for a while that I needed to take a step back. That Phuket trip, that epiphany, came just at the right time. I put down a deposit of $50,000 on one of the villas and kept making additional payments for about a year.

I went back to Phuket about nine months later. I took my son Lucas and my daughter Sophie up with me and we stayed at the Alamander Apartments in Laguna just next to the site of what would become the Sai Taan Villas complex. They were just laying the foundations of the place while we were there.

I met the project manager, an Aussie digger-type bloke from Queensland, Ron Amos. He and I got on really well. He was a good friend to have. Things have a habit of falling down in Thailand, even without tsunamis, so Ron ensured that the villa was built to the best possible standards.

The kids liked my idea of having a place away from everything we were used to in Sydney. It was a paradise, an escape from the real world as we knew it. I think part of my reason for buying the villa was because I thought it might bring me closer to my three children – not that we weren't close, but I figured it could be something else we could share, that Phuket could become a family experience. Of course, my kids are at an age now when they've got too much going on in the big smoke to go up regularly, but all three of them have been several times. When the complex was just finished, in late 2004, and I had taken ownership of the villa, I asked Lucas to go up with me for Christmas, but he rang me a few days before and said there was no surf in Phuket so he was just going to go surfing in Sydney instead. What can you do?

After a while, I started spending more time at the villa when I wasn't on tour or on a work run overseas or, as has been the case more often in recent years, when my presence in the office wasn't essential. It's a beautiful house in its own grounds, with a swimming pool and a lovely garden, inside a walled, security-manned compound. It's the perfect spot to unwind, to forget about deals and percentages and transport bills and financial woes and bidding wars and everything else in my day-to-day existence. It wasn't long before it began to feel like home. The more time I spent in Phuket, the less I liked the way I was living my life in Sydney.

I'd reached a point in the mid-2000s where I wasn't looking after myself very well, again, even though I'd been going to the health farms regularly to try and extinguish all of my old, familiar habits. I find the patterns of my life in Sydney over the past four decades are very hard to get away from. I have to be very careful. Sometimes in the office in Sydney I'll be sitting there and I'll find it very hard not to have a drink. Then, at 3 pm, I'll open a bottle of wine and I'll work until 11 or 12 pm. I shouldn't do that. Someone else might pop in, like my friend Mark Pope who has an office next door, and we'll have a few more. After that has happened with a few different people, you can end up with three or four bottles lying demolished. I've had to stop that. I've had to get myself motivated to the point where if I feel like having a drink I don't have it. For the past few years, that's what I've been doing. I try and stay away from it. Back in the day, that kind of activity was six days a week. It was just part of what you did, part of the business. Now if I have a big night it affects me for three or four days.

Travel affects me as well, which is hard to take because I love it. It's one of the best things about what I do. In the first two months of 2010 I was in Vietnam, Thailand, Canada, Tahiti, New Zealand, America, England and Australia. I've been around the world twice since then. I enjoy that. I enjoy going to places and soaking up the atmosphere and sampling the lifestyles of other people and other cultures, but the demands of travelling all the time are getting harder. On a flight to Canada or the US or the UK, four or five hours in I think it's never going to end. I'm fortunate that I can sleep fairly well on planes and I discipline myself not to drink on flights. I don't like taking sleeping pills either. I take melatonin, a natural herb. That helps.

But it's not quality sleep. When I get somewhere and check into a hotel and get two hours . . . that's quality sleep. I worry when I get off a plane and I can hardly stand up because my knees are gone. I worry about blood clots and all that stuff.

Another reason for travelling, despite the drawbacks, is that I get restless in Sydney. I have a lot of friends, many of them overseas. There are always people I can visit. In March 2010 I went to Bora Bora just to watch my friend Jimmy Buffett, who's used to playing in front of 60,000 people, play to a gathering of 90. It was awesome. I am lucky I can do that.

There are very few places I travel to where I would be lonely, not that I get lonely often. Private person probably isn't the right description of me, but there's nothing wrong with solitude once in a while. I really don't mind being with myself. A lot of people can't deal with it, but I can enjoy it. I suppose after all those years of touring and travelling and hanging out in strange cities on my own I got used to it. I enjoy a bit of peace and quiet, so I can read a book. Phuket gives me that.

Sometimes when I'm at home in Sydney I think about that, about not bowing to old habits. I have an apartment near the company's office in Surry Hills. I could just pick up the phone and call someone and go out to dinner, but more often than not I don't. I can't be bothered going out and drinking like I used to do. I love to be one on one with people, though, especially in my relationships with women. That doesn't get to happen very often. When you're on the road or you're at shows, you are surrounded by people all the time. Then when you go somewhere overseas and you're with someone and you want to spend time with them, you end up having dinners and meetings and all of a sudden you find the time has run out.

I'm a very social person, I think, but I'm choosy these days about where I go. I get invited to a lot of opening nights, a lot of receptions, those kinds of functions, but I don't go any more. You run into a lot of people at these things you really don't want to know.

That never happens to me in Phuket. Through Michael Hosking and Ron Amos I soon built up a small network of friends in Phuket. One of them, Dr Richard Cracknell, I had met in the 80s in Kauai, and he asked me to join the Hash Hound Harriers, a club that involves a bit of not too serious running and a lot of serious drinking afterwards, although I always enjoyed both in moderation. It was all very expat and male bonding, but I loved it. I don't participate now, but Dr Cracknell is the man who does his best to keep me alive over there. He keeps me focused on looking after myself.

I started to learn the Thai language, gradually, as well as the culture. When I was in Phuket the first time, in 1989, I met a lovely woman called Sano. She was a bar manager at the Chedi, where I was staying, and she also became my driver, to show me around the island for a few weeks. I learned a lot from her about the way Thailand works, how the people survive. It stuck with me and so I wanted to find out more.

On one of the first trips there after I bought the house, I went shopping in the nearby village, looking for some furniture and ornaments. In one of the shops I went to, a woodcarving store, I was always intrigued by the western music they were playing when I went in there, CDs of songs I really liked. I didn't have much in the way of vocabulary, but I did the best I could to tell the lady in the shop that I was enjoying the music. She was a beautiful, petite young woman, polite and friendly, as most Thais are. She was wearing a checked shirt and jeans and looked like a bit of a tomboy. I was taken with her. Her name was Maam.

Maam didn't speak any English, but we made some kind of connection. I found out she had five sisters. Two of the older ones ran the shop. Maam was the Cinderella of the family. She opened the shop at 6 am and closed it at 9 pm. She was the typical little sister who wasn't being treated fairly by the big sisters, but she wasn't a kid. She was thirty-two. Maam told me later that at that time she thought she was going to be a Thai spinster for the rest of her life.

Nothing much happened for a long time. I was in Phuket for a few weeks here and there and I would always visit the shop to see her. After a while, we just had a vibe about each other. I invited her to the house. She said no. She was very straight, nothing like the girls in Phuket who frequent the bars and massage parlours visited by tourists. My only other experience of Thai women was when for about a year I went out with a Thai lady who lived in New Zealand. It was nothing serious, but she was really nice.

The great things about Maam were that she was gentle and soft and Buddhist. I've always admired the Buddhist philosophy. I really dig that. Maam has a good spirit. She just feels good to be around. It was a very slow courtship. It took me about a year just to get her to come to the villa for a drink, not that she drinks much or anything like that. Maam was just what I wanted, though. I knew that. At that point in my life, soft and gentle was what I needed and she was perfect. When I let it be known that I was seeing a Thai woman, some of my friends warned me against it. They kept telling me that you have to watch Thai women because they will take you for everything you've got. Maam isn't like that at all.

She told me one day she wanted to learn English. There's a school of English in Phuket Town. She went off there for a month. She was very shy about it and wouldn't practise what she had learned, so we went to Sydney together. She got a little confidence from being there, and then when we got back she did the advanced English course at the school and she started to believe in herself more. The Cinderella syndrome slowly disappeared. I love her family now. Their attitudes have changed a little. The way they treated her wasn't deliberately malicious, it was just the way it was.

With Maam there and with my new second home very close to her, Phuket became a great escape for me. Whenever I wasn't too busy, that's where I would go. Kauai had been a bit like that to me for many years. I'd been going every year since 1983, but this time, with Phuket, there was more to it. It was about the great house and about Maam and about escaping from my rock 'n' roll circus, but also there was something really spiritual about going there. Either I was turning into a hopeless hippie or I was simply in love with the place. It was the latter, although I gave the nod to hippie culture by having the occasional joint while I had my feet up by the pool.

The villa soon became my paradise retreat. Even now, it's somewhere I can go and as soon as I get there the phone stops ringing; well, it doesn't ring as much, or maybe it rings and I simply don't answer it, because when I'm there I don't feel I always have to do that. I don't stop work altogether, but I find I can get more done in a couple of hours there than in a few days in Sydney, because there are fewer distractions, fewer inquiries, less agents' bullshit.

I found myself being more creative there and getting away from all the bad things, like cocaine and going out to lunch and getting drunk all day, ending up at home by 7 pm totally pissed and taking two days to get over it. In Phuket, there isn't the same reason to drink. I have the odd joint, but not the bad stuff. Everyone knows not to bring that stuff anywhere near the house. If cocaine became prevalent around there, I'd move somewhere else.

I've always liked nice houses, clean houses. Maybe that's a throwback to how I was brought up. One of the things I really enjoyed about having a new house in a different country, with a different culture and being technically single, was being able to do everything to it myself. I bought a lot of the furniture. My friend Michael's wife Rona is an interior designer. She had set up a business in Phuket shortly before I arrived and she helped me with some ideas and colour schemes. I bought all the silverware, cutlery, beds, chairs, vases locally, mainly because I had never seen stuff like it before.

Since then, I've tried to furnish it with little pieces from wherever I travel. The place has a hybrid Native American, African, Asian and European vibe to it. My apartment in Sydney has its good points too, although I'm never sure if being next door to the office is one of them. I like the apartment when I get there. I'm comfortable. Maam and I designed it too and put it all together so it feels a bit like home, like in Phuket. We have a lot of Thai furniture and ornaments.

Maam has her own business in Phuket now, a coffee shop not far from her sister's woodcarving shop. It took about ten months to get it going, but now it's doing well. I go and help out there sometimes when I can. The shop also sells pieces of art and books.

When I bought the villa, it was as an escape, nothing more, but after a while, since it was sitting empty at least half of the time, it seemed sensible to rent it out, so that's what I did. The overheads of keeping it going are not cheap. It comes to about $2000 a month, so I started renting it out and Maam looked after the place while there were tourists, usually Europeans, living in it. That was a positive learning curve for her. After a while, Australian friends wanted to go up and use it, so it's not unusual to spot Molly or Marcia or Richard Clapton or someone from the wonderful world of show business doing a few laps before breakfast by the pool.

During the first few years of our relationship, Maam lived in her own place and I lived in the villa, but when I started renting the place out I had to stay in hotels when I was over there. Although I had a friend who got me good rates, I still ended up paying more in hotel bills than I was getting for the villa. A real estate agent friend, Kurt Appel, solved that problem. He had a house for sale near the airport. On my way home to Sydney one time, Maam came with me to take a look at it. It was two terraced houses combined into one. I bought it for 5 million baht.

Maam and I had a lot of fun doing up that one. It has turned into a home. I only stay in the villa now if it's empty. Maam comes and stays with me at the airport house when I'm in Phuket. She has to be up at 4.30 am, though, to go and prepare her shop for opening.

I love so many things about Thailand and about Phuket in particular. I love eating Thai street food from vendors, going to markets, discovering things. Having my sixtieth birthday there was fantastic, especially since so many people came from Australia, from New Zealand, from all over the place, even Hawaii, to the party in the villa compound. Molly dressed up as Marilyn Monroe and stuck his tongue down my throat. Try forgetting that. Some of my family came along, including my sister Julie and brother Paul. I would have loved my mother to be there as well, but she is in care these days and wasn't fit to travel. The three kids came. In his speech, Lucas took great delight in telling everyone that one of the first words he learned to say was 'fuck' and he owed it all to me. Charming. Bands played into the night. Brian Cadd and Leo Sayer performed. There was fabulous food, set up in stalls and delivered on trays, and drinks of every possible variety. It was fabulous.

More than half of those who came from overseas had never been to Phuket, but from the time they spent with me they could see why I wanted to live there. About 25 per cent of those guests have been back to Phuket since then.

It's not perfect. There is rising crime. Properties have been broken into. I got robbed. I was out riding my bike. I'd been to the ATM and I had also just changed a whole lot of money and I had about $US5000 in my wallet. Yes, I know. Kick me hard. I was riding along and for some stupid reason I put my wallet and some other bits and pieces in the plastic bag I was carrying as I rode along. Two guys on a motorbike came past and ripped it out of my hand. The police came to the house and Maam helped me give a description of the bike bandits. Kurt Appel, my real estate agent, had been driving past me at the time and he was able to give a second description of the two guys. The police got them, but the money was long gone by then.

I didn't know about the Boxing Day tsunami in 2004 at the time, because I'd been on planes all day. I'd abandoned the idea of going to Phuket for Christmas after Lucas had turned down the invitation, but I was on a holiday. I was travelling by hovercraft from Hayman Island to Hamilton Island when Mark Pope rang me. He told me what had happened. I saw some of the horror on TV when I got to the airport at Hamilton Island. All I could think about was what would have happened if Lucas had said yes to the holiday in Phuket and had gone surfing.

Mark said John Watson (Silverchair, Missy Higgins), Paul Piticco (Powderfinger) and Phil Stevens (John Butler, The Waifs), three of the highest-profile artist managers in Australia, were wondering if they should put together some kind of benefit concert. They wanted me involved, for my experience, but

I think they were also wary that I would take over the running of the event. I'm not like that, really. Maybe the profile I have suggests that, but I'm only as good, at best, as the people I have around me.

Next day we had a conference call between all five of us, with the addition of Joe Segreto, and away we went. The concert blossomed quickly from a theatre show to an all-day event at Sydney Football Stadium. The three managers supplied their talent, which was joined quickly by Midnight Oil, Pete Murray, Nick Cave, the Finn brothers, the all-star band The Wrights and Kasey Chambers. On 29 January 2005, a month after the disaster that hit Indonesia, India, Sri Lanka and Thailand, taking almost 250,000 lives, the Wave Aid Benefit Concert stirred the nation.

It was a proud moment for everyone who took part, once again proving that the music industry can be a powerful tool in times of tragedy. From a professional point of view, that event got me in touch with the younger side of the industry and the local side of the industry, which I hadn't really been very close to in the twenty-first century. I'd been so busy getting the international side of things up and running that I hadn't done much in Australian music for a long time, so to be involved in that event was great. It dominated the lives of everyone involved in it for four weeks.

From the lessons we had learned from other benefit gigs, we made sure we controlled where the money raised from the concert would go. Phil Stevens wanted to do something in Sri Lanka. I wanted to do something in Phuket. I went back there for a couple of weeks about a year after the disaster. I met up with Sano, the woman I had made friends with fifteen years earlier. She took me to Khao Lak, about 80 kilometres north of Phuket, and it was decimated. She had lost her mother, father and nephew.

I had come with the intention of finding some useful way to spend the money we had allocated to helping the worst affected areas of the tsunami. It was shocking what was going on. Politicians were trying to steal the land from people who had nothing else left. Lots of families there have lived on the same land for hundreds of years, but they have nothing on paper to say that it belongs to them, so after the tsunami a lot of corrupt people in power were trying to steal it from them. Other money allocated by the government to rebuild housing simply disappeared.

I had $250,000 to spend from the proceeds of Wave Aid DVD sales. I came up with the idea of building boats, but I found out that as soon as boats were being built they were being put on the back of trailers and sold in Bangkok, so that was out. I thought of orphanages, but the culture in Thailand is very much about extended family, so there aren't many orphans.

A friend in Phuket, an American businessman called Tom McNamara, had set up a charity organisation called Phuket's Been Good to Us Foundation. It was a charity formed by many of the expats who had been there since before it was a tourist destination. He thought it would be a good idea to introduce the teaching of English in some of the local schools. All we needed were some teachers. I thought it was a great idea.

There was a school not far from my villa, in a village called Kalim, that had been washed away by the tsunami. I thought that would be a good place to start. We found Kate and Stephen Cope, an English couple who taught English. I put the money into Tom's foundation and we went from there. Now we have a number of English teachers at various schools on the island. In a place where tourism is such an integral part of the economy, it makes sense to have these kids learning English.

After my sixtieth birthday, I took my sister Julie and brother Paul to visit the school, to see how the community had rebuilt it after the disaster and to see the English program that had been put in place. Much to my surprise, all of the children gathered around us and sang happy birthday to me. If I have a happier moment in my life, I can't imagine what it will be.

22

Old Dog, New Tricks

I've never been terribly stressed about money, even when I was a few million in the hole in the early stages of Michael Chugg Entertainment. It has always been good to have money, but when there wasn't any it didn't really bother me. My gut feeling has always been that if you do something properly the money will come, a theory designed to aid my peace of mind and to send most accountants off the nearest cliff. Still, that's the modus operandi that has seen me through the past forty-five years, so it's too late to change it now.

Such a laissez faire attitude has put me in trouble in the past. When I first started in this business, every cent I made I put back in, to get the band from Tasmania to Melbourne, or to get from Melbourne to Newcastle, or to get overseas, but if you didn't have the money in the first place you had to improvise, just as a temporary measure, of course.

One European run I did with Kevin Borich in the 70s is a good example. We had a release in Germany for Kevin's album *Celebration*. We travelled to Germany and Holland to do TV shows and we went to London to record. We did the whole trip on a Diner's Club card. It took me about six months to pay it off and I never got another one, but it was a means to an end.

We had to do what we had to do. I'd worry about the money later; as long as I believed what I was doing was the right thing. Even before then, my company with Steve White, Marquee Attractions, had heavy debts for a while, but we didn't let that worry us. We worked through them and put it right.

Just because I don't worry about money doesn't mean I'm reckless with it. I still get 'the vibe', the feeling that acts as a tie-breaker when 50/50 decisions crop up, but the older I get, the more often I take a step back and think things through before I make a decision that has a fortune riding on it. Once upon a time, I might have acted first and asked questions later, but the risks I take today are more calculated. They come from experience and from consultation with my colleagues. Most importantly, they are conducted within the boundaries of the law.

I mention that because, in 2007, there was a disagreement about the proper interpretation of various agreements between Michael Chugg Entertainment and Jack Utsick. Jack was the American promoter who came to my rescue with $1 million when I needed money to promote the first Robbie Williams tour of Australia in 2001. Jack's company, World Wide Entertainment Group, one of the biggest touring companies in the

US, collapsed in 2006 amid claims that the company was a Ponzi scheme, whereby millions of dollars from new investors in WWE was used to pay off interest to previous investors in some of the company's failed projects. By then Jack and I had done many joint ventures in Australia, including tours by Yes, Martha Wainwright and LeAnn Rimes, among others.

I got the rude shock of Jack's fall from grace when I was attending the annual Pollstar music industry convention in Las Vegas in 2007. The convention is held in Las Vegas and Los Angeles on alternate years. I attend every year, for the same reasons I go to the International Live Music Conference in London, to network with all of the people who are important to my business. The American event is also a social gathering and it has been prestigious for me too. In 2001, I was named Pollstar's international promoter of the year, something of which I'm quite proud, although I've had a few awards thrown at me in the past ten years or so. The ILMC made me promoter of the year in 2005.

Word spread like wildfire among the delegates about what had happened.

The American receiver appointed to try and recover WWE's money, US attorney Michael Goldberg, was tasked with investigating Jack's investments in Australia and New Zealand.

We resolved the dispute amicably with the receiver. The terms are confidential, but everyone was happy with the results.

The receiver targeted Kevin Jacobsen as well. Jacobsen and Utsick had done many joint ventures, including the musical *Dirty Dancing*. There were other American and European and

New Zealand companies listed in the receiver's list of debtors. Celebrity Paris Hilton was on there, for not fulfilling her promotional duties on a film, *National Lampoon's Pledge This*, in which one of Jack's businesses had invested millions of dollars. It's nice to think Paris and I have something in common.

I got to know Jack quite well after that first Robbie Williams tour. He liked the rock 'n' roll lifestyle, as I did, but for different reasons. He liked hanging out with rock stars and big players because he wanted to be recognised as a big player himself, but he wasn't really cut out to be a big player. Jack was in it because he loved the glamour. He liked sailing around the Mediterranean with Andrea Bocelli, that kind of thing, but he wasn't always an astute businessman. He was a retired airline pilot who wanted to try his luck in the glamorous world of show business and came unstuck.

He did some crazy deals. I sat in his office in Miami once and listened to one of the kids on the phone booking mid-west theatre shows for Mariah Carey at $150,000 a show. This was at a time when Mariah Carey couldn't get arrested. I asked him if he had done the budget on those shows and of course he hadn't. I stopped him from doing those gigs, but I wasn't there all the time. He did a lot of dubious things. He made terrible investments in shows that were never going to make money. He was pissing his money up against the wall.

The American agents could see him coming. They might be booking a Kiss tour or a Fleetwood Mac tour and they would be a couple of gigs short, so they'd ring Jack and get him to put on shows in the middle of nowhere, cities where he was guaranteed to lose money. In one week he did two Eagles shows, two Kiss shows, two Aerosmith shows and a Fleetwood Mac show and lost $7 million. In a week! So when the receiver came in, that was all he could see – losses.

The shit hit the fan all because he didn't pay one bill and the authorities decided to investigate him. Jack had beautiful old apartments and fancy cars and houses, but all of them were in the businesses' names, so he has been a bit screwed over by all that has happened. Now he's living in Brazil and he has nothing. He has lost everything. His career is destroyed, but he hasn't been prosecuted, yet. I feel sorry for him. He's just another guy in the music business who made some big mistakes.

Utsick isn't the only promoter I had joint ventures with in the past decade. In 2005 I got involved in the East Coast Blues and Roots Festival with Peter Noble, who before that had been running the highly respected festival in Byron Bay with his partner Keven Oxford. The Bluesfest, as it is known, is a bit outside my normal range of interest, but I could see it as a growing festival and saw the opportunities to expand the format to other territories, which has worked successfully in Perth since then. It's a great festival and presented new opportunities to me and to Gaynor Crawford, who co-promotes our more roots-oriented tours with me. I had to give up Bluesfest in 2009, although not because it wasn't successful. Peter and I have radically different ways of doing things. It just couldn't work properly with the two of us on board.

Even so, after the scare of the early 2000s, my business began to start moving around 2005 and that was aided by my involvement in Bluesfest. One of the main drawcards at that year's festival was REM, who also toured with us successfully. The year began with the massively successful and rewarding Wave Aid concert. We had other landmark debut tours by

Rufus Wainwright and Damien Rice, and rising country star Keith Urban did well for us. With Matthew Lazarus-Hall's arrival at the company, we slowly started pulling ourselves out of debt and in 2006 we hit our stride business-wise and financially. The company name changed to Chugg Entertainment, which is how it remains.

I'm a rock 'n' roll guy. That, essentially, is what my life has been about. The occasional diversion into blues, roots or even country, as I have done successfully with acts such as Brooks and Dunn, Keith Urban and Tim McGraw, is to be expected now and again, but other than that my course has been set since I was fifteen. How, then, my roster of talent expanded to include a dog show, a Mexican man who talks to dogs, a troupe of tap dancers and a couple of drag queens camping it up to 'I Will Survive' was as much a surprise to me as it was to anyone who knows me.

After the success of *Long Way to the Top*, which was really as much an arena 'stage show' as it was a rock concert, Amanda and I had some ideas about expanding the theatrical end of Chugg Entertainment. We looked at doing a stage version of the hit TV show 'So You Think You Can Dance'. We spent $50,000 researching the Slim Dusty story as a live show. Amanda worked very hard on that and we had a researcher working on it.

Unfortunately, we soon learned that the country music fraternity in Australia is split into factions, so we couldn't get it to work. We couldn't get crucial players to work together on it, so we had to pull out. I was sad about that. After a year or so of banging our heads against a brick wall, I had to go and visit Joy McKean, Slim's widow, and apologise to her and tell her that it wasn't going to work. She took it very well. She understood. She had her own problems with trying to start the Slim Dusty Museum in Kempsey, New South Wales.

We looked at doing a thing on Gallipoli as an arena tour, but the politics of that got too hard as well. A lot of things didn't work out.

We reconsidered a second *Long Way to the Top*, but I don't think Australia is ready yet for a tour by 80s and 90s acts.

I was wary about theatre-type shows from the stories I had heard from other promoters, such as Garry Van Egmond, Harry M Miller and Kevin Jacobsen. Theatre didn't really interest me at all. I'd seen Jacobsen's *Beauty and the Beast* run for years in Sydney and from the royalty Disney was charging him to put it on he didn't make any money. Then you hear about the horrors of spending $6 million on producing a show and it closes in three weeks. I'd watched Kevin make $10 million one year and lose $20 million the next on theatre. Sod that, I thought. I don't know anything about it, so I'll stay out of it. That's how it was.

The change of heart developed, like many a Chugg project, in a hotel bar, this one in central London during the ILMC in 2004. While I was there chatting and drinking with agent Steve Strange and some other friends, I could hear a rather loud Aussie female voice piercing through the din. I had no idea who she was, but it turned out that she knew me, since she had gone for a job at Frontier a few years earlier and wasn't impressed with the way she was treated. She didn't have any kind words for anyone at Frontier. Her name was Liz Koops.

At the time, Liz was in London managing the comedy group The Doug Anthony Allstars. She and her partner Garry

McQuinn had a company called Backrow, which was running all of the Clear Channel/Live Nation's theatrical properties in London. The two of us got into a slanging match in that bar over a number of things, Frontier being chief among them, before I left to go to a party upstairs in the hotel.

A year later at my Surry Hills office I got a message that there was a woman waiting in reception who wanted to see me and who wouldn't go away. It was Liz. I was sweating because we had parted badly in London after I made some flippant remark as I stormed off. I thought she had come to abuse me.

Instead, she wanted to make me an offer. She had had enough, she said, of working with, as she called it, the 'Melbourne theatre mafia'. Liz was about to produce the tenth-anniversary tour of *Tap Dogs*, the highly-acclaimed dance theatre show, and wanted me to come in on it, to give it 'a rock 'n' roll edge'.

I'd had decidedly limited experience in theatre up until that point. In the late 70s, Steve White and I took on a show given to us by a promoter in New Zealand called *The Moscow Variety Spectacular*, a circus show with a cast consisting of any Russian circus performers who weren't in the official Moscow Circus. Impresario Michael Edgley was touring the real one, so he wasn't happy at all. He was all over us. The situation became very heavy.

I thought about *Tap Dogs*. It had been incredibly popular first time around and made its creator Dein Perry a star. He was coming back to do the anniversary show. I said yes. Amanda Pelman became involved as well and off we went. Dein had to go into training to revisit his demanding role in the show. I was a bit out of shape at the time, so I thought it would be a good idea to use the same trainer. Dein shed about 15 kilos and

I lost two. The main thing was that the show did great business. Suddenly theatre was more attractive than it had been with the Moscow mob.

While *Tap Dogs* went on the road, Backrow were talking to film director Stephan Elliott about a stage adaptation of his movie *The Adventures of Priscilla, Queen of the Desert*. They asked me if I would like to be involved in it. Matthew, Amanda and I went to a few *Priscilla* workshops in Sydney and liked what we saw. They had booked Star City at the Sydney Casino for the opening run. We were in. I even got to have a say in the casting and chose actor Michael Caton for the role as the lunatic old boy, Bob.

Everybody said it was going to be a dog, but everybody was wrong. It went off in Sydney. It went off in Melbourne. It went off in Auckland. I couldn't believe it, but the best was still to come. Liz and Garry got Andrew Lloyd Webber's Really Useful Company involved and in March 2009 the show opened in London's West End, at the Palace Theatre, with Tony Sheldon, Jason Donovan, Oliver Thornton and Don Gallagher in the leading roles. To be there on the opening night was one of the most exciting nights of my career.

I had been spending a bit of time in London around then and initially a lot of people didn't get *Priscilla*. They didn't quite understand what the show was about. Somehow we had to make people more aware of it. I did what I could to help. I was in the William Morris agency office in London one day and made sure everyone got tickets. When I went back the following week, one of the girls there sang a song from the show to me because they had all gone to see it a few nights before.

So obviously as soon as people saw it they knew what was going on and they loved it. By June it was a monster, the biggest show in the West End. In 2010 it's still doing great business and has led to further productions in Canada in 2010 and in New York in 2011.

Theatre, behind the scenes as well as out front, is quite different from the rock world I'm used to. You don't get your money back in a hurry, so it's a big punt. I was impressed by Backrow and how organised they were. They budgeted really well and I learned some things from them about that side of my own business. Liz liked to rattle the theatre establishment in London, too. It's a very old and very conservative set-up there and they don't like change. Liz put some of them offside by using marketing and promotional companies outside the accepted sphere. I liked that about her as well.

I was also slightly smitten by my new-found success in the theatre. I love going up to some of the established theatre producers in Australia when I see them and making the point that I'm a 100 per cent success in their domain. It makes me laugh.

I thought hard about maintaining an involvement in *Priscilla*, particularly as it moves on to other territories, because it is a big dollar commitment each time and there are no more guarantees of success, indeed fewer, in theatre, than there are in rock tours. Anyway, we're in for the long haul now, so fingers crossed. We also had success with Matthew Bourne's all-male cast version of *Swan Lake* in 2009. That show made over $750,000. We haven't ended our interest in stage shows by any means. We have a new *Tap Dogs* show planned for 2011.

And then there are the other dogs. Tara King was an executive producer for XYZ, the parent company of Channel V in

Australia. She was the person who put together the Music Max special called 'The Promoters', featuring me and based around the blues festival in Byron Bay. She did a fantastic job on that. In 2008 we got word that she was leaving XYZ. She walked into the office one day with Don Elford from Acer Arena in Sydney. She said she wanted to do more TV-to-stage stuff. She mentioned *Cesar Milan, the Dog Whisperer*, a show none of us had ever heard of. She explained the TV show to me, which is essentially Cesar Milan, a Mexican–American, showing viewers how to get their dogs to be more obedient, friendly and healthy, with a few tricks thrown in. Matthew and Tara went to Atlanta, Georgia, in 2009 to see Milan and also to see a couple of big dog shows in the US.

We did a deal with Tara to do a joint venture with the Cesar Milan show. Tara and Matthew got the rights to do it in Australia. I would never have picked it, doing a stage show that features a man telling and getting dogs to do what he wants. It's too simple and yet that is the very essence of its success. Lots of people have dogs and want to know how to get closer to them. The 2010 TV series has 11 million viewers around the world. That's a lot of potential bums on arena seats.

Tara and Mathew thought the show was a bit amateurish, but we brought him here and the show did good business and we made money, all from a guy talking to dogs and their occasionally screwed-up owners. The merchandising on a project like that is enormous, something like $35 per head, spent on singing dog collars and fur jackets and all sorts. Go figure.

We worked really hard to get the show right. Even after the tour, we re-jigged it a little to get it just right. Cesar loved it and he loved us. We did another show, a dog event called *Dog*

Olympics and Cesar came along to the launch at Sydney's Centennial Park. Actor Sam Neill and singer Diesel, among other celebrities, turned up with their dogs.

Now we've done deals all over the world with promoters to take *The Dog Whisperer* on the road. It could run and run, as they say. It has proved extremely popular in London already and now we're looking at Canada and Europe.

All of these theatre and stage projects are a nice sideline to have. They are not our core business, but we're making money from them in different parts of the world, which we don't do with rock tours.

Since we've had a pretty good strike rate since 2005, a lot of people come to us with ideas and many of them are good ones, but I'm cautious. It's hard to get shows off the ground, in this country especially. *Dirty Dancing* did well, and *Priscilla*, but apart from that it's tough. You could throw it all away in one show. *Spamalot?* No thanks. We're trying to develop other stuff on which we hold the copyright, so that once it's out there we're making money for eternity. We're starting to get out more into the big wide world, but we've passed on a lot of things too. We know how deadly theatre can be.

23

Love is All There is

I was the chief organiser of the 1956 Melbourne Olympic Games. All of the events were held in my family's backyard in Launceston and I, being the oldest sibling, decided which events my sisters and all of the kids in the neighbourhood could participate in. My brother Paul was too young to enter. I could, on a whim, disqualify, present a medal, win (quite a lot) or lose (hardly at all), commentate, pretend to be a world champion from overseas or cheer on the Australians in any of the track or field disciplines. As far as I can recall, there were no major mishaps, I collected a world record tally of gold medals on every day of competition and no scandal made its way into the newspapers. Happy days.

My sister Julie tells me that's where I first showed my organisational prowess and if she were pushed she would probably add that it's also where I mastered 'being able to boss people around'. Thankfully Julie doesn't hold a grudge. I suppose I must have let her win one of the finals.

That was the first sign of my being able to run an event and I think I did it pretty well, although I can't take all of the glory. I suspect I was acting on skills inherited from my dad. I was only nine years old at the time and hadn't done much training for the job. As far as I understood it, my father was the world authority on sport and telling people what to do. Wherever it came from, the inclination to organise stuck with me and it's that natural ability or belief in myself to motivate, delegate or boss around that got me a solid reputation and respect as a promoter early in my career. Once I had that, it was just a matter of using common sense and occasionally trusting in 'the vibe'. Those things, more often than not, are still working for me.

For all that I'm glad I chose the music industry in which to spend my working life, I still believe that I could have been a champion cyclist if I had stuck at it rather than getting myself involved in money-making scams, women and rock 'n' roll when I was fifteen. In fact, I'm sure of it. Yet I don't think I would ever have been the best sportsman in the Chugg household. The real athlete in the family was my young brother Paul. Paul was a champion ironman at state and national level when he was fourteen and fifteen years old. At sixteen, he was scheduled to represent Australia at the world surf championships in South Africa. We were all immensely proud of him.

Just prior to when he was supposed to fly out to South Africa, I was at a gig in Newcastle, New South Wales, with the band I was managing, Ida May Mack. On the way into the gig, a DJ I knew pulled up in his car and said, 'Chuggi, they're announcing on the radio that you have to ring home.' I knew right away that it was never going to be good news.

Paul had been on his way to Low Head Beach near Launceston in a Mini Minor to do surf duty with three of his mates. A car hit them and Paul went out the back window. He wasn't expected to live. After the phone call, I caught the mail train from Newcastle to Sydney. I got there about 7 am, caught a plane to Melbourne and another one to Launceston and got home about twenty-four hours after the DJ had spoken to me.

Paul was in hospital and in a bad way. He was in a coma for four and a half months. It shattered everybody in my family. When he came out of the coma, he was not the brother I had known before. He lost all of his drive, all of his will to win. The competitiveness he had, the self-belief that made him a champion, never came back. That was a tragedy for Paul, but it was tough on all of us. Dad took it particularly badly, but I was often upset by my parents' attitude towards Paul from then on. It hurt me that they would try to hide him away, as if he wasn't quite right. They loved him, but they mollycoddled him, which I didn't think was good for him.

He still lives in Launceston, as does my sister Christine. I don't get to see either of them as much as I'd like. Christine has Parkinson's disease, so she isn't able to travel easily. Paul has been to Phuket a few times. When my business became successful and money was coming in, I'd fly Dad and Paul up to Melbourne or Sydney for State of Origin games, rugby league tests and AFL finals. They loved that, my dad especially. Hanging out in the corporate box talking to sporting greats was a dream come true for him and he could hold his own with any of them. Watching him jousting with David Boon, Lou

Richards and Sam Newman at the same table . . . my god what a bunch of characters they were. Dad had coached Boonie as a swimmer before he became a superstar cricketer.

My mum moved to Perth not long after my dad died in 2002, to be closer to my sister Julie, who lives there with her family. My mum's getting on now and is in poor health. She's in care, but Julie sees her regularly and I do my best to visit her whenever I can.

Thoughts of family, friends and what I've achieved in life were uppermost in my mind during that sixtieth birthday party in Phuket. For all that it was a terrific celebration, and I'm pretty sure most people who were there had a great time, for me the party and the period around it was also a time to take stock of what my life was all about. I was glad in particular that Julie and Paul were there. It took me back to those backyard Olympics, to the wonderful, endless days at my Nan's house at First Basin and to the home in Punchbowl Road where I learned to live with the best and worst of a patriarchal household.

It was important also to have people like Michael Gudinski and Sue, Philip Jacobsen and Maxine and all manner of friends and acquaintances from every phase of my career there that night. It underlined the fact that although I've had violent disagreements with people I have worked with closely over the years, few of them would hold a grudge against me and vice-versa. I've shouted and sworn to get my own way for decades, but the people who know me well are aware that it's bluff and let me get on with it.

In the early days of my career, I had a huge inferiority complex. I had this idea, for one, that I had ripped off Michael Browning, Thorpie's and then AC/DC's manager, and stolen all of his ideas. I thought I was soaking up everybody else's professionalism and I was just a pretender. I thought I wasn't worthy of what I was doing. That went on for about ten years, but it was just about me learning the business, nothing more. That's why I love doing all of the conferences I do and lectures I do around the world, talking to young people about the industry. I want to pass on what I've learned.

Maybe my bolshie behaviour stemmed from wanting to cover up that complex I had for ten years. For many years, I used to get my way by being a bully. I was never physical exactly; I could intimidate more with my voice than I could with my fists. I used that, yelling and screaming to get my way. I also discovered that my yelling was really me covering up my mistakes, or at least trying to do that.

I've changed a lot since then. Maybe I'm more tolerant of people I used to think were dickheads. I'm trying to do less of that now. It's not good for my health, for one thing. I'm a much nicer person now than I've ever been.

Also, I'm a bit more careful and considerate in my approach to business. I don't have to be at the frontline all of the time anymore. Matthew can handle a lot of that. It's good to have someone like that alongside me. He brings bureaucracy and administration skills to the business that have never been top of my own agenda. I've lifted my game and gone corporate and let people I trust run the business. The reason I'm doing that is so that the whole thing isn't left in a mess. I want to make sure that when I go it isn't a disaster area for other people. Whether the business will go on for a long time I don't know.

One of the things I've learned to say since I left Frontier is 'no'. I don't get pressured into doing tours I don't want to do.

It's not unusual for an agent to say he'll give me one act but only on the condition that I take another act that I don't want. I still have to make those kinds of decisions every day, but now I feel less inclined to compromise.

I'm also trying to reshape my business so that it stays at the top in the twenty-first century and beyond. It's a cliché, but I've worked very hard for a long time to get where I am now and I like it here. I work with a good, talented, professional bunch of people who do such a good job that I don't have to worry every minute of the day about all the things that can go wrong on a tour, and believe me I've seen every single one of them. I'd like someone to carry on the work I have done.

I do tend to forget how old I am. The hardest thing in maintaining my level of involvement in the rock 'n' roll circus is coming to terms with the fact that I'm sixty-three years old. The energy level is still the same, but physically I can't cope like I used to. It pisses me off that I'm not forty. I have to keep reminding myself of that. Back in the days of Consolidated Rock, we used to joke that if we made it to thirty what a great life we would have had. That holds true; it would have been a great life. Yet here are Gudinski and I and Dainty and Coppel and Garry Van Egmond all still doing what we set out to do in the 60s and 70s. I'm not sure if that's a good picture or a bad picture. The only way to know would be to stop and I'm not quite ready for that.

The reason all of those promoters are still doing well is because they started at the right time. Today it's much harder to set yourself up touring big-name international acts, simply because we're still here doing it, with all of the contacts, all of the experience and to an extent the financial clout to bid for the big tours and to weather the losses when they don't work. Anyone who wanted to start up in Australia at the top level would need those things – and even then it's risky. I'd love someone to come along and prove me wrong. There are younger promoters out there doing the indie market and the world music market and the roots, country and folk markets. Good luck to them. The same goes to all of the young – or at least younger than me – people who are behind the ever-increasing festival circuit. A few of those festivals have failed, such as The Great Escape in Sydney and the touring V festival, but there are plenty of others doing good business around the country. There has never been a better time for festivals in Australia. I hope they continue to prosper.

I hope I continue to prosper too. I'm not working as long hours in the office as I was three years ago, but I'm still working pretty hard. And I still love what I do and get immense satisfaction from it. My doctor tells me I shouldn't travel as much, but if I stopped travelling I'd miss a lot of opportunities. I've built relationships all over the world because of that. I value all of those relationships, some of which have blossomed into close friendships. I wonder if my love of travel is about me escaping from myself, but I love it whatever the reason for doing it. And I love being at the top of the game. It's hard to give up, although not impossible. The reason I don't give up isn't because I want to stay at the top. It's just that when I think about it I can't come up with any good reason to stop. What else would I do? Sit on a beach? When you love what you're doing, it doesn't feel like work, and I love what I do.

I've reshaped my business in the past couple of years with an eye on the future. If you don't do that, you die. I've embraced the internet to promote and market my tours. I like also the idea of releasing albums as well as touring with the bands that make them. I've done a few deals like that and I intend to do a lot more. That is the way of my future. There are lots of overseas acts out there now who can pull a crowd and who don't have a recording or distribution deal in Australia, so it's easy for us to say, 'Give us your album, we'll get it distributed and put online and you can also sell it at the gigs we promote for you.' That's where we're heading now.

I'm not saying I want to be the CEO of a multinational recording organisation. I don't. We're doing it on a level that we can afford. It's not like Live Nation buying Madonna's touring and recording rights for squillions of dollars. I'm not interested in doing that. The way to do it is the way we're doing it, to start little. The major record companies are trying to get their feet in the door of touring in Australia, but I'm not sure that will succeed. I know how to release albums better than they know how to put on a tour. The game's on, though. It's a really exciting time for the industry.

We have a promotions company, started when I got involved in the East Coast Blues and Roots Festival in 2005. We visit radio stations and media all over regional Australia. My son Nick and his cousin Adrian work that operation. One of their prime targets is community radio. Some of these stations out in the bush might only have a couple of thousand listeners, but the vast majority of them are dedicated listeners. Most often, they will ask Nick what he is doing coming to visit them, because nobody from the big smoke takes much interest in regional radio anymore. Yet that to me is a valuable resource to have when you're competing for ticket money with a whole range of alternative entertainment.

I've been written off a number of times. The years 1995 and 1996 were pretty catastrophic for me, what with the huge losses incurred by Alternative Nation and Mighty Morphin Power Rangers and then my car crash. That and my heart attack had the potential to put me out of business. Going broke a few times didn't help, the worst being after the consecutive train wrecks of Red Hot Chili Peppers and Santana. All of these and more could have sent me under. I could have followed Philip Jacobsen's advice and put my money in the bank and lived off that, but that's just not me.

I've always worked hard and I've always tried to have fun as well. The things that make me happy are sold-out concerts, reading books, travelling, hanging out with beautiful women, doing things for people who aren't as well off as myself, teaching kids about our industry and advancing the cause of our industry. That to me is a life well spent.

The best feeling I get doing this job is one of contentment and pride when I can stand at the side of the stage in front of 77,000 people, as I did with Guns N' Roses in 1993, and watch the punters having one of the greatest days of their lives. Pulling it off is a great reward. Some of the things we have done, like Wave Aid and Live Earth, all the charity events and fundraisers, we just laughed our way through them. It's fun and there's immense pride when you pull it off.

That's the ultimate goal, that and to sell it out and make money, but that is always outweighed by the success of the event. The old man Jacobsen couldn't handle me blowing money away. It was always about making money, which is fine; we're all in it for that. My view is that it's all about doing the job properly. That has been my main motivation. It's about creating the event and putting together a team of people that you can work with and who have the same pride in what they do, whether it's the cleaner or the caretaker of the venue or the production manager or the star. That's how I've always played it. It's about teamwork. The bigger the event, the bigger the team.

American promoter Bill Graham and English promoter Harvey Goldsmith were a big influence on me. They promoted so many big tours in the US and the UK respectively in the 60s and 70s. I'd read all about them in magazines such as *Creem* and *Rolling Stone*. In late 1977, Eric Robinson and I went to Oakland Coliseum to see AC/DC's first American concert. They were opening for Ted Nugent as part of his A Day on the Green show. We were sitting backstage with Patrick Stansfield, who had done the first Woodstock as artists' liaison manager and also worked with The Rolling Stones. We were in the artists' compound and there was a little guy cleaning up with a broom and every time an artist went by they'd say hello to him. It was Bill Graham. That's what it's all about for me, hard work from the ground up, but potentially with huge rewards at the end of it.

It has been an amazing ride. Now I can afford to step back a little. I made some great money from AC/DC's *Black Ice* tour If only all tours were guaranteed to do that well. I stayed out of the limelight on that one. I took a back seat, because it wasn't my tour. It was Garry's. I can do that now. I don't have to be centre stage all of the time.

The audience for live music in Australia has grown considerably in the past ten years. When the big financial crash happened in the 90s, people stopped going to as many shows as they used to and that really knocked us around as promoters. It didn't kill us, but it could have. But the live scene in Australia now is in great shape and I don't think we can destroy it if promoters, managers and artists are honest enough and grown up enough about how to maintain that level of success. We're seeing more people at shows everywhere and in new combinations. At AC/DC, it wasn't unusual to see three generations of the one family watching the show. It's becoming that way for a lot of other acts as well, particularly the ones that first made their mark thirty or forty years ago.

There have been periods in the past where inexperience, lack of knowledge and lack of ability nearly destroyed the touring circuit. There have been dips because of greed. Now I think most people in the business are trying to make it work for everybody. That's how I feel. I'm proud of the Australian music industry and I want it to prosper. For me, it's all about advancing the musical cause. I'm lucky that I'm in a position to be able to do that and not just say it.

I'm lucky also in that after everything I've been through in life, professionally, personally and including all of the wrong decisions I've made, I can sit back and enjoy what I created. Phuket is part of that. When I'm there, I can relax more than I have done anywhere in the past fifty years. I can do more exercise. I can eat the right food and not punish myself in the way I used to. Before, if somebody offered me a drink, I'd always say yes. Now I don't. I often don't feel like it.

Maam is very good to me and good for me. She's from a different culture and has no particular interest in the music industry or in hanging out with big stars or in joining the queue to the next rock 'n' roll after-party. What we have together is something that is unique and that we can enjoy in an environment completely divorced from the world I'm so used to. We travel a lot too, when we can, to Europe or America or to other parts of Asia.

I need a companion. There are some people in life who can go for long periods of time without a serious need for company. I can handle that for a while, but not all of the time. That's where the loneliness comes in. Backstage, you are never on your own, theoretically. On the road, you're never on your own. In that world, you are a character running backwards and forwards, just like a lot of other characters. Doing that all of the time, even with people you know, doesn't mean you can't get lonely once in a while.

Sometimes in my life I have driven people away because I was afraid of getting hurt. I think that was true with Mayling; I think it was true with Lisa; I think it was true of a lot of my relationships. All of that, I believe, is related to when I lost my grandmother at the age of fourteen. I remember breaking down then and it kept coming back to me every Christmas for a long time.

I'd had no idea that some of my behaviour in later life might be related in some way to my grandmother until I started going to health farms in 1985. That's when I suddenly recognised these patterns in my behaviour that would re-occur, all of the time, like the way I got into the habit of yelling and screaming. I heard a lot of yelling and screaming as a kid. Some of it was my own, so maybe that's why I found it so easy to keep doing it.

What I've learned to do since I've been running my own company is to get away. In Thailand I can find peace. I do get lonely sometimes, but I know I can go to places like Phuket and fix that, or I can go to visit my kids. I have a grandson now – Harley, my son Nick's son – and I think that has brought all three of my children closer together. Maintaining that relationship with them is very important to me.

Sometimes I'll be sitting in some hotel in Nashville or somewhere and I'll wonder what the fuck I'm doing there and why I bother. But in the main that's still what I love doing. The patterns of my lifestyle over the past four decades are hard to get away from.

I'm very happy and very lucky. I've got three great children, a grandson, ex-wives who don't hate me and a partner who loves me, no matter that I can't be with her all of the time. I have one of the best jobs in the world and I wouldn't swap it for anything. I could look at it and think, 'Well, I've done close to 20,000 gigs in my life and made a lot of money, I may as well sit back and enjoy it.' Then I see the tours by Robbie Williams, Bob Dylan and the Billy Joel/Elton John collaboration looming on the 2011 horizon and I think, 'Why say no to that?'

The music industry is a totally different world in many ways from how it was when I gave the Launceston City Cycling Club a leg-up with £80 all those years ago, but the bands just keep on coming. Bring it on.

Index

ABBA 2, 73, 95–100, 193
Abba the Movie 96, 97
ABC television 67, 71, 256, 260, 261, 262
AC/DC 30, 51, 55, 61, 61, 73, 84, 93, 247, 261, 306, 307
A.C.E. 70, 175
acid 3, 37
Adams, Bryan 198
Adelaide Festival of Arts 40
Adventures of Priscilla, Queen of the Desert, The 293–296, 295
Aerosmith 166, 174
Albert Productions 50–52, 60, 111, 261
Albert, Ted 50, 52
Albert Studios 50, 51, 60
Alice Cooper 259

All Stars, The 55, 56, 66
Altamont 43
Alternative Nation 174–176, 249, 305
Ambo 28
Amos, Ron 271, 274
Andrew, Peter 40
Angels, The 51, 109, 120, 198
Animals, The 25
Annas, John 81
APRA 74
Aquarius 65
Argent, Jack 197
ARIA Awards 67, 217, 219, 220
Arnold, Ray 3–4, 29, 49, 59, 212
Artist Concert Tours 95
Atlantic label 52, 58, 59
ATV/Northern Songs 111, 113, 115

Auckland YMCA 181
Australasian Performing Right Association (APRA) 245
Australian Crawl 120
Australian Entertainment Exchange 71
Australian Music Week 220
Avenue Records 110
Axiom 83, 261
Azoff, Irving 209
Aztecs, The 33, 36, 55, 157, 256, 257

Backrow 292, 293, 294
Backstage Café 231
Bailey, Dr Harry 61
'Baker Street' 87
Band of Light 40
Bandstand 261
Barber, Keith 35, 39
Barber, Tony 257
Barlow, Ross 85, 197
Barnes, Jimmy 89, 119–120, 124, 198
Basement, The 244
Battles, Rebecca 173
Baxter, Jeff 'Skunk' 235
Beach Boys, The 212
Beatles, The 22, 26, 92, 95
Bee Gees, The 93, 229
Benny's Bar 120–122
Berties 31
Big Day Out (BDO) 174, 176, 251
'Billy Killed the Fish' 256
Billy Thorpe Band, The 258
Bird, John A 41
Bishop, Elvin 157
'Black & Blue' 35
Black-Eyed Bruiser 53, 55, 58, 60

Black Ice tour 306
Black Sabbath 93
Blackmore, Ron 28, 93, 94, 95
Blackwell, Chris 81
Blanchfield, John 89
Blanchflower, Chris 41
Blondie 243
Blood on the Tracks 7
Blur 228
Blurred Crusade, The 112, 113
Bohm, Adrian 157
Bois, John 41
Bolton, Tony 41, 56
Bon Jovi 5, 121, 140, 157, 158, 161–162, 166, 225, 227, 244
Bondi Lifesaver 79, 212, 256
Borich, Kevin 6, 35, 55, 70, 73, 81, 82, 84, 85, 86, 101, 106, 113, 199, 261, 264, 286
Bourne, Matthew 294–295, 301
Bowie, David 95, 242
Boyd Fleetwood, Jenny 6
Braithwaite, Daryl 198
'British Rock 'n' Roll Month' 93
Brodziak, Kenn 92, 93, 241
Brooker, Gary 259
Brooks and Dunn 290
Brown, Bryan 198
Browne, Jackson 83
Browning, Michael 6, 30–31, 33–35, 73, 84, 300
Bruce, Jack 259
Bryant, Renee 251
Buckingham, Lindsey 2, 6
Buckley, Jeff 178, 217
Buffett, Jimmy 158, 273
Bulldog 28, 31
Burke, Peter 83, 84
Burns, Ronnie 28

Bush 178
Bush Bash 198
By the Way 249

Cadd, Brian 83, 161, 279
Cannon, Freddie 113
Capitol Records 111, 112, 113
'Capricorn Dancer' 78
Captain Matchbox Whoopee Band 70
Carey, Mariah 288
Carr, Bob 217
Carrère label 111, 113
Catcher 30
Caton, Michael 293
Cave, Nick 281
Celebration 73, 78, 110, 286
Cesar Milan, the Dog Whisperer 295–296
Chain 28, 31, 35, 36
Chambers, Kasey 281
Chapman, Tracy 156
Channel 7's Christmas Concert 223
Channel V 294
Charles, Ray 249
Cheetah 51
Chelmsford Private Hospital 61
Chequers 33
Cher 35
Cherokee Studios 85
Chevrons, The 22
Chicago 212
Children of the Sun 71
Christie, Paul 81
Chugg, Barbara 23, 153
Chugg, Christine 12, 299
Chugg, Ella 15, 16
Chugg, Harley 309

Chugg, Julie 12, 283, 297–298, 300
Chugg, Lucas Alexander 166, 169, 271
Chugg, Michael 2
  Alcoholics Anonymous 189
  Aunt Margot and Beppi 32
  Auntie Barbara 23, 153
  Australian Father of the Year 165, 167–169
  born 12
  Burnie 16
  car accident 180, 188
  charities 168, 196–202
  childhood 12, 13, 144, 297–298
  Chung, Dr 235
  cycling 11–12, 18, 20–23, 298, 309
  Glen Dhu Primary School 13
  grandparents 12, 16, 144
  health farms 67, 133–137, 189, 191, 195, 272, 308,
  heart attack 229–236
  jail 178, 181–187
  Launceston 3, 11–12, 16, 19, 144
  marriages 32, 137, 138
  Melbourne Cup 19
  mother 12, 13, 17–18, 20, 153, 300
  Phuket 94, 202, 269–282, 299, 300, 307, 308
  Queechy High School 17, 19
  race-calling 21
  Radio 7EX 21
  Uncle Brian 153
Chugg, Nicholas 75–77, 100, 117, 137, 169, 171, 304, 309
Chugg, Paul 12, 283, 297–299
Chugg, Sophie Victoria 141, 156, 165–169, 271
Chugg, Victor 12, 14–16, 140, 143–144, 153–154, 299–300

Church, The 111–116, 126
City Express 109
Clapton, Richard 6, 74, 77–84, 86–89, 106, 199, 260
Clarke, Greg 268
Clarke, Paul 260
Clash, The 102, 242
Clean Up Australia 198
Clear Channel 221, 292
Cleary, Michael 123
Clinton, Bill (President) 199
cocaine 3–4, 121, 123, 136, 138, 161, 163
Cochrane, Tony 145–149, 152
Cocker, Joe 174
Cohen, Leonard 202
Cold Chisel 72, 109, 120, 123–124
Cold War Kids 252
Coldplay 202, 224
Coleman, Jonathan 219
College Lawn Hotel 31
Coloured Balls 41, 43
'Come And See Her' 51
Company Caine 34, 36
Concert of the Decade 199
Consolidated Press Entertainment 216, 224
Consolidated Rock 30–34, 50, 128, 257, 302
Consolidated Rock Concert 33
Conway, Deborah 198
Cooper, Phil 81
Cope, Kate and Steven 282
Copeland, Ian 106, 231
Copeland, Stewart 106
Coppel, Michael 70, 122, 174, 175, 218, 245, 302
'Countdown' 71, 96
Country Joe McDonald 174

Country Radio 36, 37, 41, 46, 50, 53, 56, 79
Courage, John 103
Cowbell Agency 126
Cracknell, Dr Richard 274
Crawford, Gaynor 252, 289
Crazy Horse 140
Cream 28
Creative Artists Agency 234
Creem magazine 306
Creswell, Toby 173
Crewes, Bill Rev 169
crime 211–212
Cron, Steve 184
Crouch, Jacqui 250
Crowded House 140, 191–192, 199, 200, 200, 201
    Farewell to the World concert 191, 195, 198, 200
Cure, The 126–127
Czernuszyn, Vitek 262

Daddy Cool 33, 35, 40, 45, 68
Daily Planet magazine 34
Dainty, Paul 2, 4, 59, 68, 73, 75, 82, 91–95, 101–103, 106, 108, 127, 172, 225, 231, 241–242, 302
Daltrey, Roger 259
Dandenong Town Hall 30
Dark Spaces 88
Dave Clark Five, The 26, 92
Davies, Roger 6, 34–35, 40, 41, 45, 74
Davis Jnr, Sammy 145, 149–153, 160
'Day on the Green, A' (Australia) 68–69
Day on the Green, A (US) 101, 306
de Clerk, Rodney 22
de Courcy, Brian 121, 261

de Jong, Yde 58
de Silva, Denise 173
Deakin, Peter 56
'Deep Water' 78
Definitive Events 220
Della, Harry 109, 122
Dennis, Barbara 223
Denny, Sandy 45, 181
Diamond, Neil 145
Dick, Johnny 55, 257
Diesel 198
Digamae 40, 128
Dillow, Lee 212
Dire Straits 243
Dirty Dancing 287, 296
Dirty Pool 109, 206, 207
Dixie Chicks 224
Doctor Dan 130, 132
Dog Olympics 295
Dominoes, The 22
Donegan, Lonnie 92
Donovan, Jason 293
Doobie Brothers 235
Double J 105, 117
Doug Anthony All Stars, The (DAAS) 291
Downes, Mike 257
Drugs 195 *see also* acid, cocaine, hash, marijuana, methadone
Drum Media magazine 110
Duran Duran 114, 115, 116, 121
Durant, Andy 88
Duryea, Larry 56
Dylan, Bob 140, 174, 225–227, 228, 237

Eagles, The 173, 209
East Coast Blues and Roots Festival (The Bluesfest) 289, 304

Eastick, Mal 75
Easybeats 26, 47, 49–52, 57
Echo and the Bunnymen 252
Edgley, Michael 128, 292
Edwards, Tony 151
Eizik, Zev 70, 87, 122, 175
Elford, Don 295
Elliott, Stephan 249
Elektra/Asylum label 83, 84
EMI label 52
EMI/Parlophone label 111
English, Jon 67, 74
Enjoy Yourself tour 162
Eurythmics 126
Evans, Ray 35, 36, 69, 71, 107, 121, 243
'Evie (Parts I, II and III)' 51, 54, 66

Fairport Convention 45–47, 50, 181
Faith No More 175
Farewell to Double J concert 105
Farnham, John 171, 202
Farrell, Perry 179
Ferris, Rina 267
Festival Hall 46, 56
Festival Records 52, 80, 81, 84, 88, 94
Finch, John 69, 70
Finn, Neil 191, 281
Finn, Tim 111, 281
'Fire and Rain' 68
Fleetwood Mac 2–6, 79, 95, 101–103, 242
Fleetwood, Mick 2, 6, 179
Flies, The 28
Flowers 109
Focus 58
Fountain, The 252
Fowler, John 54

Frampton, Peter 259
Francis, Michael (Danny) 158
Frankston Oval 43
Fraser, Malcolm 99
Fraternity 30
Free 259
Friction Records 127
Frontier Booking International (FBI) 106
Frontier Boy 140
Frontier Touring Company 102–103, 106, 107, 108, 116, 122, 124, 126, 127, 130, 131, 137, 138, 139, 140, 145, 148, 153, 155, 156, 160–163, 166, 174, 176, 178, 183, 188, 189, 192, 195, 210, 213, 216–219, 221–222, 225, 228, 236, 240, 248, 291, 292, 301
'FUBB (Fucked Up Beyond Belief)' 182

Gabriel, Peter 174
Gallagher, Don 293
Gallagher, Rory 59
Garbage 178
Gardner Ted 113, 174, 179, 183, 188, 229–235
Garvey, Nick 114
Garwood, Sue 28
Gary Glitter 42, 45–47, 50
Gay, Pat 135
Georgettis, Gerry 81
Get Some Fun 114, 115
'Get The Feeling' 65
Geyer, Renée 121
Gilbey, Chris 51, 52, 57, 58, 111, 197
Gillespie, Dizzy 158
Gilmore, Graeme 18–19

'Gimme All Your Lovin'' 130
Ginges, David 45, 46
Girlie Show tour 173
Girls on the Avenue 78
Go Set magazine 34
Goldberg, Michael 287
Golden Stave Foundation 168, 196–198
Goldsmith, Harvey 201–202, 217, 306
Goldstein, Merv 82
Gomez 224
'Gonna See My Baby Tonight' 35
Goodbye Tiger 78–80
Gordon, Lee 92
Gore, Al 201
Gore, Mike 145–146
Got the Vibe 139
Graham, Bill 101, 306
Gray, Macy 244
Great Australian Sound Company (GAS) 67
Great Escape, The 88
Great Escape Festival, The 303
Greening Australia 201
Groop, The 83
Gudinski, Michael 6, 28–31, 33, 35, 36, 40, 69, 70, 75, 89, 102, 106, 107, 125, 137, 138, 146, 148–149, 152, 157, 158, 159, 160, 161, 172, 173, 174, 176, 178–179, 184, 188–189, 202, 209, 210, 215, 218, 219, 221–223, 243, 245, 249, 300, 302
'Guitar Band' 55
Guns N' Roses 6, 145, 157, 166, 170–171, 174, 305
Gunston, Norman 69
'Gypsy Queen' 41

Hair 68
Hallett, Rob 114
Hallstrom, Sir Edward 167
Hammersmith Odeon 115
Hancock, Herbie 157
Harbour Agency 40, 102, 103, 106–109, 122, 124, 127, 158, 162, 192, 193
Hard Road 50–52, 53, 55, 57, 66
Harrigan, John 157
hash 34, 56, 147, 158, 159, 161, 163
Healing Force 31
Hearn, Ray 109
Hearts on the Nightline 86–87, 88
Hebbes, Peter 197
Hedges, Steve 108
Hegerty, Michael 81
'Hello, Hello, I'm Back Again' 41
Hell's Angels 36
Hely, Alan 84
Henderson, Brian 262
Hendrix, Jimi 28
Herbert, Daryl 220
Hero 56
heroin 3, 56, 60, 61
Hewitt, Colleen 157
Heymann, Susan 223, 252
Hi Fi Bar 244
Highland, John 29
Highway To Hell 7
Hilton, Grant 121–122, 123
Hilton, Paris 288
Hines, Marcia 68–69, 73–74, 88, 261
Hoadley's Battle of the Sounds 65
Hoadley's Battle of the Sounds (TAS) 128
Hogarth, Tony 67, 68
Homebake Festival 202, 251

Hoodoo Gurus 106, 126
Hopewell, Martin 126
Hoppe, Ossy 265
Hordern Pavilion 46
Hosking, Michael 270, 274
Howard, Kathy 73, 74, 108, 112, 127, 217, 219
Huey, Mike 83
Huffam, Ian 228
'Hungry Like the Wolf' 114
Hunters and Collectors 198
Hush 63–69, 71

Ian Saxon and the Sound 157
Idol, Billy 6, 140
Iggy Pop 145, 158–159
'I'm Getting Better' 157
'I'm Not Like Everybody Else' 111
Individuals 114
International Live Music Conference 227, 270, 287
INXS 120
Ironside, Colleen 108, 109, 192
Isaak, Chris 178
Island Records 81
'It's All Happening' 257

Jackson Five, The 93
Jacobsen, Amber 261
Jacobsen, Kevin 157, 229, 261, 287, 291
Jacobsen, Philip 40, 44, 69, 70, 94, 107, 126, 137, 138, 162, 172, 183, 188–189, 210, 213, 215, 221, 224, 249, 269, 300, 305
James, Ian 218
Jands 45, 46, 95
Jane's Addiction 179
Jarvis, Wane 'Swampy' 29

Jesus Christ Superstar 49–51, 60, 68
Jet 263
Jigsaw Productions 157
Jimmy and the Boys 110–111
Joel, Billy 6, 83, 139–140, 157, 243
John, Elton 243, 249
Johnston, Russ 56
Jonathon's Disco 35
Jones, Bob 6, 43
Jones, Greg 122, 123
Jones, Ignatius 110–111
Jones, Valentine 257
Joseph, Bill 28, 69, 70
Joseph's Coat 45
Joye, Col 260
Joylene Hairmouth 110

Karagiannis, Michael 224–226
Kelly, Paul 198
Kernaghan, Lee 107
Kevin Borich Express 4, 6, 85, 86, 101
Key, Phil 35, 40
Kiernan, Ian 198
Kilbey, Steve 112, 115, 16
Killers, The 245
King, Tara 294–295
Kinks, The 111
Knight brothers 30
Ko, Mayling 166–167, 172, 173, 187, 192–195, 219, 222, 265, 308
Kooks, The 252
Koops, Liz 291–294
Koppes, Peter 112
Korda, Peter 222–223

La De Das 35, 36, 39, 50, 53, 65, 70, 72
Labriola, Gary 152

Lang, Tom 202
Lazarus-Hall, Matthew 250, 252, 290
Le Bon, Simon 115
Lees, Vivian 174, 251
'Legs' 130
Leighton, Scott 223
Let It Be agency 40, 41, 43
Light, Rob 234
Little Pattie 261
Little Richard 242
Little River Band 4, 73, 101, 107, 108, 112
Live Aid 198
Live Earth 307
Live Nation 292, 304
Living in the 70s 70
Livingston, Dr Larry 217
Lloyd, Ian 84
Lloyd Webber, Andrew 293
Lock Up Your Mothers 258
Lollapalooza 179
Lonely One 110–111
'Long Tall Glasses (I Can Dance)' 94
Long Way To The Top (LWTTT)
  LWTTT2 262
  television show 255–256, 264
  tour 62, 260–264, 266, 290, 291
Lory, David 217, 219
Los Angeles County Jail 177, 183–187
'Love Game, The' 56
Love Police (label) 226
'Lovecats, The' 126
Loved Ones, The 22, 28
Lovegrove, Vince 30
Loyde, Lobby 3, 43, 44, 256

Maam 275–280, 307
McBride, Reggie 83

McDonald, John 110
McGraw, Tim
McKean, Joy 291
Mack, Ida Mae/May 28, 30, 31, 298
McKenna Mendelson Mainline 211
Mack, Lonnie 157
McLennan, Diane 81
McNamara, Tom 281
McPherson, Sally 167
McQuinn, Garry 292
McVie, Christine 2
McVie, John 2
Maddah, AJ 251
Madder Lake 28, 41
Madigan, Graham 'Scrooge' 42, 46
Madonna 173, 304
mafia 146
'Magic Mushroom' 29
Maloney, Vince 257
Manfred Mann 26, 92
Manzil Room, The 121
Marcia Shines 68
marijuana 3, 37, 38, 136
   'Durban poison' 37
Mario's Restaurant 140
Marquee Attractions 69, 70, 73, 74, 102, 108, 286
Martin, Dean 149
Master's Apprentices, The 30, 261
Matchbox 20 218
Max Merritt and the Meteors 36, 113
May, Ricky 147
Mayer, John 224
Mazzone, Mick 160, 162
MCG 173
Megadeth 244, 251
Melbourne music scene 60s 28–32

Meldrum, Ian 'Molly' 34, 38, 71, 96, 173, 279
Mellencamp, John Cougar 162, 166
Men at Work 113, 120, 174, 179
Mental As Anything 120
Mercury (label) 86
Mercury, Freddy 54
methadone 57, 59
Mi Sex 113
Michael Chugg Management (MCM) 108, 114, 126, 167, 209, 223, 224, 261, 285, 287, 290, 291
Midnight Oil 69, 105, 113, 123, 124, 198, 281
Mighty Morphin Power Rangers 176, 305
Milan, Cesar 296
Miller, Harry M 47, 92, 121, 241, 291
Minnelli, Liza 145, 149–151, 160
Minogue, Kylie 162, 166, 260
Models, The 126
mods 27
Mondo Rock 126
Moneypenny Services 250
Monster Trucks 230
Moomba Festival 98
Morgan, Warren 'Pig' 55, 264
Morocco 264–266
Morris, Gary 124
Moscow Variety Spectacular, The 292
'Most People I Know (Think That I'm Crazy)' 7, 37
Most People I Know (think that I'm crazy) (book) 258
Mostyn, Patti 95, 147
Mötley Crüe 166
Mudvayne 251

Muir, Rod 41, 128–130, 133
Mulray, Doug 198
Mulry, Ted 51
Murphy, Chris 77
Murray, Pete 281
Mushroom Records 35, 70, 89, 193, 218, 221, 258, 260
　Mushroom Publishing 106, 218
Myponga Festival 43
Mystery Jets 252

Nails, Rusty 219
Narara Festival '83 120, 122
Narara Festival '84 125, 126
Narara Hilton 123
Narrabeen Surf Club 33
National Lampoon's Pledge This 288
National Parks and Wildlife Foundation 198
Naylor, Tony 28
Nellis, Con 127, 128, 166, 173, 187, 219, 229–234
'New City Lights' 84
New Music Seminar 217
New South Wales Bushfire concert 198
New South Wales Community Disaster Relief Fund 198
new wave music 102
Newcastle Earthquake Appeal concert 198
Newton Faulkner 224
Newton-John, Olivia 35, 179
Nichols, Judy 95
Nicks, Stevie 2, 6
No Doubt 178, 224
No Turning Back 85
Noble, Peter 289

Norton, Richard 6
Not Like Everybody Else 111
Nucleus 70, 107
Nugent, Ted 85, 306
Numan, Gary 108

O'Donnell, Mark 81
Odyssey Festival 43
Of Skins and Heart 111, 112
O'Keefe, Johnny 33, 41, 260
Old Sydney Town 122–123
Olympic Games 194
On the Street magazine 109–110
Orbison, Roy 26, 92
Orchestral Manoeuvres in the Dark 140
Oxford, Keven 289
Oxley, Jeremy 115
Oz label 130
Oz Rock International Incorporated 82

Pacific Circle Music Convention (PCMC) 217–220, 223, 249
Packer, Kerry 216, 221, 222, 224–226, 239
Paddington Town Hall 67
Page, Jimmy 178
Parkinson, Doug 31
Parlophone (label) 111
Parry, Chris 127
Past Hits and Previews 86
Patterson, Syd 20
Pearl Jam 125, 126, 247, 252
Peel, Ronnie 55
Pelman, Amanda 202, 260, 292, 293
Pennywise 227
Pepsi 159

Perfect Circle, A 227
Perry, Dein 293
Perth Entertainment Centre 100
Peters, Nigel 270
Phuket's Been Good To Us Foundation 282
Pinda, John 40
Pink 35
Pirana 35, 36, 71
Piticco, Paul 280
Pitts, Nick 193–194
Plant, Robert 178
Ploog, Richard 112
Police, The 6, 101–103, 106, 107, 116, 117, 131, 132, 194, 242
Polydor (label) 52, 57
Polygram Australia 85, 86
Pope, Jon 171, 173
Pope, Mark 202, 272
Porter, Robie 69
Powderfinger 200
Premier Artists agency 40, 69, 70, 102, 106, 109, 122, 127, 193, 213, 223
Procol Harum 259
'Promoters, The' 295
Propaganda 72
Pub Rock 70
punk music 101–102

Queen 54, 121
'Quick on the Draw' 72
Quill, Greg 37, 41, 79

Radiators, The 110
Radio Stations
  2SM 41, 42, 117, 199
  3XY 35, 36, 40–44
  Fox FM 105
  2JJJ 105
  K-Rock 83
  2MMM 105, 128
Radiohead 222
Rafferty, Gerry 87
Ramones, The 102
Raso, Tommasina 127, 137, 162
Rat Pack 149
Raven, Bruce 112
Ravenscroft, Raphael 87
Ray Brown and the Whispers 157
Ray, Johnny 242
Really Useful Company 293
Red Hot Chili Peppers 174–175, 178, 249, 305
Reed, Lou 55, 175, 243
Regatta de Blanc tour 102
Reisner, Liselotte (Lilo) 31–34, 37, 41, 57, 66, 71, 75, 77, 78, 101, 117–118, 141, 169, 269
REM 145, 289
Rex Hotel 110
Riccobono, Fifa 53, 60, 61
Rice, Damien 290
Richard, Cliff 92
Ridgefarm Studios 114
Righi, Sam 107, 109, 124, 138, 188, 213, 221
Rimes, LeAnn 287
Rio 114
Risby, Col 257
Ritz Ballroom 33
Rix, Peter 63–68, 73, 88, 89, 122, 123, 125, 127, 168–169, 199, 239
Robbins, Christie 235
Roberts, Elliot 178
Roberts, Peter 35, 40
Robinson, Eric 44, 45, 95, 122, 124, 173, 260, 306

'Rock and Roll Ballroom of the Air, The' 67
Rockarena tour 4, 101, 102, 231
Rocky Horror Show 111
Rodgers, Paul 259
Rodrigo and Gabriela 224, 244, 252
Rogers, Akiko 231
Rolling Stone magazine 306
Rolling Stones, The 25, 92, 93, 259, 265, 306
Rolling Thunder 147, 156
Ronstadt, Linda 95, 242
Rooney, Peter 4
Rose, Axl 170–172
Rose Tattoo 51, 114, 120, 124
Rosebud festival 35, 43
Rosene, Ken 131–132
Rowe, Normie 261, 262
Roxy Music 68
Rudolph, Renee 223, 252
Rumours
   album 7
   tour 6
Rylands, Billy 56

Sabbath Bloody Sabbath 93
Saddington, Wendy 36
Saffron, Abe 212
'Sail On *Dr Dan*' 130
St John, Jeff 35
Salomone, Ross 85
Sanctuary Cove 145–148
Sano 275
Santana 4, 101, 174, 250, 269, 305
'Save a Prayer' 114
Saxon, Ian 137, 139, 147, 155–164
Saxon, Lloyd 163
Sayer, Leo 68, 92, 93, 94, 107, 279

Schafer, Tim 85, 86
Scott, Bon 30
Screaming Lord Sutch 257
Sebastian, John 174
Sebastian's Disco 30
Sebel Townhouse 96–98, 125, 165, 168, 197
Seekers, The 26, 92
Seger, Bob 85
Segreto, Joe 202, 251, 281
Sex and Thugs and Rock 'n' Roll: a year in Kings Cross 258
Sex Pistols 178
Shadows, The 92
Shakespeare, William 51
Shaman 250
'Sharp Dressed Man' 130
sharpies 27, 43
Sheldon, Tony 293
Shepherd, Dr Bruce 168
Shepherd Centre 168
Sheraton Marquee Hotel 87
Sherbert 35, 71, 74
'She's So Fine' 51
Shorrock, Glenn 261
'Show Must Go On, The' 94
Sidney Myer Music Bowl 38, 56, 99, 100
Silver Clef 197
Silver Studs, The 69
Simple Minds 126
Sinatra, Frank 143–153, 159, 160, 162
   Sinatra, Barbara 150, 152, 153, 160
   Sinatra Jnr, Frank 150
'Since You've Been Gone' 266
Sing When You're Winning 228
Skyhooks 70
Slash 170–171

Slattery, Lisa 117–118, 121, 124, 127, 133, 137, 141, 162, 165–169, 172, 218, 308
Slim Dusty 291
Sloane, Mac 20–21
Smith, Dallas 87
Smith, Joe 84
Smith, Lance 139
Smith, Stan 'the Man' 211–212
Smith, Trevor 36, 37, 40, 44, 67, 68, 173
Snow Patrol 244
Snow, Phoebe 157
So You Think You Can Dance 290
Solidarity 89
Solo Premier 77
'Sorry' 51
Sound Relief 202
Soundwave Festival 251
Southern Contemporary Rock Assembly 157
Spectrum 36, 40, 45, 70
Split Enz 106, 113, 198
Springfield, Rick 68
Spry, Garry 28
Squeeze (Australia) 107
Squeeze (UK) 106, 107, 116
Stagecoach, The 33
Starfish 115
Stars, The 72, 88, 199
Status Quo 68, 92, 93, 225
Steely Dan 235
'Steppin' Across the Line' 83
Stevens, Cat 93
Stevens, Phil 281
Stevie Wright Band, The 56
Stewart, Rod 85
Sting 102, 117, 145, 166, 178, 198, 227

Stivala, Frank 69, 70, 107, 137
Stone Temple Pilots 175
Strange, Steve 292
Stranglers, The 102, 242
Sunbury Pop Festival 35–37, 54, 259
Sunbury 72 (1972) 40, 46, 79, 120, 157
Sunbury 73 (1973) 41–43
Sunnyboys 112, 114, 116, 126
Sunrise agency 34, 40, 46, 50, 71, 79
Supernaut 63, 71
Swan Lake 295
Sweeney, John 29
Sweeney, Norm 29
Sweet, The 63
Sydney Children's Hospital Foundation 196, 200
Sydney City Mission 198
Sydney Festival 199
Sydney Live Earth concert 201
Synchronicity tour 131, 194

Tag, John 110
Take That 228
Talking Heads 102, 126
Taman Shud 35
Tanelorn Festival 112–113
Tangier 256, 265, 266
Tap Dogs 293
Taranto, Brian 226, 227
Taylor, Jim 85, 257
Taylor, Matt 41
Teddy Boy's Picnic 111
Tempo Records 73
10cc 75
'They Won't Let My Girlfriend Talk To Me' 111
Thing, The 65
Thomas, Deborah 264

Thomas, Grant 122, 191, 195
Thompson Carol 84
'Thorn in the Saddle' 83
Thornton, Oliver 294
Thorpe, Billy 30–33, 35–39, 46, 71, 79, 113, 157, 178–180, 184, 188, 222, 255–268
Thorpe, Lauren 258
Thorpe, Lynne 71, 258, 264, 266, 267, 268
Thorpe, Rusty 258
Thumpin' Tum 30
Ticketek 250
Time On Earth 201
Time Out of Mind 225
Toi, Teddy 257
Tolhurst, Kerryn 41
Torv, Jaan 41
'Transpac Slide, The' 129–130
'Treaty' 193–194
Tripp, Phil 219
Tully, Caroline 223
Turner, Tina 35, 179
Twilights, The 22

U2 121
'Ultimate Event, The' 149–155, 159
Ultimate Rock Symphony 259, 264
'Under the Milky Way' 115–116
'Unguarded Moment, The' 112
Unwritten Law 227
Urban, Keith 290–291
Use Your Illusion tour 170
Utsick, Jack 229–230, 286–289

V Festival 302
Valentines, The 30
Van Egmond, Garry 247, 291, 302, 306

Vanda, Harry 47, 49–53, 55–57, 60, 65
Vedder, Eddie 125
Vega, Suzanne 157
Victorian Bushfires Appeal 202
Victoria's Discotheque 31

Wainwright, Martha 252, 287
Wainwright, Rufus 290
Waits, Tom 121
'Walk, The' 126
Walker, Clinton 260
Walker, Phil 33
Walters, Barbara 82
Ward, Rachel 198
Warner Brothers 65, 88
'Waterloo' 97
Watson, Chris 160
Watson, John 280
Watson, John 'Bluey' 257
Wave Aid Benefit Concert 202, 281–282, 289, 305
Wayne, George 83
Weisman, Elliot 146, 149, 152
West, Ken 174, 251
Wheatley, Glenn 107
'When the Heat's Off' 83–84
Whiskey A Go-Go, 33
White House 199
White, Margaret 71–72, 75
White, Stan 71
White, Steve 68, 73, 107, 108, 286, 292
'Who Can It Be Now?' 113
Who, The 25, 259
Wilkins, Richard 'Dicky' 147
William Morris Agency 230, 293
Williams, Robbie 107, 114, 124, 126, 138, 139, 171

Williams, Robbie (talent) 228–229, 236–237, 247, 249, 286, 288, 309
Willis, Rod 109
Wilson-Piper, Marty 112
Winston, Frankie 131–133, 137–138, 167
Wishbone Ash 68, 92, 182
Wizard Records 67–69
Woodruff, John 109, 122, 206, 207
Woodstock 40, 43, 173, 306
Worldwide Entertainment Group 229, 286–287
Wright, Gary 85
Wright, Stevie 47, 49–62, 65, 66, 68, 70, 71, 106, 111, 198, 199, 261, 263, 264
Wrights, The 281

Xray Touring 228
XYZ (company) 294

Yardbirds, The 25
Yellowcard 251
Yes 287
'Yesterday's Hero' 56
Yothu Yindi 193, 218
You Am I 200, 263
Young, Angus 55
Young, George 47, 49–53, 55–57, 60, 65
Young, John Paul 51, 56, 60, 261
Young, Malcolm 55
Young, Neil 140, 166, 178, 241
Yunupingu, Mandawuy 193, 218

Zenyatta Mondatta 116
Zito, Richie 83
ZZ Top 137, 140